THE SLEEP OF REASON

The Sleep of REASON

Fantasy and reality
from the Victorian age
to the First World War

DEREK JARRETT

Weidenfeld and Nicolson
London

CONTENTS

Introduction 1

1 Paradise lost 8

2 Aspects of Antichrist 22

3 The harrowing of hell 39

4 Other gods before me 56

5 The coming of the Lord 72

6 The uses of fantasy 92

7 Watchers upon the high towers 112

8 The triumph of fiction 128

9 All truth is change 143

10 The power of evil 161

11 The waste land 177

Postscript 199

Notes 202

Index 221

INTRODUCTION

In 1936, a few months before the centenary of Queen Victoria's accession, Sir Charles Ensor in *The Oxford History of England* gave his verdict on her reign. 'No one will ever understand Victorian England,' he wrote, 'who does not appreciate that among highly civilized, in contradistinction to more primitive, countries it was one of the most religious the world has known ... hell and heaven seemed as certain as tomorrow's sunrise and the Last Judgement as real as the week's balance sheet.' It was a slightly condescending observation and it seemed to suggest that by confusing dream and reality, fact and fantasy, the Victorians had slipped back into the credulous superstitions of a primitive society instead of advancing towards the rationalism of a highly civilized one. For all their energy and in spite of their enormous achievements they had been in some sense asleep, lost in dreams of eternal bliss and nightmares of endless torment. By contrast Ensor's own enlightened generation was of course awake, living in the real world rather than in an imagined one and knowing that sunrise was more certain than hell and heaven. His readers could only conclude that in the course of ninety-nine painful years the human mind had come of age and put away childish things. Fantasy had been banished and reality reigned.

Many years earlier, as the eighteenth century's supposed Age of Reason drew to its close, the Spanish painter Francisco Goya had portrayed *El sueño de la razon*, the sleep of reason, in which the dreamer was surrounded by dark creatures of the night. 'Imagination deserted by reason begets impossible monsters,' he had explained, 'United with reason she is the mother of all the arts and the source of their wonders.' Was it a premonition of what was to come? Were the Victorians and their American contemporaries doomed to sleep the sleep of reason and beget impossible monsters? Certainly not in their own view. On

1

the contrary, they knew it was the sceptics who slept. On one side of the Atlantic Henry Francis Lyte looked forward confidently to the moment when 'Heaven's morning breaks and earth's vain shadows flee', while on the other Henry Wadsworth Longfellow declared that life was real precisely because the grave was not its goal. 'Tell me not in mournful numbers, Life is but an empty dream,' he cried, 'For the soul is dead that slumbers, And things are not what they seem.' The sleep of the soul, the sleep that was death to all true wisdom, was the same as the sleep of reason because reason came from God and was God. The dark creatures of the night were the vain and shadowy imaginings of the atheists, empty materialistic dreams which mistook appearance for reality and conjured up unreal nightmares without meaning and without purpose. For all his civilized condescension Ensor had achieved only an understatement. The English-speaking world of the nineteenth century did not put immortality on the same plane of reality as mortality but on a far higher one. All that was open to doubt was whether tomorrow's sunrise was as certain as hell and heaven, whether the week's balance sheet was as real as the Last Judgement.

There was nothing new about this. The Victorians were not an eccentric and aberrant generation which had strayed from the paths of rational thought under the influence of some self-injected dose of piety. Centuries ago Christianity had inherited from the ancient world the idea that reality was invisible and beyond man's ken. Lyte's phrase about earth's vain shadows was in direct line of descent from Plato's picture of the human race as men chained at the mouth of a cave and able only to peer into its depths at shadows cast by the real world which lay unseen behind them. This view of things extended even to the insubstantial world of fantasy to which Ensor wanted to consign heaven and hell. Since the source of all human imagining was the unseen world of ultimate reality it followed that all fantasies other than those of the insane could spring only from that world. Samuel Taylor Coleridge's famous definition of imagination as 'a repetition in the finite mind of the eternal act of creation in the infinite' was made only a few years after the appearance of Goya's drawing, while his subsequent remark that poetic genius had good sense as its body and the imagination as its soul was an echo of Goya's insistence on the need for imagination to be united with reason. The notion that outward appearances might be more real than ideas in the mind of God was not only an unthinkable thought:

2

it was also an unimaginable fantasy.

Yet in the course of a century or so the unthinkable came to be thought, the unimaginable imagined. For the first time in human history the invisible was no longer the necessary framework within which truths about the visible world could be discerned. Fantasy and reality changed places. It was clearly one of history's great turning points and well worth our study. But how should we study it? Some see it as a chapter in the history of religion, which at best is rather like investigating truancy by looking at the children who still go to school. At worst it is more like charting a voyage into outer space by examining the launching pad. Others would have us call it a chapter in the history of ideas, which usually means fitting allegedly significant thinkers and their allegedly significant thoughts into a kind of intellectual ladder up which the human race is supposed to have climbed. Unfortunately most such ladders tell us more about the retrospective thought of those who assemble them than about the creative thought of those who are said to be their rungs. In any case the change with which we are concerned was not a series of disjointed debates taking place at some rarefied philosophical level. It was a continuous and collective and often very painful human experience. Most of those who took part in it moved not from thought to thought but from fantasy to fantasy. They modulated the imagination into a new key rather than coaxing the intellect into a new philosophy. Although thinking has sometimes been regarded as the most respectable activity of the human mind imagining has always been far more prevalent and far more potent.

Can there be such a thing as the history of the human imagination? Some have tried to write it along Freudian lines, exposing and dissecting the fantasies of the dead in the way the psycho-analyst exposes and dissects those of his patients. This approach has its uses for the biographer, who deals only with the fantasies of an individual, but it has seldom been effective in the hands of the historian and it certainly seems unsuited to an investigation which must take account of millions of people on both sides of the Atlantic from the accession of Queen Victoria to the First World War. More promising is Jungian psychoanalysis with its notion of the collective unconscious and its emphasis on myths and universal archetypes. Jung's impact on literary critics has certainly been greater than that of Freud. And since the psychoanalyst and the literary critic are both in the business of assessing fantasies the historian of fantasy should perhaps look to their

3

disciplines. For the truth of the matter is that if hell and heaven and the Last Judgement were myths, mere products of the human imagination as Ensor seemed to suggest, then they did not simply vanish at reason's touch in the way dreams die when the dreamer awakes. Their place was taken by other myths, less pious but just as powerful. The prescribed fantasies of religion were replaced by secret fantasies confessed on the psycho-analyst's couch or more respectable ones engendered by popular fiction. The fact that thousands of people refused to believe that God was real is one side of the coin: the fact that almost as many refused to believe that Sherlock Holmes was fictitious is the other.

Once we have the courage or the impertinence to put God and Sherlock Holmes on the same plane things begin to fall into place. Holmes established his claim to be an archetype pretty convincingly in 1894, when he came back to life after he had been sent to his death over the Reichenbach Falls. Arthur Conan Doyle was forced to realize then that the great detective had an existence outside that of his creator. There are also literary critics who give the text or structure of a piece of fiction a reality which transcends the consciousness of its author and may even make a study of his or her intentions irrelevant. Others view creativity in a way which looks back beyond Coleridge to his mediaeval predecessors. When Coleridge spoke of imagination he distinguished it from fancy, an inferior faculty which could only juggle with images conveyed to it by the senses. 'Fancy has no other counters to play with,' he wrote, 'but fixities and definites'. Mediaeval thinkers put it the other way round, contrasting 'Imaginatio', a humble faculty of copying and imitation, with 'Phantasia', something truly creative. But Phantasia could not conceive anything God had not imagined, any more than Coleridge's finite imagination could outdo the eternal act of creation it was repeating. In both cases the lower faculty is merely mechanical while the higher one mirrors something outside itself. The layman or the Freudian may think of fantasy as something which begins and ends within one mind but the critic and the Jungian give it a wider meaning.

In *The Sign of Four*, his second public appearance, Holmes looked out on the 'dreary, dismal, unprofitable world' and exclaimed that 'no qualities save those which are commonplace have any function upon earth.' Shortly afterwards he advised Watson to read Winwood Reade's *The Martyrdom of Man*, which he said was one of the most remarkable books ever written. It ended with a vision of a world

4

drained of meaning and reduced to the commonplace because it had lost its faith. 'A season of mental anguish is at hand,' Reade wrote, 'and through this we must pass in order that our posterity may rise. The soul must be sacrificed; the hope in immortality must die. A sweet and charming illusion must be taken from the human race, as youth and beauty vanish never to return.' Did he really think that a world without the hope of life after death would be one from which youth and beauty had vanished for ever? Did he look to a future in which the finality of the grave would cast its shadow even over the years of hope and vigour? Perhaps not; but the fact that he felt it necessary to indulge in such rhetoric showed how important the sweet and charming illusion was. Goya had suggested that imagination could not survive without reason but Reade knew that for most of his readers reason could not survive without the conventional images of Christianity. If heaven and hell were unreal then reality itself could have no meaning. And no one understood this better than Holmes, perhaps because he had come to remedy the situation and trade old myths for new. It was certainly ironic that one of the few people to appreciate the significance of Reade's epitaph on fantasy should himself have been a fantasy.

The Martyrdom of Man appeared in 1872, rather more than halfway through Queen Victoria's reign. A few months before its publication a powerfully built young man wearing a shooting-coat and a wide-awake hat dived into the Thames from the parapet of London Bridge and rescued a man who had fallen overboard from the Woolwich steamer. 'Here is the sort of Christianity which all of us, little and great, learned and unlearned, can read as we run,' enthused the *Daily Telegraph* in a leading article, 'the gallant fellow going through the air like an angel in a shooting-coat and wide-awake'. It later transpired that the young man was a swimming instructor who owned the Wellington Baths in Leeds. The man he had rescued was his brother, also a swimming instructor, and the incident had been a publicity stunt. The *Daily Telegraph* was much mocked yet its talk of angels was of more than passing significance. Angels and archangels and all the company of heaven were part of the illusion which Reade saw as being under threat but they also had a status of their own which might enable them to outlive it. It was possible to reject conventional Christianity and still believe in 'guardian angels', just as half a century later even the irreligious talked of the Angels of Mons who were said to have come to the aid of British soldiers in Flanders. Powerfully built young angels in shooting-coats were especially desirable: if the imagination could not accept the fantastic as real it could at least turn the real into the fantastic.

No newspaper hailed Holmes as an angel in a deer-stalker and he was never called upon to investigate the mysterious affair at Mons. Yet there was a basic human need which linked the great detective with the enterprising swimming instructor and also linked Winwood Reade's traumatic vision with the traumatic realities of the First World War. It was the need to believe in heroism and self-sacrifice, in man's readiness to fight the good fight. Even Reade's farewell to conventional fantasies was couched in the form of a challenge, a summons to sacrifice: one generation must pass bravely through a season of mental anguish in order that its children and its children's children might rise to higher things. Holmes was 'an expert singlestick player, boxer and swordsman' and if he worshipped a god at all it was the god of battle. On the eve of the First World War, when Watson felt that 'God's curse hung heavy over a degenerate world', Holmes assured him that the English would turn from that world and purge themselves in battle: 'There's an east wind coming, such a wind as never blew on England yet. It will be cold and bitter, Watson, and a good many of us may wither before its blast. But it's God's wind none the less, and a cleaner, better, stronger land will lie in the sunshine when the storm has cleared.'

The relationship here between fantasy and reality was more complex and also more surprising than in the case of the Last Judgement and the week's balance sheet. The fantasy was that in 1914, before the appalling realities of war had made themselves apparent, a detective told his friend that the coming conflict had been sent by God to make England cleaner and better and stronger. The reality was that Sir Arthur Conan Doyle passed this message to the British and American reading public not on the eve of the war but three years into it, when millions of his countrymen had already been driven like cattle to be killed or maimed and when the same thing was about to happen to the young men of the United States. However unpleasant the fantasy may seem the reality is a great deal worse. Yet Doyle was only doing what he thought to be his duty, as were thousands of others who preached the need for more slaughter. Reality had become so obscene that it needed fantasy to make it bearable. And all the professional myth-makers of society, from the pundits of popular fiction to the potentates of church and state, hastened to clothe the senseless killing in garments of pride. What was the God of the Christians to do? The truth was that if by some miracle he could have made the rulers of the warring nations follow Christ's precepts the values of civilized society might have been saved. The myth was that if he had done so the world would have been cursed and degenerate, dishonoured and disgraced. It was a harsh and terrible myth which defaced and distorted the image of God to suit the needs of men. The image of God never fully recovered. The First World War succeeded in doing what all the sneers and disbelief of the nineteenth-century sceptics had failed to do. It was not the war to end wars but it was perhaps the illusion to end illusions.

1 PARADISE LOST

THE VICTORIAN MIND INHERITED THE FEARS AND uncertainties of a revolutionary age. Lord Melbourne, British Prime Minister at the time of Queen Victoria's accession in 1837, had been thirteen when the fall of the French monarchy in 1792 had ushered in a quarter of a century of bloodshed and devastation. Martin Van Buren, the American President, had been ten. Future ages would see worse things but to Melbourne and Van Buren and their generation it seemed they had lived through the world's greatest cataclysm, 'the day when heaven was falling, the hour when earth's foundations fled'. In the real world they had had some success in shoring up earth's foundations but in the world of the imagination heaven's intentions still gave rise to anxiety. In retrospect the Victorians may seem to have been walking serenely in the paths of righteousness but in 1837 there was more concern about God's absence than delight in his presence. Certainly few of the young queen's subjects and even fewer of their American contemporaries thought in terms of a new dawn of godliness and piety.

To many it seemed that darkness was already closing in, a darkness which foreshadowed the end of the Christian era. Paradise had perhaps already been lost. The world of their forefathers, a simple innocent world close to God, was slipping away. The revolutionary upheavals of the 1790s had brought war and violence and terror, shaking to its foundations the optimistic and rational view of mankind which had inspired them. It was a time of strange irrational fears, fears which coloured the early Victorian imagination and helped to shape its concepts of fantasy and reality. Men and women were not as yet worried by the thought that God might not exist but some of them were very worried indeed by the thought that he might have turned his face from them, perhaps for ever. A clergyman in Birmingham

warned his congregation that 'the spirit of infidelity and atheism manifested during the French Revolution' was still at work, separating
man from God and helping Antichrist to take over the earth. 'Beloved
brethren, perilous times are come,' he concluded.

The young Gladstone, twenty-seven years old and Member of Parliament for Newark, used the same adjective: Victoria had been left
a perilous legacy, he noted in his diary on the day of her accession.
Her predecessor, King William IV, had died muttering anxiously, 'The
church! The church!' A few months later, standing in St Peter's in
Rome, Gladstone lamented the rift between the Roman Catholic and
Protestant churches. Unless God himself did something about it the
state of Christendom could only get worse: it was 'in every human
sense hopeless'. The Church of England was particularly under threat
because some of its most eminent clerics seemed to be tending towards
Catholicism just when popular fear of Rome was at its height. Sydney
Smith, man of letters and Canon of St Paul's Cathedral, declared
that it was the new queen's duty to avoid anti-Catholic prejudice
and not to 'mistake fanaticism for religion.' Tennyson, who was also
twenty-seven when the Victorian age began, had already written
'Morte d'Arthur', in which he had seen his dead friend Arthur Hallam
in the guise of an undying king miraculously healed. Now, in the
first winter of the new queen's reign, he felt the need to put the poem
into a contemporary setting where men mourned the decay of faith
and the passing of the old forms of worship. In the countryside people
could remember going to the water's edge on Easter morning to watch
'the angels who were at the resurrection' playing in the sun; but such
bright visions were now fading into the hard light of day. Wordsworth
was not the only one to feel that 'there hath pass'd away a glory
from the earth'.

Wordsworth's lost paradise was the world of his own childhood.
Others, especially poets and artists, idealized the childhood of their
nation or their race, evoking images of ancient times when men and
women had supposedly lived close to the glory and the magic of nature
and had not yet been corrupted by the gross and greedy ways of
an increasingly materialistic age. Architects made their contribution
to the current nostalgia, disguising factories and railway stations as
castles or cathedrals. Aspiring politicians wove fantasies about the
past in order to attack the present. And through it all, in art and
in literature and in society's view of itself, the same theme kept recurring: a world that had once known God naturally and instinctively

had somehow lost touch with him. John Keble, whose verse best seller *The Christian Year* had evoked the former world with enormous success, was unsparing in his attacks on the present one. He had already preached an uncompromising sermon accusing the British of 'direct disavowal of the sovereignty of God' and now he and his supporters were suggesting that the country was farther from God than it had been in the Catholic Middle Ages. The group of young churchmen he gathered round him in Oxford soon came near to splitting the Church of England apart as debate over the lost paradise moved from nostalgia to theological confrontation. The Victorian age opened not in pious confidence but in anxious uncertainty.

As well as the threatened divisions within the Church there was the widening gulf between scientific research and revealed religion. Charles Lyell's *Principles of Geology*, which came out at the same time as Keble's sermon, paid careful respect to the Christian view of creation. 'In whatever direction we pursue our researches, whether in time or space,' Lyell wrote, 'we discover everywhere the clear proofs of a Creative Intelligence, and of His foresight, wisdom and power.' Such homage did not save the book from being attacked by the orthodox because it questioned the chronology laid down by the Book of Genesis. Parson Holmes, the irascible clergyman in Tennyson's 'Morte d'Arthur', singled out 'geology and schism' as twin evils which were separating mankind from God and sapping the foundations of faith. How was God to be regained, how would he once again manifest himself? Tennyson dreamed of a world reassured by miracle, of a mighty wind blowing King Arthur's ship to shore while the waiting crowds cried out in ecstasy: 'Arthur is come again: he cannot die'. The once and future king, stepping effortlessly from the days of chivalry into the nineteenth century 'like a modern gentleman of stateliest port', would re-establish man's communion with God and restore the glory that had passed away.

Parson Holmes did not share the dream and real-life parsons were even less ready to countenance it. They had a different picture of God's coming, one which rested on biblical authority and was to influence the Victorian mind even more powerfully than the fashionable nostalgia for the days of chivalry. The Book of Revelation had predicted long ago that mankind's drift into unbelief would result in the seven vials of God's wrath being poured out upon the earth while the Four Horsemen of the Apocalypse – Death, Famine, War and Pestilence – rode out to ravage mankind. God would not return as a kindly mediaeval monarch in latter-day disguise but on the wings of the storm, ushering in his reign by delivering a faithless generation over to Antichrist. Interpretation of this prophecy had never been easy and the exact sequence of events which it foretold was still a matter for argument; but by the time Queen Victoria came to her throne most commentators were agreed that the French Revolution had marked the pouring out of the first vial. The Rev. Edward Bishop Elliott, fellow of Trinity College Cambridge, proved the point in a massive work in four volumes which went through three triumphant editions in as many years. There was but a short time left, he warned, before the end of all things.

It seemed that across the Channel in Europe three of the four horsemen were already saddled. The French Revolution had plunged the continent into twenty years of war and it had also led to civil strife and appalling barbarity not only in France but in other countries as well. The fiendish atrocities and obscenities committed in Spain had led Goya to produce the series of drawings for which 'The Sleep of Reason' had been intended as a frontispiece. To some Christians it seemed it was the angels who slept while monsters continued to walk the earth. Many parts of Europe were still subject to the sort of superstitious tyranny which was later summed up by Gladstone as 'the negation of God erected into a system of government'. There was widespread starvation and by the 1830s there was cholera as well. 'The sword, famine and *the Pestilence* are represented in the Holy Scriptures as peculiar judgements on the sins, and particularly the national sins, of men,' wrote the Rev. William Marsh, 'We have, then, nothing to dread as men but a continuance in sin and unbelief; and we have nothing to dread as Britons but a perseverance in those national crimes which would be visited with national judgements.' Even Parson Holmes, when he had finished berating the geologists and the schismatics, had to admit that the real danger came from outside: if there was little faith left at home there was none at all abroad.

Englishmen in their complacency had always known this. Whilst Europe had been divided between the superstition of the Roman Catholics and the fanaticism of the extreme Protestants, the Church of England prided itself on holding the balance between authority and enthusiasm, between the stability given by an established church and the right of individuals to interpret the scriptures for themselves. Revolution had resulted from kingly and priestly tyranny and European states and European churches had fallen like ninepins before the

11

onslaught of atheism and rationalism. Only the British and their American cousins had stood firm. An impartial observer might think this had something to do with the oceans which had prevented the revolutionary armies from getting to the English-speaking peoples but the English-speaking peoples themselves did not doubt that it was because of their superior piety and good sense. The European nations had moved from superstition to blasphemy and back within a generation and it was hardly surprising that God had turned his face from them.

By 1841 Marsh was beginning to fear that the British had neglected his warning and were risking divine retribution. Soon God's patience would be at an end and the whole world with it. The Chartists, agitators for working-class rights and parliamentary reform, had just set up a church in Birmingham and Marsh warned his Birmingham congregation that this blasphemy signified the coming of Antichrist. 'What is Chartism but opposition to all human government?' he thundered in a sermon later published as *Antichrist detected*, 'What is Socialism but opposition to all moral and religious control, or Infidelity under its most dangerous form?' Both were insidious manifestations of Antichrist, 'approaching their victims in the garb of philanthropy while leaving unrestrained all the sinful passions of man'. The holocaust threatened in the Book of Revelation could not be long delayed.

Rumour had it that London rather than Birmingham would be the first to be punished. Early in 1842 word went round that the city was to be engulfed by an earthquake on 16 March and a week before the appointed day the credulous were reporting that St Paul's Cathedral had already sunk five feet. Printed notices were circulated, stamped with the royal arms, announcing that the event had been officially postponed for a week. They served only to amuse the few rather than to reassure the many. Streams of people fled before the approaching catastrophe and hotels in Brighton reported that 'numbers of families of the middle and upper classes have arrived to avoid its consequences'. On the day itself 'frantic cries, incessant appeals to Heaven for deliverance, heart-rending supplications for assistance' were heard from the poorer quarters while 'large bodies of respectable inhabitants' went up to Hampstead and Highgate in order to watch 'the demolition of the leviathan city'. Unfortunately, recorded *The Times*, 'the darkness of the day and the thickness of the atmosphere prevented it being seen.' When the weather improved it became clear that the earth had not opened up, the city had not after all been consumed by the fires of hell.

12

It was sad that a sense of the absence of God should find expression in prophecies of punishment, in visions not of heaven but of hell. Not since the Middle Ages had there been such an obsession with the Devil and his works. Earthquakes, even those which did not happen, were seen not simply as natural disasters but as hell's incursions. Even the geologists, impious questioners of the Book of Genesis, agreed that the earth beneath their feet was the abode of fire as well as the abode of the dead. Londoners had this underlined for them by Dr John Cumming, an eloquent prophet of apocalypse who drew audiences of many thousands to his lectures on the approaching end of the world:

The fire, which I told you geologists have admitted and which the Scripture confirms, to be a large ocean of restless and liquid lava, that rolls and heaves in the innermost recesses of the earth, of which our volcanoes are but the safety-valves and our earthquakes as the reverberations of its ceaseless waves lashing its desolate and dreary shores, shall burst forth at a thousand orifices; the gases that compose our atmosphere shall ignite and the earth shall melt; Christ's people shall be taken up into the air a certain distance while the wicked shall be left on earth, the living punished on it, the dead buried beneath it.

In many ways the picture was a conventional one. The Christian imagination had for centuries placed a lake of fire at the centre of the infernal regions and Milton in *Paradise Lost* had depicted its flames as giving out 'no light, but rather darkness visible'. The point was driven home by Father Pinamonti's *Hell Opened to Christians*, a seventeenth-century work which was still being brought out in the 1840s by the Catholic Book Society. The damned souls were in total darkness, Pinamonti insisted, and were denied the comfort that light could bring, yet in the darkness all the horrors and torments of hell were fully visible. And the agent of torment, the element in which the damned would writhe for evermore, was fire – 'fire bed, fire food, fire drink', as one outraged critic of the doctrine put it. Nor did it need either theologians or geologists to point out that darkness and fire were not incompatible: miners had always known it and the appalling accidents that happened when fire took command below ground showed that the imagined subterranean world and the real one had something in common. It only remained to put actors on to the stage, to fill out Cumming's depopulated fiery gulf with tormentors and tormented.

This was done, at any rate as far as the real underground world

13

was concerned, early in June 1842. With the earthquake scare still fresh in the minds of Londoners the House of Commons debated a report on the employment of children in mines and factories. Members soon learned that the earth under them was indeed a place of suffering where children were chained and tortured. 'I went into the pit at seven years of age,' said one of them, 'when I drew by the girdle and chain, the skin was broken and the blood ran down. If we said anything they would beat us. I have seen many draw at six. They must do it, or be beat. They cannot straighten their backs during the day.' The passages along which he and other children had to draw cartloads of coal, in foul air and in total darkness, were deep underground and were sometimes less than two feet high. It was there-fore essential, said those who understood the requirements of the job (and they included clergymen as well as doctors), that children should start work young so that they could become suitably deformed while the bones were still soft. Lord Ashley, presenting the report, gave details of the treatment received by Edmund Kershaw, whom the parish authorities of Castleton in Lancashire had apprenticed to a nearby collier:

His back and loins were beaten to a jelly; his head, which was almost cleared of hair on the scalp, had the marks of many old wounds ... One of the bones in one arm was broken below the elbow, and seemed to have been so for some time. The boy, on being brought before the magistrate, was unable to sit or stand and was placed on the floor in the office. It appeared that the boy's arm had been broken by a blow with an iron rail, and the fracture had never been set, and that he had been kept at work for several weeks with his arm in that condition. It was admitted – what an admission! – by the master that he had been in the habit of beating the boy with a flat piece of wood, in which a nail was driven and projected about half an inch ... The boy had been starved for want of food and his body presented all the marks of emaciation. This brutal master had kept him at work as a waggoner until he was no longer of any use, and then sent him home in a cart to his mother, who was a poor widow residing in Rochdale.

The world revealed by the report was strikingly similar to the one depicted in *Hell Opened to Christians*. The only difference was that in the latter the sufferers were being punished while in the former they were merely being employed. However, the one might well lead to the other. Ashley was especially eloquent about the ignorance of the children: they were benighted spiritually as well as physically. They had never known God, they were not taught their catechism, so how

14

could they avoid hellfire? The darkness they knew in life might be
followed by an even deeper darkness after death.

Darkest of all was the view of God and of man which such a train
of thought revealed. Indeed, the least justifiable thing in Ashley's outburst was the use of the word 'brutal', for the cruelties he described
were uniquely human. No brute beast could have been capable of
them. 'What are men better than sheep or goats,' Tennyson's King
Arthur had asked, 'If, knowing God, they lift not hands of prayer?'
By the same token what were men better than tigers or vipers if,
knowing the cruelties sanctioned by God for the punishment of sinners,
they did not emulate them? Christianity had long ago relegated the
brute creation to an inferior place in God's scheme of things: only
human beings had souls, only human beings would go to heaven or
to hell. And only human beings practised cruelty for its own sake.
Why? Had the human mind created images of evil or had it been
created by them? Did the earthly torturers create the fiends of hell
or were they inspired by them? Had human compassion given itself
over to the underworld or was the underworld rising, in mental if
not in geological terms, in order to engulf the senses of mankind?

The apocalyptic scenario, like the infernal one, required human
participation. This was especially true of war, the third of the four
horsemen. And the fear in the summer of 1842 was not just of foreign
war but of something far worse. Even as Parliament debated the report
strikes broke out in the Staffordshire pits and by the middle of August,
when the Chartists met in Manchester, one of their leaders was convinced that 'the spread of the strike would and must be followed by
a general outbreak'. '1842 was the year in which more energy was
hurled against the authorities than in any other of the nineteenth
century', one historian has written, 'It was the nearest thing to a
general strike that the century saw.' God-fearing Christians echoed
Marsh's words: 'What is Chartism but opposition to all human government? What is Socialism but opposition to all moral and religious
control?' First reactions to Ashley's revelations were of shock and
shame and horror but as the threat of revolution grew a reaction
set in. He was arraigned for his sensationalism and for his indelicacy
– it was intolerable, said his critics, that such disgusting things should
be published in the newspapers to distress susceptible ladies – and
clergymen who had at first thought that there might be something
unchristian in the way the children were treated soon came to see
that the really sinful thing was working-class insubordination.

15

Antichrist was where he always had been, down among the discontented in the infernal regions, only too ready to clamber out and distress the susceptible.

While the British contemplated the possibility of a man-made apocalypse, an Armageddon of working-class revolt, America was promised divine intervention. William Miller, a farmer from Low Hampton in New York State, gathered a large following around him when he announced that Jesus Christ would come to earth between 21 March 1843 and 21 March 1844. The righteous would be 'caught up to meet the Lord in the air', while the wicked would have their bodies destroyed by fire and their souls 'shut up in the pit of woe until their resurrection unto damnation'. Once the earth had been cleansed by fire Christ and his saints would take possession of it and rule it for ever. Camp meetings – ecstatic outdoor services which were a special feature of American Christianity – were held all across the United States and it was reckoned that more than half a million Americans were devoutly awaiting the coming of their Lord. The *New York Tribune* published a special extra number on 2 March 1843 explaining the prophecies of the Book of Daniel and the Book of Revelation and concluding that 'the Lord has most plainly showed us that we are living in the days of the voice of the seventh angel ... This sound of the last trump, at which the dead will rise and BE JUDGED we now expect to hear. Reader, slight not the Lord's warning. Improve the present moment. PREPARE TO MEET THY GOD!'

'The time, as I have calculated it, is now filled up,' said Miller on 25 March 1844, 'and I expect every moment to see the Saviour descend from heaven'. But the skies failed to open and the prophet had to tell his followers that 'he confessed his error and acknowledged his disappointment'. Then his friend Samuel Snow made a new calculation showing that Christ would come on the tenth day of the seventh month of the current Jewish year – Tuesday 22 October 1844 in Christian terms – and once more excitement mounted. Crops were left unharvested, shops and offices put up their shutters, people resigned from their jobs and gave their money away in order to prepare for the great day:

Many have become maniacs, wasting their property and leaving their families to suffer in indigence. The religious community seems, as it were, convulsed to its centre. Nor is it strange or wonderful if the credulous, from the signs of the times, should become alarmed or apprehensive of the approach of

16

some dread event or revolution. All is fanaticism, feigned or real ... If an intelligent stranger should now land in this country he might suppose that they were on the verge of a revolutionary outbreak.

What they were in fact on the verge of, what they had to face up to once the great day had come and gone, was less dramatic but ultimately more damaging. Every cosmic non-event, every doomsday that failed to arrive, was another nail in the coffin of a God who was apparently unable to give substance to the visions he had inspired or to the predictions he was supposed to have prompted. The prophets and those who believed them were caught in a descending spiral of despair. Their sense of loss at the absence of God convinced them that the end was nigh; the end's stubborn refusal to arrive intensified the sense of loss, even of betrayal. Nevertheless the spate of prophecies continued unabated and unabashed. They were now regarded by many as the only way to keep Christians in a proper state of readiness, to 'awaken the unbelieving and profane'. If they were not heeded by those few nations which had so far not committed 'national crimes', then what hope was there for mankind? In a twilight world of blasphemy and unbelief, with no prayers to make the heavens relent, the darkness would continue to deepen.

And it was Christianity, for so long the proudest of the world's religions, which had caused the gods to turn away. For many thousands of years, in all kinds of societies from the most primitive to the most advanced, religious observance had preserved the universe. Men had acted out the required rituals, offered up the necessary sacrifices and prayers, and in return the gods had lit up the heavens and replenished the earth. In ancient Mexico the priests had promised that the sun would continue to rise as long as sufficient human blood was poured out upon the altars. Their will had been done and the sun had not failed. Elsewhere, in remote and secret regions, prayer wheels had turned tirelessly in the knowledge that if they stopped the thread of existence would snap and nothingness would blot out the meaning of the world. Gods had been replaced by other gods – or perhaps had merely changed their names – as their followers had migrated or been conquered or converted. But always there had been worship, always there had been the sustaining breath of prayer to hold up the sky. Now, for the first time in human history, there were thousands upon thousands of men and women who denied the need for any gods at all. By spawning open unbelief Christianity had undermined

17

not just its own foundations but the whole world's delicate balance between fantasy and reality, faith and knowledge.

Sixty years later, in *Peter Pan*, J.M. Barrie produced the appropriate image. The fairy Tinkerbell lay dying and the children in the audience were told that they could only save her by affirming their belief in fairies. It is not recorded that any audience ever remained silent but it is interesting to wonder what would have happened if one had. Would Tinkerbell have died and if so why? Because Barrie was right, because supernatural beings only existed as long as they were believed in, or because the uncaring audience must be punished for its silence? As with fairies, so with gods: if silence on earth produced silence in heaven was it from necessity or from choice? Was God dead for lack of belief in him or had he merely turned away from an uncaring humanity? For God's audience in the 1840s, deeply divided as to whether it should shout its belief, this issue of choice or necessity was a painful one. If God was absent out of choice, because unbelief had offended him, then the surrounding darkness was the darkness of his anger and would lift only when enough people affirmed their belief; but if he was absent from necessity, because he had never been anything more than man's yearning for him, then the darkness of superstition would be dispelled only by enlightened unbelief. Either way the drama could not proceed, the shades of night could not give way to a new dawn, until the members of the audience agreed among themselves. In this situation Goya's recommended union of reason and imagination would be hard to bring about.

There were many for whom the prospect of empty untenanted skies was too appalling to contemplate. It was the worst of all possible cosmic tragedies, something which could only be conveyed by the metaphor of God's death. A German thinker called Jean Paul Richter – like Winwood Reade a great favourite of Sherlock Holmes – had already proclaimed that God was dead and mankind orphaned. In March 1844, just as God was failing to keep the first of the appointments made for him by William Miller, the same proclamation was heard again, this time from France. Gérard de Nerval's poem 'Le Christ aux Oliviers' described Christ on the eve of his crucifixion staring into the void and realizing that his father who had once been in heaven was now dead, with the result that the coming sacrifice on the cross would achieve nothing. The trumpet would not sound, the dead would not be raised, the promised apocalyptic drama would never take place. The whole world, the whole universe, could only grow colder and darker.

Others detected not darkness but dawn. One of the most influential was George Jacob Holyoake, a London atheist who started a magazine called *The Reasoner or Herald of Progress* in June 1846. 'The last census informs us that Great Britain is afflicted by no fewer than 23,000 clergymen,' he complained in his first editorial, 'centres of 23,000 local associations which in effect, so think we, cripple the moral energies of men, humiliate their native spirit and divert them from independence and social amelioration, chaining the spirit of progress to musty records and drivelling dogmas – and not one Association rears its head against this vast organized error!' He was quick to publicize American atheism, telling how in Boston 'the disciples of Thomas Paine, Infidels by profession' had offered the free use of their hall to a Christian anti-slavery lecturer who had been ostracized by all the Christian communities there. 'Boston is professedly a Christian city,' the lecturer had commented, 'hence I blush while I am constrained to acknowledge the superior humanity of what is called Infidelity.'

As the exponents of atheism and rationalism came more and more into the open the beleaguered believers needed to find out what proportion of the audience they formed. Holyoake's interpretation of the 1841 census was fallible since neither that nor any previous census had taken a count of religious services and attendances. When one was taken in 1851 it only covered England and Wales and it showed that there were 34,467 places of worship, 14,077 belonging to the Church of England and 20,390 belonging to other denominations. Out of a population of nearly eighteen million there were some ten and three quarter million church attendances on the Sunday chosen for the count but these covered morning, afternoon and evening services and many people attended more than once, so that the number of individual worshippers was clearly much less. However, taking into account those who worked on Sundays or were for other reasons prevented from going to church – the census officials put them at four tenths of the total population – it was a respectable figure. And there were clearly many people who did not attend church but still believed in God and would shout out their belief if and when the moment came. The figures for Scotland, though less reliable and more belated, suggested that about sixty per cent of the population worshipped regularly. In Ireland the fierce dissension between Catholics and Protestants bore witness to the intensity of religious fervour on both sides.

19

The Almighty need not languish and die because of any uncaring silence on the part of his British audience.

America was another matter. The constitution of the United States expressly forbade any established church and many people in Britain imagined that American religion was a matter of frenzy and fanaticism, what one historian has called 'the swamp fire of religious conversion, the emotionalism of rural America'. On the other hand Charles Dickens, by no means an admirer of the United States, insisted that the Americans were no more fanatical than the British. 'I have beheld religious scenes in some of our populous towns which can hardly be surpassed by an American camp meeting,' he wrote, 'and I am not aware that any instance of superstitious imposture on the one hand and superstitious credulity on the other has had its origin in the United States which we cannot parallel.' Others sought more precise information and *Painter's Church of England Gazette* estimated shortly after Queen Victoria's accession that there were about one and three quarter million communicant members of recognized churches in the United States, ranging from the Episcopal Church, an American version of the Church of England, to Methodists, Baptists, Congregationalists and Presbyterians. The American census of 1840 showed the population to be just over seventeen million, so these communicants represented about a tenth of the total. So, whether Dickens was right or wrong, the shout for God from America would have to go up also from the unrecognized, from strange sects, from camp meetings, from the followings of itinerant preachers.

It seemed that the moment of truth could not be long delayed. Early in 1847 Holyoake published a letter from a correspondent in Paris who proclaimed that in Communism, 'the Religion of the Future', Europe was keeping all that was best in the old faith while abandoning the dark imaginings that still held sway in Britain and in America. 'Communism abroad rests mainly on the essential maxims of Christianity, which would hardly be safe with you, where there is danger of being dragged into all the absurdities tacked on to them.' At the beginning of September *The Times*, usually quick to dismiss talk of revolution, published a leading article on the Communist threat in France. There was real danger, it warned solemnly, of 'disasters to which no living man can assign a termination.'

In November 1847 the Congress of the Communist League, meeting in London, gave Karl Marx and Friedrich Engels the task of drawing up the *Communist Manifesto*, printed in England and then published in Europe as successive revolutions broke out there during the spring and summer of 1848. Capitalist society, declared Marx and Engels, was like 'a sorcerer who is no longer able to control the powers of the nether world whom he has called up with his spells'. The potentates of Christianity had frightened ordinary men and women for centuries with talk of hellish torments; now it was time for them to be buried under the debris in which they had traded. 'What the bourgeoisie produces above all are its own gravediggers,' concluded the *Manifesto*. Whatever the God of the Christians had done in the past, however cleverly he had rolled back stones and slipped from sepulchres and appeared in visions to his disciples, his days were now numbered. The gravediggers of bourgeois society were also the gravediggers of God. The surrounding darkness was the darkness before the dawn of a bright new world purged of superstition and unreason.

Meanwhile another voice had spoken of deepening darkness, of shadows that would flee, of a morning that would soon break. On Sunday evening 5 September 1847, the day before *The Times* published its prediction of revolution and disaster, the Rev. Henry Frances Lyte preached what was to be his last sermon in his church at Brixham in Devon. It was not an especially distinguished sermon because he was mortally ill and speech was not easy. But in his pocket he had a sheet of paper on which he had written out a hymn which he showed to members of his congregation after the service. It was called 'Abide with me' and it was to prove one of the most enduring messages of comfort that the English-speaking world had ever known. While Holyoake and Marx and Engels gestured their sections of the audience into silence, stifling the shout of affirmation that might yet save a dying God, Lyte's hymn sang out in unquenchable praise and trust. With men like this to believe in him there was life in the old God yet.

2 ASPECTS OF ANTICHRIST

ON FRIDAY 3 SEPTEMBER 1847, AS LYTE PREPARED
the final draft of his hymn, Londoners living in the streets around
Euston station woke up to find that an immense quantity of human
remains had been dumped outside their homes. The station was being
extended and debris of all kinds was being tipped into the excavations.
The gravediggers from some overcrowded burial ground – suspicion
fell on those from St Pancras – had seized the opportunity to get
rid of their unwanted dead in order to make more money. In many
London burial grounds the corpses were piled upon one another to
within a few inches of the surface to make the land yield more in
fees. Coffins were often dug up once the mourners had left and sold,
either as firewood or for re-use. Once the dead were out of their coffins
they were horribly at the mercy of the living: Parliament was told
of two St Pancras gravediggers who had been seen hacking a body
apart and cramming the pieces into a shallow hole. There was often
only a thin covering of earth between the dead and the living. August
had seen an angry meeting of the Anti-Interment in Towns Association, as well as a gruesome lecture by a medical man describing the
injurious effects of the metropolitan graveyards. Now *The Times* produced equally gruesome details of this latest exhumation:

Large numbers were drawn to the spot and not only were human bones
found in large quantities but pieces of flesh were picked up. The children
who were there amused themselves by raking over the soil for the purpose
of finding teeth of which great numbers were picked up. The reporter who
was present had a whole handful shown him, the urchin who had picked
them up telling him that he should take them to a dentist's and sell them.

The Euston scandal provoked a spate of angry letters. 'Day by
day, year by year,' wrote one outraged citizen, 'we go on displacing

one generation, only yet partially returned to the dust, to make room for another ... the narrow slip of earth is sold over and over again ere the bones of its rightful owner are unclothed of their flesh.' The London Cemetery Company saw its chance and ran a series of advertisements for its splendidly appointed establishments at Highgate, Kentish Town and Nunhead. 'A part of each cemetery remains unconsecrated,' it added, conscious that some potential patrons had little time for Christian hopes. While 'Abide with me' grew more popular, affirming that death would dispel earth's vain shadows and reveal the glories of heaven, sceptics saw such fantasies as cruel and childish delusions. 'One might as well take lodgings over a cooking establishment in the Cannibal Islands,' remarked Holyoake in *The Reasoner*, commenting on the idea that those in heaven would be able to watch the smoke of torment rising from hell. 'The quiet sense of submission to annihilation is infinitely preferable,' he concluded.

It had also to be admitted that the last verse of 'Abide with me', with its picture of heaven's morning breaking at the moment of death, was not entirely orthodox. Christianity taught that only the saints would be taken directly to heaven when they died, while ordinary mortals waited in the graveyards for their bodies to be resurrected at the Day of Judgement. Lyte's hymn seemed at odds with this doctrine on two counts: he hoped to go straight from his death-bed to eternal bliss and he hoped that his soul would be accorded this privilege irrespective of his body's decay. Longfellow's 'Psalm of Life', as popular in America as 'Abide with me' was to become in Britain, went further, implying that the body was itself part of those earthly appearances which eternity would reveal as being unreal:

> Life is real! Life is earnest!
> And the grave is not its goal;
> Dust thou art, to dust returnest,
> Was not spoken of the soul.

Nevertheless the Anglican creed spoke of the resurrection of the body and most Christians thought of heaven as being inhabited by real people and not by disembodied souls. Mrs Elizabeth Stone, in a popular book on the subject, pointed out that whereas devotees of other religions might burn their dead Christians had to ensure that burial was carried out 'consistently with the revealed doctrine of the resurrection of the body'. 'Yes, *this body*,' she continued, 'waiting, sleeping, changed – this human chrysalis shall waken.' Some took

23

the prospect even more literally. Sabine Baring-Gould, author of 'Onward, Christian soldiers', was shocked to find that his parishioners in Yorkshire insisted on putting a candle and a coin in every coffin, the former to light the corpse's way to heaven and the latter to pay its toll at the gate. The doctrine of the resurrection of the body found expression in customs of this kind, primitive though they might seem, just as it found expression in the horror with which the practices of the gravediggers were regarded. They were seen not just as unhygienic but as sacrilegious. Instead of merely containing putrefying flesh, dangerous to health and divorced from the person who had once inhabited it, the coffin housed a sleeping human being destined for some kind of physical resurrection and possibly already under the protection of the angels or demons associated with its eventual fate. That being or its protectors might take revenge on anyone who disturbed the body. Christianity might have blunted the fear of death but it had certainly not blunted the fear of the dead.

Fear and fascination were closely linked. It could well be argued that the horror story was a specifically Christian literary genre. Other religions had devils and monsters and ghosts but Christianity excelled in tales in which visitors from the next world were actual corpses rather than mere spirits. No other religion led men to write with such ghoulish glee about the walking dead, the opening vault, the cold cadaverous hands closing around the throat. The power of such images sprang, like the hopes of the devout, from the doctrine of the resurrection of the body. The stench of the charnel-house mingled, usually quite pleasurably, with the odour of sanctity. In America there were no urban burial grounds, no horrific juxtaposition of the living and the dead, but in spite of this – or perhaps because of it – Edgar Allan Poe's strange tales of the undead became increasingly popular while in Britain *Varney the Vampire* enjoyed an enormous success when it was published in monthly parts between 1845 and 1847. Dr Mayo, founder of the medical school at the Middlesex Hospital, wrote an article for *Blackwood's Magazine* in April 1847 in which he tried to scotch the vampire myth. The supposed vampires were simply people in comatose or cataleptic states who had been buried alive. He quoted one case of a youth who was thought to have become a vampire and was therefore exhumed. To their horror his relatives found him lying as if alive, colour in his cheeks and a ghastly smile on his lips. They prayed for him and hacked off his head, whereupon he writhed and screamed most horribly. It was not the curse of the vampire that was departing from him, Mayo said grimly, it was life itself. And the same was true of all the other poor wretches who had been disinterred down the centuries in order to have stakes driven through their hearts while the fresh blood gushed and spurted.

It was a timely article which seemed to endorse Holyoake's prediction of the coming triumph of reason over superstition. Yet Mayo left some awkward questions unanswered. How had these supposed vampires been identified? If all the rigmarole of vampirism was imagined, the scratching at the window and the monstrous bat-like form and the punctures in the neck, why was it only the relatives and neighbours of the prematurely buried who imagined it? And how did they know which graves to go to? Did the prematurely buried have telepathic powers, seeking release or revenge by projecting a vampire image on to those who had entombed them? Or was there some strange force in the minds of the living which led them to fill the dark void of death with evil creatures? The idea of hell rising to engulf the human mind might be a superstition but the idea of the human mind immersing itself in hell was a fact. Nor were Christian fantasies the only ones to influence popular thinking. Alongside the advertisements for the hygienic and enlightened services of the London Cemetery Company were other and stranger announcements. 'TO CAPTAINS and others GOING TO SEA,' proclaimed one, 'A CHILD'S CAUL to be DISPOSED OF, in perfect condition.' Seamen had long believed that a caul, the membrane sometimes found on a baby's head at birth, was a sure safeguard against drowning. In the autumn of 1847, as Holyoake and Lyte put forward their differing visions of the morning that was about to break, this superstition was still powerful enough to ensure a steady sale for cauls at ten guineas or more. Even a newspaper as respectable as *The Times* advertised at least one a fortnight. Holyoake's belief in the reasonableness of mankind seemed as much a matter of faith as Lyte's confidence in the mercies of God.

Each awaited the dawn in his own way. Lyte did his best to live out what was left of his life in the spirit of his hymn. 'O for more of entire dependence on Him!' he wrote, 'Entire confidence in Him! Conformity to the will and image of the Lord is no easy attainment and it takes much hammering to bend us to it.' Two months later he died, searching passionately for the vision he had conjured up in his verses. It was to be hoped that it was granted. Holyoake on the other hand looked for an actual earthly daybreak, a tempestuous dawn which would dispel the shadow of human tyranny as well as the imagined dominion of the divine. Revolution in one country would lead to universal change, just as *The Times* had predicted, and all the old hierarchies would crumble. But *The Times* had now regained its composure and was assuring its readers that there would be no revolution in France. On 24 February 1848 it published a leading article declaring that no insurrection could possibly succeed in Paris. 'We suspect, however,' it continued, 'that no serious popular insurrection is even probable ... If lives are lost in this miserable brawl the reckoning will lie heavily on those who inconsiderately commenced an agitation which they had no power to bring to a successful termination.'

The pronouncement was singularly ill-timed, for the French monarchy had already fallen after fighting in the streets of Paris had left insurrectionary forces in control. Revolutions followed in Hungary, Austria, Prussia and Italy. By the end of March it seemed that the old Europe of priests and kings and noblemen was on the point of collapse. In *The Reasoner* Holyoake mocked *The Times* for its failure to comprehend the new dawn of reason which was sweeping away old superstitions. He also took the opportunity to mock the Earl of Arundel, a Catholic who spoke in Parliament in defence of papal efforts to re-establish the Jesuit order in England. 'Were honourable members aware', Arundel asked, 'of the atheistical and infidel publications which were sold at a cheap rate among the lower classes?' He brandished a copy of the rationalist *Northern Star*, containing advertisements for such subversive tracts as *Discussions on the Bible* and *Socialism made easy*, and declared that the Church of England desperately needed Jesuit help in combating such horrors. Most Englishmen associated the Jesuits with Catholic bigotry and the torture chambers of the Inquisition, so that Holyoake was able to make considerable capital out of the confrontation, especially when Arundel declined to produce any arguments in support of his point of view. Even the *English Review*, a piously orthodox journal, referred scathingly to 'sophistries put forth by the Romanists under shelter of Lord Arundel's name' and predicted that the papacy would be overthrown altogether if it did not yield to revolutionary demands.

Arundel was not to be deflected. He continued to attack European revolutionaries and British radicals alike, proclaiming that they were 'rebels to their God'. He was not old enough to remember the way in which Antichrist had been manifested in the 1790s, but many who were shared his fears. Lord Brougham, once a trenchant critic of

Britain's wars against revolutionary France, now came forward to deplore the new uprisings: 'I everywhere observe all the elements of mischief; and turn which way we will the repose of the world seems in peril.' He went on to allege that Parisians had already put out reports of the overthrow of Queen Victoria and the setting up of a godless republic in Britain. Dr Cumming, preparing for publication his immensely popular lectures on the approaching end of the world, warned that the seventh and final vial of God's wrath was now being poured out and that the 'People's Charter', the cherished manifesto of British radicals, was the Devil's work, 'a war-cry of rebellion, a code of treason, a prescription for crime on a large scale'. The bright new dawn was in truth a deepening apocalyptic darkness.

It was true that Holyoake's sunrise was by now a little clouded. All across Europe revolutionary movements split into warring factions while the brave new world of rational conduct dissolved into unreasoning violence. In Britain the radicals marched not to triumph but to disaster. Rebels in Ireland failed dismally, making their last sad stand in a cabbage patch in County Tipperary, while the Chartist petition to Parliament was ridiculed and rejected. Pitched battles between police and Chartists followed, resulting in hundreds of arrests and the virtual extinction of the radical movement for more than a decade. 'Every species of folly and wickedness seems to have been let loose to riot on the earth,' wrote Charles Greville as the year 1848 came to an end. It was not just the god of the Christians who was absenting himself but the supposed goddess of reason as well. A lifetime ago, in the calm and confident world of the eighteenth-century philosophers, it had been possible to believe in her: man had seemed then to be a rational being who had only to remodel society and government along rational lines in order to be permanently and rationally happy. The French Revolution had changed all that: Goya had not been the only one to think that reason had slept while madness spawned monsters. 'There was a time when I believed in the persuadability of man,' the poet Robert Southey had written in 1797, 'and had the mania for man-mending. Experience has taught me better ... The ablest physician can do little in the great lazar-house of society, it is a pest house that infects all within its atmosphere.' Even if Holyoake's readers were rationally motivated they were almost certainly outnumbered by those who were at home in the dark world of the vampire or were ready to see shrivelled membranes as a charm against drowning.

27

The man whose predictions had been vindicated by the year's events was neither George Holyoake nor the editor of *The Times* but Karl Marx, who had always insisted that mankind was moving not to some rationalist utopia but to bloodshed and violence, to a world in which only conflict could bring progress. Few of god's defenders in 1848 had read the *Communist Manifesto* and fewer still understood the thinking which lay behind it, but most knew there was something called 'German metaphysics', an ominous iceberg of which Marx's dialectical materialism was but the ugly tip. It was this strange new philosophy, monstrous and shapeless and half-hidden, which was increasingly seen as the real danger. It was the darkness of German unreason, not the light of reason shining from France, which now threatened to engulf God. The clerics and thinkers who formed his first line of defence hastened to proclaim themselves rationalists in order to form a common front against the metaphysicians.

In October 1849 the *Edinburgh Review* published an article called 'Reason and Faith; their Claims and Conflicts' by Henry Rogers, who was a teacher of logic as well as a Christian apologist. 'We fear that many young minds in our day are exposed to the danger of falling into one or other of the prevailing forms of unbelief, and especially that of pantheistic mysticism, from rashly meditating in the cloudy regions of German philosophy,' Rogers warned. A young man would do well to shun German philosophers, he declared sternly, 'at least till he has matured and disciplined his mind'. Only then could he be sure of reconciling reason and faith in a properly Christian manner: 'God has created two great lights – the greater light to rule man's busy day – and that is Reason; and the lesser to rule his contemplative night – and that is Faith. But Faith itself shines only so long as she reflects some faint illumination from the brighter orb.' Some writers still had their doubts about following the dictates of reason – the Unitarian J.R. Beard thought that the 1848 revolutions sprang from 'the combined influence of Rationalism and Pantheistic Philosophy, which has gone far to blight and uproot the positive religious convictions of France as well as Germany' – but most were convinced that German metaphysics was the greater danger. The *English Review* launched two attacks on it, one attributing recent subversion of the faith in Britain to its influence and the other explaining how 'that character, literary, moral and social, which we may denominate the German mind' had done more to undermine true religion than even 'the audacity of Voltaire'.

Yet German philosophy was a good deal more religious than Voltaire had ever been. Just as Christians considered sinning or not sinning more important than abstract reasoning or scientific observation, so German thinkers from Kant to Hegel thought moral values more important than physical appearances. They insisted that life was about the imperative commands that came from the will, not about the abstract patterns that came from the intellect. Eighteenth-century rationalists who had traced such patterns had imagined that they were explaining everything, that the rational nature of man reflected the rational nature of the universe. This was the delusion that had bred disillusion and brought violence and suffering on an enormous scale instead of the ideal world of which the philosophers had dreamed. Man must learn to see life as something dynamic, something continually re-moulded by the will of God, rather than the two-dimensional backcloth painted by the rationalists. Just as a man's fate was shaped by the inner commandments of the individual will, so the fate of mankind would be shaped by the universal commandments of God.

Instead of revealing himself once and for all and then retiring to remote eternity God was now seen as unremittingly involved in human affairs. He was Antichrist's constant and cunning antagonist. History, said Hegel, was the march of God in the world. It was not a steady upward march, as the rationalists had imagined, but a series of conflicts. The Greeks had sought truth by a process called dialectic, the clash of thesis and antithesis in order to produce synthesis, and Hegel thought that history worked in the same way. So far from digging God's grave the German thinkers had given him a new and vital role. But was it the same god? Certainly Marx's materialist version of Hegel's dialectic saw history as moulded not by a personal god but by blind economic necessity and it could be argued that the god of the earlier German thinkers was a similarly uncaring juggernaut. And he was all the more dangerous because he was born of conviction rather than doubt. He existed on a moral plane rather than an intellectual one and so to the orthodox his adherents seemed not merely misguided but heretical. For the prophets of apocalypse the matter was even simpler: like all false gods this one was a manifestation of Antichrist. One of Dr Cumming's reasons for predicting the end of the world was the fact that 'Germany and America are over-run with fanaticism of the most hideous description.' German metaphysicians had succeeded where French revolutionaries had failed: they had

29

infiltrated the English-speaking world and corrupted a large part of it.

The most prominent American disciples of the German philosophers were the Transcendentalists, a group of Boston intellectuals led by Ralph Waldo Emerson. Emerson sought what he called 'the ideal' and set more store by consciousness than by appearance. 'The idealist takes his departure from his consciousness,' he wrote in 1843, 'and reckons the world as an appearance ... Mind is the only reality, of which men and all other natures are better or worse reflectors.' Since there was no established church in America it was left to the Roman Catholics to sniff out heresy: in a withering article called 'Protestantism ends in Transcendentalism' Orestes Brownson, a Roman Catholic journalist, predicted that the new religion would end by overthrowing Protestantism altogether. By claiming to put everyone in direct touch with the universal it did away with the need for ministers, for sacraments, for intermediaries of any kind.

Even less interested in intermediaries were the utopian communities which had been a feature of American life since the beginning of the century and were now proliferating at an astonishing rate. More than fifty such settlements were set up in the 1840s, far more than had appeared in any other decade, and most were concentrated in New York and neighbouring states. The latest was the Oneida community, established in New York State in February 1848 by John Noyes and his band of Bible Communists after they had been chased from Vermont by a hostile crowd. These sects looked forward – like Holyoake's correspondent in Paris they saw Communism as 'the Religion of the Future' – but they also looked back to the ideals of the early Christian church. 'The apostasy of the United States from their original principles in respect of slavery affords precisely the illustration that is needed,' wrote John Noyes, 'to set forth the backsliding of Christendom from the standard of original Christianity.' And like the early Christians the new sects had their martyrs. In 1844 the Mormon prophet Joseph Smith and his brother were shot dead by a mob which invaded the jail where they were being held. The murderers were acquitted and bands of rioters ranged through Illinois burning Mormon homes. *The Times*, always ready to castigate American lawlessness, was able to lick its lips over 'the threatened crusade for the extermination of the Mormonites'. It was worth remembering that when the Mormons had undertaken missions in England in 1837 and again in 1840 they had not been persecuted, even though their success had been sufficiently spectacular to make a body of Anglican clergy petition Parliament to act against them. It was difficult to know whether the hideous American fanaticism which Cumming detected came from the sects or from their persecutors.

At the beginning of 1848 the British sent a champion of orthodoxy to America. He was not a cleric but an astronomer, Professor John Pringle Nichol of Glasgow University, and he gave a series of lectures at the New York Mercantile Library Association premises in January and February. The *New York Tribune* sent Oliver Dyer, its expert phonographic writer, to take down every word the professor uttered. The poet Edward Young had once said that Christian devotion was 'the daughter of astronomy' and Nichol bore this out. Ignoring pantheism and metaphysics, ignoring the claims of the sects and the communities to have a direct and intimate relationship with infinity, he put God back on his throne and man back in his place as a humble and distant worshipper:

O what a world is this! Change rising above change, cycle growing out of cycle in majestic procession ... what must be the Creator, the Preserver, the Guide of all! He at whose bidding these phantasms come from nothingness and again disappear, whose Name – amid all things – alone is EXISTENCE – I AM THAT I AM! The All-Encompasser; the All-Sustainer! He enwraps, he upholds all those gorgeous Heavens! Reverentially before Him – humbly grateful that in the course of His beneficial arrangement He has permitted such intimation of His glory to reach us – let us conclude in the rapt language of the Psalmist: *How manifold, oh God, are thy works, by wisdom Thou hast made them all!*

A few blocks away, in the New York Society Library building, another lecturer was presenting a different picture of God's creation. During the previous summer and autumn, while Lyte had been walking the hills above Brixham composing 'Abide with me', Edgar Allan Poe had been pacing the heights above the Harlem river working out a view of the universe based on the doctrine of the inner consciousness. Now, on 3 February 1848, he made his ideas public in the form of a lecture on 'The Cosmogony of the Universe'. It was a cold night, the audience was sparse and Poe was profoundly disappointed, even though the *Tribune* said next morning that his lecture had been 'characterized by the strong analytical powers and intense capacity of imagination which distinguish him'. Some of his insights into the nature of the universe were startling – he declared, a lifetime before Einstein, that space and time were the same thing – while others were merely

31

idiosyncratic. But it was his unrepentant pantheism, his insistence that God was everywhere and that everything was God, which gave his lecture its driving force. He went further, proclaiming that every human being partook of divinity. 'This Heart Divine – what is it? *It is our own.* Each soul is, in part, its own God – its own creation.' Forty years earlier Wordsworth had suggested that there was life before birth: 'trailing clouds of glory do we come, From God, who is our home'. This idea had recently been incorporated into Christian belief by the Mormons and now Poe made it the keystone of his philosophy. 'We live out a youth peculiarly haunted by such dreams,' he said, referring to man's sense of the infinite, 'and yet never mistaking them for dreams. As Memories we know them. *During our youth* the distinction is too clear to deceive us even for a moment.' As the beginning, so the end: all would one day return to be part of the godhead. 'The sense of individual identity will be gradually merged in the general consciousness – Man, ceasing imperceptibly to feel himself Man, will at length attain that awfully triumphant epoch when he shall recognize his existence as that of Jehovah.'

So far it was only Cumming and the apocalyptic fanatics who saw the United States as the stamping-ground of Antichrist but they were soon to be joined by Samuel Wilberforce, Bishop of Oxford, who included American heresies among those which represented 'the first stealing over the sky of the lurid lights which shall be shed profusely around the great Antichrist.' He condemned pantheism roundly – 'the human soul cannot bear to be told that God is nowhere, but can be cajoled by the artful concealment of the same lie under the assertion that God is everywhere' – but he reserved his fiercest denunciations for American spiritualism, which he regarded as the final blasphemy. Spiritualism, even more than Poe's pantheism or the Bible Communism of the Oneida community, was the American version of the 1848 revolutions. It was in March 1848, as thrones tottered and Marx consigned the bourgeois God to the gravediggers, that the spirit of a dead man was said to have communicated with Katherine and Margaretta Fox in their cottage at Hydesville near New York. The Fox sisters later confessed that they had produced the so-called 'spirit rappings' themselves, but no amount of confessions or exposures could stop spiritualism's triumphant progress. One of its earliest historians, compiling her account 'at the command and under the supervision of the Wise and Mighty Beings through whose Instrumentality the Spiritual Telegraph of the Nineteenth Century has been constructed' was told that the house at Hydesville had been chosen 'as one peculiarly suited to their purpose from the fact of its being charged with the aura requisite to make it a battery for the working of the telegraph'.

Spiritualism brought to a climax the long reaction against the rationalism of the eighteenth century. The wise and mighty beings had apparently transformed the unreasonable into the reasonable, the supernatural into the natural. The greatest of all reasons for disbelieving in God, the conviction that there was nothing outside material existence, had now lost its power. Lyte's distinction between the glory of heaven and the vanity of earthly things, like Longfellow's insistence that the only reality lay beyond the grave, now stood vindicated. The spirit world might not be quite the heaven which the pious looked for but it was at least a life after death, a proof that the atheists had been wrong about the most important thing of all. If spiritualism could stand up to investigation the years of cold unbelief could perhaps be brought to an end. Whatever reservations orthodox Christians might have about earlier manifestations of unreason, about the metaphysics of the Germans or the enthusiasms of the Americans, they would surely now unite with spiritualists to confound the sceptics and demonstrate the immortality of the soul.

The orthodox did nothing of the sort. Long before Bishop Wilberforce launched his denunciations Christians feared that spiritualist manifestations were the work of Antichrist. Mrs Fox's first reaction, once she was convinced that the rappings were supernatural, was to worry in case her children had been possessed by an evil spirit. Just as Hamlet had concluded that his father's ghost came from hell or from purgatory so Christians throughout the ages had assumed that only the dead who were themselves troubled would have need to trouble the living. 'Do you think it's all a fraud and the spirits do not appear?' asked Hall Caine when Dante Gabriel Rossetti advised him not to go to a spiritualist séance. 'No,' Rossetti replied, 'but they're evil spirits – devils – and they're allowed to torment and deceive people.' As the son of a lifelong student of the occult and the nephew of the man who introduced the vampire into English literature, Rossetti very much wanted to get in touch with the dead, especially after his wife's suicide and her subsequent exhumation. Nevertheless he shunned spiritualism as a modern form of necromancy. *The Spirit World*, a spiritualist journal launched in London in May 1853, took such charges in its stride: 'If there are bad spirits there may be good,' it observed, 'equally powerful for good as the others for evil.' The comparison with past sorcerers was a gently ironic weapon in the hands of sceptics – 'all our present degenerate mediums would have to hide their heads in the presence of Cagliostro,' said Senator Shields of Illinois when he asked Congress to investigate spiritualism – but it was a very real one in the hands of ecclesiastical authority. When the medium Daniel Home went to Rome he was arraigned before the Inquisition and expelled from the city as a necromancer.

Nor did spiritualists always want to unite with Christians. 'Spiritualism is the acknowledgement of a fact, not the enunciation of a creed,' declared the London *Spiritual Herald* in April 1856. The American spiritualist Eliab Capron also refused to talk in terms of religious experience or divine intervention, even though his wife had been cured of an illness by a medium exerting healing powers at a distance and without her knowledge. He found that no two spirits agreed about the nature of truth and he thought they were in no better position than mortals to know whether or not God existed. 'I see nothing in the new revelations that would of necessity lead an atheist to change his views,' he concluded. Many of the spirits were American Indians who knew little of Christianity and who tended to manifest themselves, perhaps not entirely coincidentally, after the publication of Longfellow's *Hiawatha* in 1855 had highlighted the Indian's mysterious affinity with elemental forces. Meanwhile in the summer of 1852 dead John Murray sought out John Spear, a medium who was also a clergyman, in order to deliver 'important instructions to the inhabitants of the earth'. Mortals must stop regarding Jesus as a god and they must also give up heaven and hell. 'All goes on in infinite progression,' Murray explained, 'that poor, foolish, unwise man – he goes into a lower state; and there are those ready to welcome him, to teach him; and, as rapidly as possible, to raise him from that estate to a higher and more perfect condition.'

This confounding of the virtuous and the wicked was particularly galling to the devout. 'A miserable debauchee like Poe, who lived without the thought of a Redeemer, dies and straightway through a "medium" announces himself to be in glory!' cried *Blackwood's Magazine* indignantly when Edgar Allan Poe manifested himself in a spiritualist séance shortly after his death in 1849. If there was indeed an 'infinite progression' then Poe had vaulted infinity with deplorable ease. Clearly there was no tedious delay in the grave, no waiting for the Last Trumpet, no eventual emergence of an incorruptible body. Heaven's morning would break at the moment of death just as Lyte had hoped and it would break for saint and sinner alike, welcoming them as disembodied souls and freeing them from the physical frame and its supposedly sinful appetites. There would be no raging Antichrist, no apocalyptic horsemen, no bursting of bodies from graves, no coming of Christ in glory to judge both the quick and the dead, none of the spectacular cosmic happenings that Dr Cumming and Bishop Wilberforce predicted. It was hardly surprising that both men saw spiritualism as being itself a manifestation of Antichrist and a sign of his imminent arrival.

Nevertheless they were in the minority, not only because of their apocalyptic predictions but also because of their view of the afterlife. Tennyson's *In Memoriam*, published in London in May 1850 before spiritualism had made much impact in Britain, rested on a view of the next world which was even less orthodox than the hopes expressed in 'Abide with me'. Far from being mere suspended dust, trapped in cold earth until time should end, the dead were already in glory and could enter the hearts and minds of the living. Tennyson was convinced that his dead friend Arthur Hallam could see into his inmost soul, could 'look me through and through', and he decided – after some understandable hesitation – that this prospect must be welcomed. The poem quickly became a best seller and Tennyson was able to get married on the strength of it: his fiancée's father had opposed the match for ten years but now at last the success of *In Memoriam* made him give in. The Queen and her husband Prince Albert read the poem eagerly and before the end of the year Tennyson was made Poet Laureate. When the Queen opened the Great Exhibition in Hyde Park a few months later *The Times* remarked that the scene was like the coming Day of Judgement, 'that day when all ages and climes shall be gathered round the throne of their MAKER'. It did not, however, venture to rebuke the Poet Laureate for releasing the dead from their coffins in advance of that momentous occasion. Popular belief and enlightened opinion were anticipating the spiritualists and turning away from the darker aspects of Christian orthodoxy.

When the British and the French attacked Sebastopol at the beginning of the Crimean War Dr Cumming's friends pointed out excitedly that in Greek the word 'Sebastopol' meant what 'Armageddon' meant in Hebrew. Even *The Times* admitted that 'in the turmoil and excitement of the fight many fancied they beheld the preliminary skirmishes

35

which were to lead us to the grand battle of Armageddon'. According to the Book of Revelation this last great combat would take place when 'the spirits of devils, working miracles, go forth unto the kings of the earth and of the whole world to gather them to the battle of that great day of God Almighty'. In April 1855 one of Elizabeth Barrett Browning's friends wrote to ask whether she thought Cumming was right. 'That *you* should ask me about "Armageddon" is most assuredly a sign of the times,' she replied, 'I don't, for the rest, like Dr Cumming. His books seem to me very narrow ... The end of the world is probably the end of a dispensation. What I expect is a great development of Christianity in opposition to the churches'. England in particular, she thought, would need to be shaken out of its smugness: 'I begin to think that nothing will do for England but a good revolution and a "besom of destruction" used dauntlessly.' In August of that year, after attending a séance conducted by Daniel Home, she wrote to tell her sister that spiritualism would be at the heart of the new dispensation:

You may be quite sure that these things are developing themselves, even here in England, more and more, though the secret of them is being kept in order to avoid the derision of a sceptical public. Lord Stanley said to Sir Edward Lytton, a few days back, that the government should appoint a committee of investigation so as to get as far as possible at the facts ... A very little patience and we shall not speak such things in a whisper: *for it is but the beginning*.

There was no committee of investigation but an impressive number of influential people in London society were converted to spiritualism. In August 1860 Thackeray's *Cornhill Magazine* printed an article called 'Stranger than Fiction' describing a séance held by Daniel Home at the London house of the President of the Board of Trade, Thomas Milner-Gibson. It told how Home had been miraculously raised four or five feet above his chair and then placed in a horizontal position – 'he said he felt as if he had been turned in the gentlest manner as a child is turned in the arms of a nurse' – before floating backwards and forwards in the air for several minutes. All this had taken place in the presence of eight or nine distinguished ladies and gentlemen. It was hard to believe that the spirits were merely communicating with the living. They seemed much more concerned to overawe the living by showing off their supernatural powers. Cumming did not doubt that they were emissaries of Antichrist seeking to infiltrate the ranks of the powerful: he had recently published yet another apocalyptic best seller saying that the growth of spiritualism in Boston and other American cities showed how close was the end of all things. Another of Antichrist's tentacles, the Roman Catholic Church, had made its latest bid for dominion by re-establishing the popish hierarchy in England in 1850 and by holding its first Plenary Council in the United States in 1852. And for good measure there had been 'a star of almost supernatural brilliancy' over the Holy Land in 1857. It was small wonder that another prophet, P.S. Desprez, published two triumphant editions of *Apocalypse Fulfilled* to prove that the Second Coming had already taken place.

In February 1861 the *Revue des Deux Mondes* in Paris published an article by Edmond Schérer proclaiming the death of God. 'I cannot think of these things,' he said, speaking of current varieties of unbelief, 'without remembering that voice which rang out long ago across the deep to tell man that the great God Pan was dead ... Now the voice sounds once more in the world, telling us of the end of another age, of the last moments of another God. The absolute is dead in the souls of men: who will bring it back to life?' *The Times* had recently recommended the *Revue des Deux Mondes* to its readers as being 'the only periodical publication in France pretending to anything like independence', but this was more like irresponsibility than independence. It was time for all men of weight and influence to unite in defence of orthodoxy, especially as a group of Anglican clerics had recently published *Essays and Reviews*, a collection of articles which propagated many of the dangerous German heresies. A formal denunciation of the book by the Archbishop of Canterbury was published on the day after Schérer's article appeared. Bishop Wilberforce arranged for the publication of a volume of replies and it was in the preface to this work, written in December 1861, that he provided a postscript to Schérer's epitaph on God by announcing the arrival of Antichrist. It could be no mere coincidence, he thundered, that so many insolent objections to Holy Writ were being put forward at the same time:

Much more true is the explanation which sees in it the first stealing over the sky of the lurid lights which shall be shed profusely around the great Antichrist. For these difficulties gather their strength from a spirit of lawless rejection of all authority, from a daring claim for the unassisted human intellect to be able to discover, measure and explain all things ... Thus the pride of man's heart is flattered to the utmost; thus the old whisper, 'Ye shall be as gods,' disguises itself in newest utterances. Such a state of the human mind may be traced with more or less distinctiveness during this century everywhere in Christendom. It may be seen speculating in German metaphysics, fluttering in French literature, blaspheming in American spiritualism.

It was perhaps unfortunate that the bishop's indignation should culminate in a denunciation of spiritualism at this particular moment. Thirty miles away, in the Blue Room at Windsor Castle, Prince Albert lay dying. The end came at a quarter to eleven on the night of 14 December and for Queen Victoria it was the end of the world. 'My life as a happy one is ended,' she told her uncle Leopold, 'the world is gone for me!' She found consolation in a view of the afterlife that owed more to *In Memoriam* and to the spiritualists than to Christian orthodoxy. 'He is near me,' she cried desperately, 'his spirit will guide and inspire me!' Dr Cumming was quick to adjust his views and within a matter of days he had preached and published two sermons under the title *From Life to Life*. The spirit of the dead Prince Albert was indeed able to speak to the living, he declared, and all the Queen's subjects must 'let the voice that comes from a shroud be heard.' 'It is generally understood,' *The Spiritual Magazine* announced in October 1864, 'that Her Majesty holds constant communion with the spirit of Prince Albert. A statement to the same effect has been widely circulated by the Continental and American press.' The widowing of Queen Victoria, rather than her accession, was the real beginning of the Victorian age. It opened with talk of Antichrist's triumph and God's death but what was really in prospect was the painful dismembering of the image of Antichrist and the equally painful recasting of the image of God.

3 THE HARROWING OF HELL

On 30 March 1842, at Jefferson in the state of Georgia, Crawford W. Long gave sulphuric ether to James Venables before removing a tumour from his neck. The operation was a success and the patient felt no pain. Long used ether in several more operations during the next few months but did not communicate his discovery to the medical world. In 1844 at Hartford in Connecticut Horace Wells, a dentist, inhaled nitrous oxide before having a tooth extracted. He felt no pain and he suggested to his partner W.T.G. Morton that the technique could be used in major surgery; but Morton was more interested in ether, which he administered on 16 October 1846 at the Massachusetts General Hospital during an operation performed by John Collins Warren. The operation was successful and within a month an account of it was given to the American Academy of Sciences and published in the *Boston Medical and Surgical Journal*. Long and Wells contested Morton's claim to have pioneered the new painless surgery and Wells continued his experiments until he became addicted to chloroform. Early in 1848, while under its influence, he created a disturbance in New York and was locked up in the city prison, where he committed suicide.

Up to this time the only known form of painless surgery had been that undertaken under hypnosis or 'Mesmeric Sleep', which was by no means infallible. A strikingly successful operation was performed in March 1844 at Sedgley in Staffordshire. It was an amputation, the removal of a finger, and the room was thronged with 'medical and other gentlemen'. 'The cutting of the flaps and the dividing of the bone by the nippers was watched with breathless anxiety by all present,' reported the *Wolverhampton Chronicle*, 'but not a muscle quivered, nor did a sigh escape, nor any single thing occur to betray the slightest sensation. During the dressing the hand was suspended

39

over the table in a cataleptic state without any further support.' Even though such results could be achieved in cases where patients were susceptible to hypnotism, for most people surgery of any kind meant appalling suffering. But now at last, as medical men took in the good news from Boston, anaesthesia became a reality on both sides of the Atlantic. By January 1847 the distinguished obstetrician Professor James Simpson of Edinburgh was giving ether to relieve the pain of childbirth. Later in the year he and other doctors switched to chloroform as being safer and more effective. In 1853 it was administered to Queen Victoria when Prince Leopold was born. With startling suddenness there had taken place a revolution in medical practice, a revolution which the American physician Weir Mitchell summed up as 'the death of pain'.

The phrase was a good deal too sweeping. The agony of surgery was only a fraction, albeit a ghastly fraction, of man's inheritance of pain. The immemorial burden of human suffering could not be so easily lifted. But at least a start had been made. Doctors were quick to see that if surgery was less painful it would be more painstaking. Speed was no longer paramount, so that more care could be taken and the chances of success greatly improved. Short-term alleviation of pain meant long-term alleviation of suffering. Even more important was the new attitude to pain which anaesthetics brought. 'They altogether destroy,' proclaimed the *Westminster Review*, 'the old belief in physical suffering having an expiatory purpose.' Such suffering need no longer be regarded as a necessary and ultimately beneficial aspect of the human condition but as an enemy to be conquered. War had been declared and the first battle won.

On the face of things it would seem that Christians must be on the side of the doctors both in the battle and in the war. Christ had been concerned to relieve suffering, sometimes by means which seemed miraculous, and he had told his followers that by faith they would do the same. For centuries Christians had claimed that their religion was a caring and compassionate one which contrasted with the callous inhumanity of the heathen. 'Barbarian', which had once meant anybody outside the world of Greece and Rome, now meant anybody outside Christian civilization; and 'barbarity', savage and unmitigated cruelty, was the distinguishing mark of such people. It was also, in Protestant eyes, the distinguishing mark of Roman Catholicism. The British had had two Catholic monarchs since the Reformation, Mary Tudor and James II. Mary was known as 'Bloody Mary' and James

40

was known for the 'Bloody Assizes', while Protestant cruelties in other reigns were unremembered.

Unfortunately there were those even in the Protestant English-speaking world who used Christianity as an excuse for the deliberate and savage infliction of pain. 'John McCue of Augusta county in Virginia, a Presbyterian preacher, frequently on the Lord's day tied up his slaves and whipped them,' reported *The Times* in February 1841, 'and left them bound while he went to the meeting house and preached, and after his return repeated the scourging.' Mrs Pence, also of Virginia, did the same except that she put a 'negro plaster' of salt, pepper and vinegar on the raw backs of her slave girls to make the pain fiercer while she went to church 'demure as a nun' between their first and their second floggings. When asked whether it was fitting to do this on a Sunday she pointed out that if she whipped them on any other day she would lose a day's work. It was important to make proper use of the sabbath. 'Their backs get well enough by Monday morning,' she concluded crisply. A few months later the United States census returns showed that there were about two and a half million slaves, well over a sixth of the nation's population, who were liable to be treated in this way. In May 1846 the negro abolitionist Frederick Douglass told a shocked London audience that slavery was 'identified with religion and exposes those who denounce it to the charge of infidelity'. 'The church and the slave prison stand next to each other,' he added, 'the groans and cries of the heartbroken slave are often drowned in the pious devotions of his religious master.'

The accusations were thrown back at the accusers. When a posse of Kentucky slavers crossed into Ohio in December 1844 and beat up several respectable citizens whom they suspected of sheltering runaway slaves, burning down their houses for good measure, the *New York Sun* insisted that the affair was prompted by the rabid anti-slavery propaganda put out by misguided Christians in London. *Punch* replied with a wry comment on President Polk's inauguration in 1845: 'It is not generally known – and the touching circumstance ought to be published to the whole world – that the Bible on which Mr Polk took the presidential oath was very handsomely bound for the purpose in the skin of a negro.' The revelation, macabre though it was, did at least suggest that there were skins sufficiently unscarred to be used for bookbinding. According to one historian visitors to the southern states seldom told of 'anything but the most inconsequential whipping, nothing like, indeed, what the traditional English

41

schoolboy expected and endured in many of the public schools in those days.' In 1842, as if anticipating this countercharge, Charles Dickens dealt both with the whipping of slaves and with the birching of schoolboys in *American Notes*, a book which gave great offence across the Atlantic. He attacked the 'foul growth and tangled root' of American life, giving as instances of it not only the horrifying treatment of negroes but also the appalling insolence and arrogance of white American youngsters, which he attributed to the fact that they were not properly birched.

British attitudes to corporal punishment had extremely tangled roots. The birch, as Phillipe Ariès has remarked, was 'above all an opportunity for the boy being flogged to exercise self-control, the first duty of an English gentleman.' Nor was stoicism under the rod a gentleman's monopoly. At all levels of society it was thought right to beat children frequently and severely, not only because the Bible advised it but also because it did them good by teaching them to endure pain. Dr Johnson's schoolmaster told him that he whipped him to save him from the gallows but he might equally well have said that he did it to steel him against the surgeon's knife. In a world in which pain was unavoidable fortitude was not merely a virtue but a necessity. Initiation rites, ceremonies in which boys were ritually tortured in order to prepare them to be warriors, were far older than Christianity. By advising the mortification of the flesh against the assaults of Satan, rather than the brave endurance of the wounds of combat, Christianity merely produced variations on a theme. It was perhaps strange that a religion which made a virtue out of relieving pain should also make a virtue out of its well-meaning infliction and its dutiful acceptance. While Mr McCue and Mrs Pence whipped their slaves in order to make sure that they remained their inferiors, British schoolmasters whipped their charges in order to make sure that they became their equals.

Both kinds of infliction could quote biblical authority, for the stark truth was that pain was approved and endorsed by God. 'I will greatly multiply thy sorrow and thy conception,' he had told Eve angrily after she had persuaded Adam to eat the forbidden fruit, 'in sorrow thou shalt bring forth children.' Could such sorrow be lightly dispelled? If Professor Simpson did away with it by the use of chloroform was he flying in the face of God? The pangs of childbirth were only a beginning: 'we know that the whole creation groaneth and travaileth in pain until now,' St Paul had written. Pain had been the key to

God's plan for the world ever since Adam and Eve had offended him. The agony his son had suffered upon the cross had brought the chance of redemption – hence St Paul's 'until now' – but it had not been universally accepted. There was still sin in the world and so there must still be pain. Indeed Christ taught that pain in this world might be the only way to avoid far greater pain in the next. 'If thy hand offend thee, cut it off,' he advised, 'it is better for thee to enter into life maimed than having two hands to go into hell, into the fire that never shall be quenched.' There was added point to the advice now that the hand could be amputated painlessly, especially since there was no evidence that chloroform would be available in hell. There pain still reigned supreme, just as it had reigned when Christ had redeemed the world. It was difficult to believe that the torture of God's son would have been efficacious had it been carried out under a general anaesthetic.

Yet it was equally difficult to believe that God revelled in human suffering or would resent the relief which anaesthetics had brought. The Greeks had thought of all life's afflictions as being wished on mankind by Zeus himself: the king of the gods had sent Pandora down to earth knowing full well that she would open her box and let loose every evil upon the world. The Christian myths which fleshed out the skeletal account given in Genesis were more respectful. Milton summed them up in *Paradise Lost* when he pictured Satan buying his way out of hell by promising sin and death that they would henceforth have dominion over mankind. It was not just sin but pain and suffering as well, 'death and all our woe', that had come into the world once Eve had eaten the apple. God had seen to it that all evil and all pain were confined securely in hell but Satan's rebellion had led first to their being released and then to their being let loose upon mankind as retribution for sin. Hell was the source of present and temporal pains as well as the home of future and eternal ones.

But there was also a belief, admittedly based on extremely slender scriptural evidence, that between his death and his resurrection Christ had gone down into hell in order to secure the release of all those who had had the misfortune to be born between Adam's original sin and the redemption of mankind. The harrowing of hell, as this divine gesture was called, was a concession wrung from Satan by the power of the cross as an instrument of torture. Christ had been able to defy the foul fiend not merely because he was God but because of the agony of his death. And for nearly two thousand years, in fact and

43

in fiction, Christians had held out the cross as a sure defence against the forces of hell. 'We wrestle,' St Paul had said, 'not against flesh and blood, but against principalities and powers, against the rulers of the darkness of this world.' Yet it was flesh and blood, the torn flesh and the spilt blood of an incarnate God, which could defeat those powers and dispel that darkness. Hell was the kingdom of pain, actual bodily pain, and its tribute could only be paid in its own currency. It must have been created by God, in order to be available as a place of punishment for the fallen angels, and so he must have decreed its laws. He had had a share in the birth of pain, but the harrowing of hell, like the crucifixion itself, suggested that it was a share he had cause to regret. Now that the death of pain was in prospect, now that man was moving in for the kill, God would surely wish to play his part.

As anaesthetics and spiritualism crossed the Atlantic the scene was set for this new harrowing of hell. It was not so much a matter of changing the nature of God as of seeing it clearly for the first time. Just as God had once saved man from being hell's victim so man would now rescue God from being hell's master. The responsibility for creating evil and ordaining pain, loaded upon God by superstitious Christians of the past, must be lifted by enlightened Christians of the present. Frances Power Cobbe, an eager though unorthodox Christian journalist, spelled out the challenge: 'the current teaching of our present divines shall grow unendurable and we shall insist that to the All Righteous All Merciful God shall be attributed no longer deeds and modes of government we should abhor as unjust and cruel from a despot of the earth.' The inspiration for the campaign against hell came from America: it was there that the frontiers of pain's domain had been rolled back and the notion of bodily resurrection dispelled. But the campaign itself could not be fought in America because there was nothing to fight, no established church whose dogmas could be challenged. Hell's destruction must be achieved in the old world or not at all.

Predictably enough the first shot was fired by George Holyoake. It was fired not against the Church of England but against Roman Catholicism, which he saw as 'the predominant religious influence of Europe and the great enemy of philosophy and freedom'. In the spring of 1850, just as Tennyson published his bland and sanitized vision of the hereafter in *In Memoriam*, Holyoake ran a series of articles in *The Reasoner* in which he summarized Pinamonti's *Hell Opened to*

Christians. There was nothing bland or sanitized here: Holyoake gave his readers all the horror of the original, with its emphasis not only on the fires of torment but also on the filth and the stench of the bottomless pit: 'as in dead bodies worms are engendered from putrefaction, so in the damned there arises a perpetual remorse from the corruption of sin.' 'Its effects on the imagination of children and sympathetic women are appalling to contemplate,' Holyoake commented, 'To these brimstonian tortures Roman Catholics consign all who do not believe in Popery; and Protestants all who do not believe in the Bible; so that, if both churches are right, a very small portion of the human race have any chance of going to heaven.'

Anglicans were genuinely worried by the attacks on hell and by the problem of God's apparent responsibility for sin and for its punishment. The anonymous author of *The Bible History of Satan* tried to solve it by denying that the Prince of Darkness was a fallen angel at all. 'It is infinitely more likely,' he declared, 'that the Devil has existed from eternity as an evil spirit.' In the end God would destroy him and there would be no more evil. 'Reason may cavil at the delay,' he concluded, 'but cannot deny the omnipotence of the act, and must admit that God's toleration of sin for a season is self-imposed, and not from external necessity.' Catholics made no concessions. In Dublin Father Furniss published *The Sight of Hell*, one of a series of tracts for children. It told of one little girl who was wearing a bonnet of fire for ever because she had been too fond of pretty clothes while she was alive. 'It is pressed down close over her head,' Furniss assured his young readers, 'it burns into the skin, it scorches the bone of the skull and makes it smoke.' In another fiery dungeon he found a boy whose eyeballs were alight, bursting out of his head with a noise like a kettle on the boil, while his blood was liquid fire which ate into the very marrow of his bones. When questioned the lad admitted that he deserved this punishment because he had frequented dance halls and theatres. More than four million of these tracts were printed and the publishers reported that *The Sight of Hell* sold particularly well because of 'attacks by enemies of the Church'. Furniss's biographer declared that the tracts would be found 'of incalculable utility for school and family use', especially now that the doctrine of hell was being questioned by 'whatever is unsound and vague in the Protestant mind'.

In the eyes of the orthodox, Catholic and Anglican alike, the unsoundness and vagueness of the Protestant mind came indubitably from Germany. Progressive thinkers were equally sure that German philosophy and German biblical criticism constituted the best defence against papal tyranny. The Americans might well save themselves, as many German Catholics had done, by setting up their own Catholic church. The *New York Herald* proclaimed proudly that republicanism bred a spirit of freedom, in religious as in secular matters, and that there might soon be an independent Catholic church in the United States with its own American pope. But if Protestant Europe was to escape what one contributor to *Essays and Reviews* called 'those shadows of the twelfth century which with ominous recurrence are closing round us', it must look to Germany for its salvation.

At first *Essays and Reviews* was favourably received. 'We cannot but honour,' wrote the *Spectator* in April 1860, 'the men who have so courageously set the example of "open teaching" in the Church of England'. It was the atheist Frederic Harrison, writing in the September issue of the *Westminster Review*, who deliberately goaded the ecclesiastical authorities into taking action against the book. 'No fair mind can close this volume,' he claimed, 'without feeling it to be at bottom in direct antagonism to the whole system of popular belief.' It replaced the orthodox doctrine of hell with 'idealized damnation' and it showed that Anglican intellectual circles were 'honeycombed with disbelief'. Why then had it not been condemned? 'Nowhere,' he continued, 'has there been seen or heard a sign of official repudiation. These professors, tutors, principals and masters still hold their chairs and retain their influence. No authorized rebuke has been put forward.' Stung by Harrison's mockery, Bishop Wilberforce reviewed the book in the *Quarterly Review* for January 1861 and declared that its contributors were heretics. 'Holding their views, they cannot, consistently with moral honesty, maintain their posts as clergymen of the Established Church'. He then set to work to make sure that the Church condemned the book and punished its authors.

Once again it was Edmond Schérer in the *Revue des Deux Mondes* who saw the significance of what was going on. In May 1861, just three months after his announcement of the death of God, he published an article called 'The Crisis of Protestantism in England'. 'Do you know what pre-occupies and excites the English at this moment?' he wrote, 'It is not Armstrong guns or armour-plated warships or the affairs of China or the Lebanon; it is not the budget or the famine in India; it is not even Garibaldi or the crisis in the cotton industry. It is a book, a book whose innocuous title, *Essays and Reviews*, gives no hint of the tempest it has unleashed.' In his view the storm was about the part which myth and fantasy should play in religion. Roman Catholicism accepted them because it knew that man could not live by reason alone. The Church of England, poised between Catholicism and Protestantism, had managed hitherto to combine the religion of myth and the religion of reason. Now it was being forced to choose and the choice was about the nature of religious myths as well as the nature of supposedly rational doctrines. It was the future of Christianity, not just the future of the Church of England, which was at stake.

Also at stake was the future of hell. At the outset it had played a minor part in the argument. All that had been said in *Essays and Reviews* was that 'we must entertain a hope that there shall be found, after the great adjudication, receptacles where the stunted may become strong and the perverted be restored'. It was a kindly and comparatively harmless suggestion, certainly not as destructive of Christian doctrine as many other things in the book, but it quickly became the thing upon which the whole volume was judged. Henry Bristow Wilson, the man who had written it, was one of the only two contributors who were parish priests and thus subject to the authority of the bishops. The other was Rowland Williams, who had denied that the Bible was literally true or divinely inspired. Both were found guilty by a church court and suspended from their benefices for a year. 'This apparently interminable case', as *The Times* called it, was then referred to the Judicial Committee of the Privy Council, headed by the Lord Chancellor, which mulled it over for eight months. Edward Pusey, Professor of Hebrew at Oxford and a doughty champion of Anglican dogma, kept hell in the public eye by telling how a man had plucked his sleeve in a crowded street and told him: 'Dr Pusey, I have been burning in hell the last hour for that lie I told you.' He had then gone to the man's house and discovered he had died an hour earlier. Nevertheless the Lord Chancellor's Committee finally reversed the sentences in February 1864. Little was heard about Williams but much about the Committee's ruling that Wilson must be acquitted because the doctrine of eternal punishment formed no part of the teaching of the Church of England. 'He dismissed hell with costs,' said the *Spectator* of the Lord Chancellor in words quickly taken up by other journals, 'and took away from orthodox members of the Church of England their last hope of everlasting damnation'.

Orthodox members of the Church of England determined to fight to the last for their unforgiving God. *The Times* insisted that the two defendants had only escaped 'by the skin of their teeth' and that there was no parish in the country which would not throw them out if they dared to preach such heresies. Wilberforce persuaded Convocation to pronounce a 'synodical condemnation' of *Essays and Reviews*, while Pusey set up a committee which sent out to all Anglican clergy a declaration of belief in eternal punishment. Less than half of the clergy signed and some wrote in fury to the newspapers saying that they would resist this 'hateful tyranny' and throw the document into the waste-paper basket. John Keble wrote *A Litany of Our Lord's Warnings for the Present Distress*, addressed to 'all those whose hearts are aching at the recent decision of the Privy Council touching the eternal punishment of the wicked'. How many souls would be damned, he wondered, now that priests could lie to their flocks and tell them there was a chance of the wicked escaping the eternal flames? 'Only think what men and women risk as it is,' he shuddered, 'knowing as they do our Lord's awful words and as yet untaught how to explain them away; what will it be when the Evil One has met them and put this word into their mouths?' Keble followed up his tract with a letter to *The Times* demanding an inquiry into the powers of the Privy Council. 'Men are free to think they should have a Church without dogma,' he concluded, 'but they are also free to think they should have one *with* dogma.'

The final humiliation of hell's defenders took place in the House of Lords on Friday 15 July 1864 and was brought about by Lord Houghton, who combined outward piety with an encyclopaedic knowledge of pornography and had been nominated by Thomas Carlyle for the office of 'Perpetual President of the Heaven and Hell Amalgamation Society'. Houghton asked whether Convocation had any right to make its much-publicized 'synodical condemnation', whereupon the Lord Chancellor replied that Convocation was a futile body which had only recently been allowed to resume business after being suspended for more than a century. Its ridiculous pronouncements had no significance and if it continued to make them it would have to be suspended again 'to check its eccentricities'. The Church of England was by law established and so the law must have the last word. Pusey preached a final defiant sermon, declaring that the fires of hell burned for evermore, and there the matter rested until 1876, when the Privy Council once again quashed an ecclesiastical decision. The Rev. Flavel Smith Cook had been supported by the church courts when he refused

Communion to a certain Henry Jenkins because he did not believe in the Devil. The Privy Council ruled that belief in the Devil was no part of Anglican doctrine and ordered Cook to administer the sacrament. As the Prince of Darkness went the way of eternal torment hell's new harrowers could celebrate total victory.

But had they been fighting on the wrong field of battle? Harrison's initial challenge had not been about legal decisions but about 'the whole system of popular belief'. The Lord Chancellor for all his powers could not do much about popular belief. Tennyson had edged it along a little with his *In Memoriam*, but even he could not entirely shake off older and cruder visions of the hereafter. A few weeks after the poem's publication he and his bride found themselves in a house full of strange nocturnal noises. When they were told it was haunted by the spirit of a murdered child they left hurriedly. Their own first child was accidentally strangled at birth and died unbaptized. 'I thy father love thee and weep over thee,' said Tennyson sadly, 'though thou hast no place in the universe.' Popular belief – and Tennyson's belief too, it seemed – still feared that only sacramental technicalities could admit a human soul to the divine mercy. And the end of the story mirrored its beginning: when the Privy Council decided against Cook his parishioners presented him with a testimonial, paid his legal costs and made it clear to Jenkins that he must not insist on receiving Communion. A quarter of a century of controversy had done a lot at the legal level but very little at the level of popular belief.

Nor had spiritualism changed conventional attitudes as much as might have been expected. When the London *Spirit World* was set up in May 1853 its very first issue told how Mrs Hayden, the American medium who had recently arrived in England, had been put in touch with her dead child. 'The Good Shepherd has taken into his ever loving arms the sweet innocent lambkin,' she had been assured, 'that you may follow to the fold of heavenly love.' Although the orthodox clearly knew more about the parameters of paradise – Queen Victoria's chaplain published a useful little book called *The Recognition of Friends in Heaven*, while the Rev. Richard Shimeall of New York plotted heaven's exact astronomical position – the spiritualists were not far behind. They also received accounts which came close to traditional visions of posthumous punishment. When the Tsar of Russia died in 1855 the spirits told their mortal contacts that he had been shut up in an iron cage to curb his haughtiness.

In addition spiritualists showed a ghoulish interest in the corpses whose total irrelevance they had originally proclaimed. In 1860 the *Spiritual Magazine* printed with some excitement a piece about 'singular displacement of coffins in a vault in a burying ground', even though the events described had taken place forty years earlier and thousands of miles away on the island of Barbados. It could have been the work of no human hand, the journal declared solemnly, pointing out that two of the bodies had been those of suicides. A later issue contained a report on a vault in Wiltshire where the coffin of the local squire had turned itself round and risen several feet in the air. In view of such revelations it was not surprising that the advent of spiritualism did little or nothing to check the growing popularity of tales of horror about vampires and other manifestations of the undead. Soon the National Association of Spiritualists in London was proudly exhibiting casts of spirit hands and spirit feet. These had remained intact even after the spirit limbs had dissolved and disappeared – 'a thing manifestly impossible had they encased any human limb'. 'This corruptible must put on incorruption,' St Paul had written in explanation of the resurrection of the body. Now it seemed that the supposedly disembodied spirits were doing just that. What had begun as a challenge to orthodoxy had now become suspiciously like an endorsement of it.

Meanwhile pain was an unconscionable time dying. The anaesthetists might be smothering it but there were many who had an interest in keeping it alive. Sarah Potter, keeper of a whipping brothel in Chelsea, was arrested in July 1863 while the future of hell was still unresolved. She fell foul of the authorities because she forced her girls to let her clients flog them, but in most of these places it was the client who suffered the pain. It had been said of Theresa Berkley, queen of the profession, that 'her instruments of torture were more numerous than those of any other governess ... at her shop, whoever went with plenty of money could be tortured till he had a belly full.' By the time she died in 1836 there were at least ten such establishments in London and the number increased during the next quarter of a century. The 1860s and early 1870s also saw an impressive number of pornographic or semi-pornographic works portraying flagellation in schoolrooms and in bedrooms with equal and impartial gusto. It was Henry Salt, an old Etonian with considerable experience of the birch, who pointed out that 'Spare the rod and spoil the child' had been said not by King Solomon in the Bible but by a lascivious lady in an erotic seventeenth-century poem. 'Love is a boy, by poets styl'd,

Then spare the rod and spoil the child,' she had told her lover when he seemed reluctant to submit to aphrodisiac flagellation.

It was not only the grimly sadistic rulers of the great English public schools who needed Salt's reminder. The Wiltshire curate Francis Kilvert was the gentlest of men and yet he could commend a little girl's parents who 'very wisely have not spared her nor the rod' while remarking of another child whose bottom he glimpsed while she was on a swing that 'her flesh was plump and smooth and in excellent whipping condition'. Nor did he spare his own flesh: 'I sat down in my bath upon a sheet of thick ice which broke in the middle into large pieces,' he wrote one Christmas morning, 'whilst sharp points and jagged edges stuck all round the sides of the tub like chevaux de frise, not particularly comforting to the naked thighs and loins, for the keen ice cut like broken glass.' While disciplinarians and ascetics made sure that the pains of this world survived the advent of anaesthetics, theological subtleties did the same for the pains of hell. If bodily pain could be killed by deadening the mind, wrote Gerard Manley Hopkins, then it must exist in the mind irrespective of the body. God could therefore inflict bodily torture on souls in hell even though their actual bodies had been consumed by worms or by fire.

Even English law could not dispense with hell as easily as the Lord Chancellor might think. In 1860, just as the row over *Essays and Reviews* was getting under way, Mrs Maden of Rochdale in Lancashire sued her stepfather for damages because he had refused to let her take her piano with her when she left his house to marry an atheist of whom he disapproved. She had become an atheist herself and for this reason the judge in the county court would not let her take the oath or proceed with her case. It would he a mockery, he said, because she did not believe in hell. How could the court possibly accept the evidence of someone who did not know that she would be tortured for ever if she failed to tell the truth? The Rochdale Secular Society, encouraged by the publicity given to the case in *The Reasoner* and in Parliament, raised money for a re-trial and then for an appeal. At every level the original ruling was upheld: those who did not believe in hell could not give evidence and so could not have recourse to the law. Holyoake's friend Sir John Trelawny brought a Bill before Parliament to allow atheists to affirm instead of taking the oath, but he was told he was endangering the whole fabric of society and so consideration of his measure was adjourned indefinitely. The same thing happened in 1862 and 1863, after which he gave up the attempt.

On Sunday 1 July 1860, as Mrs Maden embarked on her attempt to recover her piano, Arthur Munby went to Oxford for the day. He was a Cambridge man, an unsuccessful barrister who worked at the London office of the Ecclesiastical Commissioners, but he had friends in Oxford who were quick to welcome him and tell him about the dramatic confrontation which had taken place there at the previous day's meeting of the British Association for the Advancement of Science. Bishop Wilberforce, seeking to ridicule Darwin's theory of evolution, had asked Professor Huxley whether he would rather have a man or an ape for an ancestor. Huxley had replied that an ape would be preferable to a man like Wilberforce who sought to obscure scientific truth with religious prejudice. Munby's friends assured him that this was the end as far as belief in the literal truth of the Bible was concerned – 'defence is no longer possible – the controversy has been pushed to the last point and that will soon be given up' – but Munby insisted that even if science excluded God from the natural world he personally would still regard him as supreme in the moral world. 'Even if Love be not Power, I will yet believe in Love: I must and will have a Father in Heaven, and a Christ too, if I have even to create them out of old memories and tottering beliefs. In religion, at least, let us be allowed to live through the Imagination if we can find no stronger aliment.' Three weeks later, when he came home one evening to discover that he had been robbed of some silver and a favourite coat, Munby found that he needed a God of retribution as well as a God of love. 'I feel a magnanimous pity for the miscreant,' he noted in his diary, 'I will enjoy my triumphs over him if he is caught: and if not I know – blessed thought! – that he will suffer for his doings in a future world.'

Munby was typical of the many thousands of devout Christians on both sides of the Atlantic who saw the publication of *The Origin of Species* in 1859 as a threat to their faith. The challenge to the Book of Genesis, the suggestion that man was the descendant of an ape rather than the image of God, was the most obviously alarming thing in the book but not necessarily the most fundamental. More important was Darwin's insistence on competition and conflict as the instruments of all evolution and progress. Karl Marx welcomed this as 'a basis in natural science for the class struggle in history' and Lord Houghton's young protégé Algernon Charles Swinburne went further, proclaiming that 'if we would be at one with nature let us continually do evil with all our might'. Herbert Spencer had already declared in 1852 that 'the survival of the fittest' was the determinant of human as well as animal evolution and even *In Memoriam* had lamented that God and nature were at strife, the one the image of perfect love and the other 'red in tooth and claw', indifferent to the fate either of individuals or of species. Darwin's book was not so much a sudden bombshell as part of a continuing cannonade.

It was perhaps surprising that the traditional view of pain as the offspring of hell should have stood up to this bombardment for so long. Christian myth, like the myth of Pandora and her box, envisaged a painless golden age in which men and women had basked before all the woes bottled up in hell had been released upon them. It was now becoming clear that such a golden age was a blank impossibility. Pain was not so much an added evil as a basic necessity, an essential warning system without which no species could have evolved or survived. Nature was red in tooth and claw because it could not be otherwise. 'What a book a devil's chaplain might write,' remarked Darwin in 1856, 'on the clumsy, wasteful, blundering, low and horribly cruel works of nature!' When *The Origin of Species* appeared some thought that it was indeed diabolically inspired, but in fact no devil would have had any reason to be proud of it. It did not describe the cruelty which had resulted from Satan's success in tempting mankind but the cruelty which must have existed before that event took place, the cruelty which had underpinned the allegedly idyllic world of God's original creation. And if pain had not come from hell why should it be thought that it would return there? Suffering and happiness were complementary and constituent parts of human life – of all life – rather than moral absolutes to be separated out like wheat and chaff in some great winnowing operation at the end of all things.

But the world of the imagination, the world in which Munby built a god out of old memories and took satisfaction from the thought of a petty thief writhing in hell, was almost totally unaffected by abstract reasoning or by scientific observation. It was also unaffected by decisions of the Privy Council or the House of Lords. On the afternoon of Friday 15 July 1864, as Lord Houghton confronted Bishop Wilberforce, Munby took a stroll in St James's Park with one of the park keepers who showed him the outcasts of London, the starving and the homeless, who lay motionless on the grass. Gustave Doré's illustrated edition of Dante's *Inferno* had recently been published in England and it was the sinners in hell who came into Munby's mind. 'I looked and looked,' he wrote in horror, 'it was Dante and Virgil gazing on the damned; and still they did not move.' Charles Dodgson, who was soon to achieve fame under the name of Lewis Carroll, was also in London that afternoon playing croquet in George Macdonald's garden in the Kensington Road. In his mind was another croquet game in a dream world of unreason where, as Alice remarked, 'they're dreadfully fond of beheading people'. Nor were Houghton's own private imaginings free from the visions of torment which he condemned in public. He had recently introduced Swinburne to the writings of the Marquis de Sade, only to be told that de Sade's torture chambers with their 'loaded iron whips and elaborately ingenious racks and horses' were less exciting than 'the simple common birch rod and daily whipping block' which Swinburne had known at Eton.

An age enlightened enough to scout belief in eternal punishment and the Prince of Darkness should surely be able to banish such images. Frances Power Cobbe, one of those who had first pointed the way to the conquest of hell, certainly thought that the intellect had finally penetrated and dispelled the darkness which lay at the edges of thought. She wrote a glowing review of Albert Réville's disproof of the Devil's existence when it was translated into English in 1871, pointing out that belief in evil as a positive force, rather than as the absence of good, was as silly as belief in positive lightness as opposed to the absence of weight. And yet she knew, for all her brave words, that there were areas in the human mind where reason still slept and where monsters came forth and strode across the world as confidently as ever they had done in Goya's day. She therefore developed the idea of Unconscious Cerebration, one of the neglected masterpieces of Victorian ingenuity, which stood Freudian psycho-analysis on its head a generation before it was born.

Her theory was put forward in two articles in *Macmillan's Magazine* in November 1870 and April 1871. She first showed that a great deal of thinking was done unconsciously, particularly when the thinker was asleep. When he woke he could remember names or words or tunes which he had tried in vain to recall the night before. Some people found they had performed necessary tasks, often menial tasks, without being conscious of what they had done. 'But our Familiar is a great deal more than a walking dictionary, a housemaid, a *valet de place* or a barrel-organ man,' Miss Cobbe continued, 'He is a novelist who can spin more romances than Dumas.' The world of fantasy and dreams was unbelievably rich and yet it was outside the control of the conscious self. It was a world of violence, often of obscenity, a world in which the Devil and hell might well seem more real than God and heaven. 'The small share occupied by the Moral Law in the dream world is a significant fact,' proclaimed Miss Cobbe, 'Our dream-selves, like the Undines of German folk-lore, have no Souls, no Responsibility and no Hereafter.'

The assumption that the lack of moral responsibility ruled out the possibility of personal immortality was the vital stage in the argument. Men and women might be 'such stuff as dreams are made on', but 'in that "stuff" there enters not the noblest element of our nature, that Moral Will which allies us, not to the world of passing shadows, but to the great Eternal Will in whose life it is our hope that we shall live for ever.' 'We are not centaurs, rider and steed in one,' Miss Cobbe concluded triumphantly, 'but horsemen'. Each conscious human being, able to reason and make moral decisions, sat astride an unconscious thinking machine which would eventually sink and die. And the separability of rider and steed was in itself the proof of immortality. The survival of the conscious reasoning mind would bear witness to the reality of the god it worshipped, just as the death of unconscious fantasies would demonstrate the emptiness of the demons they had conjured up. It was a comforting prospect, a fitting tailpiece for the uplifting story of hell's destruction. Heaven was of course intact and undamaged because it was the inspiration and destination of the rider, not the foul fantasy of the steed. Bad imaginings came from the unconscious and were mortal, good imaginings came from the conscious and would inherit eternity. To sceptics the distinction sounded like wishful thinking but for Miss Cobbe it had to be real because the mind that rode was itself more real than the instinctive mechanism that was ridden. It was as well she did not live to see Sigmund Freud turn her riders into steeds and her steeds into riders.

4 OTHER GODS BEFORE ME

THE WARNING THAT EDMOND SCHÉRER DELIVERED IN 1861 when he spoke of a mighty voice announcing 'the end of another age, the last moments of another God', referred to an incident during the reign of the Emperor Tiberius. The crew and passengers of a ship sailing near the isles of Paxi had heard a loud voice, seemingly supernatural, crying that the great god Pan was dead. Tiberius had ordered an inquiry but no satisfactory explanation had emerged and Christians had been quick to assume that the heavens had been announcing the passing of Christ's pagan predecessor. It seems rather more probable that the travellers had overheard a ritual lament intoned by worshippers on the islands. Schérer's experience was less dramatic, less authenticated, but it was not entirely self-induced. There were certainly laments to be heard, whether human or divine, and there were heralds eager to proclaim a new dispensation. If the opening of the Christian era had meant great Pan's death then its close might bring about his rebirth.

A few months earlier Thackeray's *Cornhill Magazine* had printed a full-page picture of Pan to accompany Elizabeth Barrett Browning's poem 'A Musical Instrument'. The legs were suitably hairy and hooved, a reminder that here was a being who defied Miss Cobbe's separation of rider from steed, but of Pan's lusty and archetypal genitals there was no sign. If this was the symbol of the lewd unconscious mind, the bringer of pagan ecstasy, then it seemed to lack the means of bringing either lewdness or ecstasy to a suitable consummation. In her poem Mrs Browning was concerned not with Pan's sexuality but with the changes he wrought in those who worshipped him. 'Half a beast is the great god Pan,' she declared, telling how the faun-like god tore a reed from the bed of the river in order to make music so piercing sweet that the sun forgot to set. A poet was like a reed, she concluded: Pan blew through him and touched him with his magic but in order to do so he had to tear out his soul as surely as he drew the pith from the reed. The poet would never again live a conventional life, 'as a reed with the reeds of the river', and the true gods, the gods who put virtue above ecstasy, would have to 'sigh for the cost and pain'.

A rather different view of the magic and the pain of paganism was given in a novel which Nathaniel Hawthorne published in London and in Boston in the spring of 1860. He called it *The Marble Faun* and it was published under this title in America, though his London publishers thought it too fanciful and brought out their edition under the rather more solemn title *Transformation*. Hawthorne was not too fond of living respectably with the other reeds in the river: after four laborious years as American consul in Liverpool he gave in his resignation in 1857 and set off for Italy. There he found what he called 'a sort of poetic or fairy precinct where actualities would not be so terribly insisted upon as they are, and must needs be, in America'. He dismissed his native land as 'a country where there is no shadow, no antiquity, no mystery, no picturesque and gloomy wrong, nor anything but a commonplace prosperity'. He did not encounter the great god Pan in Italy but he did develop a great affection for a marble faun which he saw in Rome and which seemed to him to have 'a strain of honest wildness'. What if 'this race of fauns, the most delightful of all that antiquity imagined,' had somehow become 'intermingled with the human race'? What would happen when a wild creature, half man and half faun, was confronted with conventional Christian morality? The reverse, presumably, of what happened in Mrs Browning's parable: the reed would lose its magic but regain its pith so that it could be bedded down comfortably among the other reeds while the false gods who put ecstasy above virtue were suitably chagrined.

Hawthorne's answer was not so neat. There was nothing comfortable about the Christianity which bore down upon Count Donatello, the faun of his title, and upon the girl he loved. It came in the form of a threatening figure in monk's garb who spoke of heavy sins and harsh penances and continued to haunt the couple even after Donatello had seemingly killed him in an outburst of that 'honest wildness' which Hawthorne admired in his marble counterpart. Christian morality, aided by some sinister supernatural happenings, then managed to strip Donatello of his honest wildness and saddle him with an unaccustomed and overwhelming burden of guilt. At the end of the book one of the other characters hazarded the guess that the transformed Donatello, having sinned and repented, was nearer to paradise than the faun had been. But in the faun's world from which Donatello had come there were gods who sighed for the cost and pain. And it was this world that Hawthorne painted in glowing colours while the passages concerning Christianity had about them, as the *New York Tribune* remarked, 'the stifling air of the charnel-house'. In some ways Hawthorne's parable echoed Elizabeth Barrett Browning's instead of reversing it: the process whereby Christianity made a godly man out of a pagan seemed as ruthless and as destructive as the process whereby Pan made music from a reed.

Christians had long had rather more than a sneaking affection for the pagan gods. Even Milton had been unable to resist bringing in Pan to lead the dance of eternal spring in the Garden of Eden in *Paradise Lost*, though in *Paradise Regained* he had returned to the orthodox view and made Satan reveal Pan and other pagan gods as devils in disguise. Schiller's *The Gods of Greece*, one of the earliest German attacks on eighteenth-century rationalism, had accused Christianity of shattering the bond with nature which the Greeks had forged. In 1806, when Wordsworth tired of being a reed in the river, when he yearned to break free from the sordid world of getting and spending, his cry was to be 'a pagan suckled in a creed outworn'. Wordsworth was not alone: an idealized view of nature and a nostalgia for paganism were recurring themes in the literature of the first half of the nineteenth century. Then, from the late 1850s onward, the pagan gods began to move into other fields. 'Half a beast is the great god Pan' was poetic fancy but 'half a beast did God make man' now seemed to be scientific fact. The Old Testament idea of man being God's image had relegated both animals and animal gods to the same inferior plane: from being part of great Pan's image the goat became for the Jews the scapegoat, an unclean creature on whom they loaded their sins before driving it into the wilderness to die. But now Darwin made such separation infinitely more difficult, infinitely less justifiable. Pan's spell was no longer confined to literary allusions or to imagined pipings heard by the river.

Nor was it just a matter of Pan and the other gods of Greece and Rome. If Darwin was right, if mankind sprang not from a single creative moment but from great vistas of evolutionary time, then the relationship between human beings and God was not just a matter of the few centuries of Jewish history chronicled in the Bible. If men and women stood above the beasts of the field, lords over them because made in God's image, then everything they had ever believed or envisaged or worshipped must have gone into the making. Pagan rituals and strange superstitions, whether of the past or of the present, were not denials of God but stages in the process by which he had come to be understood. Jehovah's insistence that his people should have no other gods before him needed reconsideration. There had been true gods before him and there might well be true gods after him. Man's image of God had evolved with man and was still evolving. Bishop Heber's popular missionary hymn still sang confidently of lands where only man was vile, where the heathen in his blindness bowed down to wood and stone, but the study of anthropology and comparative religion, inevitable concomitants of evolutionary theory, were soon to make such contemptuous dismissal of other cultures impossible. At one level Darwin had demonstrated the irrelevance of a few Jewish creation myths; at another and more important level he had shown the relevance of the myths of all mankind.

Friedrich Max Müller, probably the greatest of all scholars in the field of comparative religion, had been working in Oxford for several years and in 1860 his name was put forward for the recently created and highly prestigious chair of Sanskrit. Pusey was one of his supporters, not because Christianity had anything to learn from other religions but because the highest possible level of scholarship must be enlisted in order to penetrate and convert the heathen mind. However, Max Müller was associated with those German metaphysicians whom Bishop Wilberforce denounced as heralds of Antichrist and so his rival, a man of considerably less distinction, was elected to the chair in December 1860. Another and seemingly slighter reminder of eastern religions appeared in 1859 entitled *The Rubáiyát of Omar Khayyám*, a small volume of seventy-five quatrains translated anonymously from an eleventh-century Persian poet. Their message was not merely pagan but openly irreligious: God had enmeshed men in sin and so all they could do was to drown the memory of the divine impertinence in wine. 'I often wonder what the vintners buy,' mused Khayyám, 'One half so precious as the goods they sell.' The book proved astonishingly popular and as edition succeeded edition it became clear that these verses were more influential than all the new scholarship in opening up perspectives beyond those of Christianity.

It nevertheless remained true that for most British readers the only

59

religious ideas outside the Bible were those enshrined in the mythology of Greece and Rome. They knew about Pan and his attendant fauns and satyrs but very few of them knew about Cernunnos, the Pan-like horned god who had once been worshipped in Britain. Some of them still danced round a pole on May morning but they did not care to be reminded that it had once been a phallic symbol. Some scholars even suggested that Christ's cross had been such a symbol but they got short shrift from the devout. 'I have said that the phallic origin attributed to the cross is destitute of evidence,' wrote Sabine Baring-Gould angrily in 1868 in his *Curious Myths of the Middle Ages*, 'In a work like this, which will be in the hands of general readers, it is impossible to enter into the subject.' There was no disguising the pagan nature of celebrations such as the Horned Dance at Abbot's Bromley in Staffordshire or the Puck Fair at Killorglin in County Kerry, where a he-goat presided over a drunken saturnalia, but most of those who took part in them were folklore enthusiasts rather than lusty devotees of the old fertility cults. Any reversion to paganism which took place among the Victorians was likely to be an intellectual game rather than a physical reality.

Things might have been different in the United States, where horizons were wider and where the old gods were closer at hand. To the south was Mexico with its relics of the most bloodthirsty of all pagan religions, to the west a host of indigenous Indian cultures. After working closely with Emerson and other transcendentalists Henry David Thoreau spent more than two years living alone in a hut on the shores of Walden Pond in an attempt to reach to the heart of nature and find what gods reigned there. He hoped that from America's forests and wildernesses would come images more powerful and more universal than those of Greece and Rome. 'Mythology is the crop which the Old World bore before its soil was exhausted,' he wrote, 'The West is preparing to add its fables to those of the East.' But *Walden, or Life in the Woods*, which came out in 1854, was certainly no storehouse of fables. Thoreau reached out for the spirit of the woods but showed little interest in those who had populated them with gods and demi-gods before the coming of the white man. His own response to the natural world was ambivalent, poised between the instincts of the hunter and the aspirations of the transcendentalist intellectual. 'I found in myself, and still find,' he wrote, 'an instinct toward a higher, or, as it is named, spiritual life, as do most men, and another toward a primitive rank and savage one, and I reverence them both.

60

I love the wild not less than the good. The wildness and adventure that are in fishing still recommend it to me.' It was a somewhat cautious confession of bloodlust, milder than most Indian braves or most devotees of Pan would have produced, and it was hardly the stuff of a new mythology.

Three years earlier Henry Lewis Morgan, later to be known as the father of American anthropology, had published an account of Iroquois beliefs based partly on the researches of Ely Samuel Parker, son of a Tonawanda Seneca chief and later an Iroquois supreme chief in his own right; but this kind of collaboration was rare and the book long remained unique. In 1855 Longfellow's *Hiawatha* gave a sympathetic picture of Indian nature worship but ended by suggesting that its true destiny lay in conversion to the Christian faith. In the eyes of most white Americans Indian culture was not something to be studied but something to be destroyed: in 1866 General Patrick Connors declared that Indians must be 'hunted like wolves' and his soldiers had orders to kill all males over the age of twelve. Lands guaranteed to Indian tribes were invaded, usually in search of gold, and when the Indians fought back their bravery in battle was reviled as murderous savagery. Meanwhile the war against Mexico had also brought in land which was rich in gold, as well as its own crop of stories of heroism. It was left to an Englishman, Edward Burnett Taylor, to give the first scientific account of Mexico in *Anahuac, or Mexico and the Mexicans, Ancient and Modern*, published in 1861. The only fables the Americans contributed to the world's store concerned their own exploits rather than the cultures they had fought against. They did indeed seem to be more interested in what Hawthorne called 'commonplace prosperity' than in 'poetic or fairy precincts'.

They were therefore especially pleasing to Frances Power Cobbe, who had always hoped that the study of comparative religion would lead to the genteel gods of the riders and not to the hairy gods of the steeds. Her great hero was Theodore Parker, a Boston clergyman who rejected Christian orthodoxy and saw all the world's religions and all the world's myths as revelations of one universal truth. The *Massachusetts Quarterly Review*, which he and Emerson established in 1847, discussed religion and philosophy in an impressively wide context but said little about such indelicate gods as Pan. Emerson kept a close eye on what was going on in Europe and made sure that he was always supplied with Max Müller's latest work. His journals and notebooks were preoccupied with Greek mythology, which he

said was 'more catholic than any other' and therefore of central importance in the modern world. He related it to Greek thought, showing
how 'the Greeks wrote their metaphysics in names and attributes of
gods', but he left Pan and Dionysus, the gods of unreason, out of
his exposition. Miss Cobbe told how some disciples of Theodore Parker
had given their son Greek myths to read before they introduced him
to the Bible, thus making him 'without exception the most religious
boy I ever knew', but she was reluctant to probe the fertility cults
from which such myths sprang. In a review of James Fergusson's
Tree and Serpent Worship she remarked that 'the ever-recurring connection between the Tree and the Serpent, the beautiful and beneficent
vegetable and the noxious reptile, is well-nigh incomprehensible.' She
would not entertain the possibility that both were phallic symbols
and declared instead that the book demonstrated 'the moral unity
of our race'.

One American who did conjure up the great god Pan was Edmund
Clarence Stedman, a poet who was also a stockbroker. His poem 'Pan
in Wall Street' showed the god in an unusually playful mood, bringing
the New York financiers thoughts of 'ancient, sweet-do-nothing days'
and encouraging a newsboy and a peanut girl to dance together in
the streets. Shortly before publishing the poem Stedman received a
letter from his friend Bayard Taylor who was travelling in Europe
and had met Swinburne, an altogether more passionate devotee of
the horned god. 'What I admire in him – yet admire with a feeling
of pain,' wrote Taylor, 'is the mad, unrestrained preponderance of
the imagination. It is a god-like quality, but he sometimes uses it
like a devil. He told me some things unspeakably shocking... his
aberration of ideas is horrible.' When young Henry Adams was in
London in 1862 as secretary to his father, who was American minister,
he met Swinburne at one of Lord Houghton's house parties. 'The
idea that one has actually met a real genius dawns slowly on a Boston
mind,' he wrote, 'but it made entry at last.' Like Taylor, he was both
horrified and fascinated by what he heard: Swinburne's invocation
of the old gods was very different from the rarefied pantheism of the
American intellectuals. 'One felt the horror of Longfellow and Emerson,' Adams recorded, 'at the wild Walpurgis night of Swinburne's
talk.'

Swinburne's public reputation as a pagan was based on *Poems and
Ballads*, which he published in 1866. The most notorious poem in
the volume was 'Dolores', a hymn to a bloodthirsty pagan goddess

whom he addressed as 'Our Lady of Pain', begging her to 'come down and redeem us from virtue'. It was this prayer for redemption from virtue which stuck in the gullet of most reviewers. John Morley in the *Saturday Review* said that it revealed Swinburne as either 'the apostle of a crushing iron-shod despair' or 'the libidinous laureate of a pack of satyrs'. Most readers took the latter view and a gentleman in Dublin wrote threatening castration if the poems were not withdrawn. 'He would way-lay me,' Swinburne wrote in some amusement, 'slip my head in a bag, and remove the obnoxious organs; he had seen his gamekeeper do it with cats'. Later Swinburne was encouraged to hear that his young cousin had been so severely birched for reading 'Dolores' that the blood had 'soaked through his shirt and the seat of his breeches in patches and stripes, to the wild delight of the junior male members of the household'. It was an auspicious beginning for his new religion, he told Rossetti, for like any other faith it needed the blood of the martyrs to make it grow.

But this libidinous laureate, this red-blooded poet of revived paganism, was not all he seemed. There was more despair than libido in his make-up and he spoke darkly of 'the diabolic government of this worst of all possible worlds'. His Satanism was ostentatious – his friends received letters promising to meet them 'by the grace of Satan, Deo Nolente' – but it betrayed little of the ecstasy which might have been expected of a worshipper of the old gods. When Rossetti and Burton arranged for Adah Menken, his real-life Dolores, to knock on his door and say that she had come for the night he showed no desire to take her to his bed. When she died a few months later he said it was 'a great shock to me and a real grief', but by that time he was seeking consolation of another kind in a whipping brothel in St John's Wood. Even this was a second best: his private correspondence made it clear that his real longing was for the strictness of the schoolroom rather than the excitements of the bawdy-house. Morley came to the heart of the matter when he said that Swinburne's poems would have been more effective if they had 'vindicated passion, and the strong and large and rightful pleasures of sense, against the narrow and inhuman tyranny of shrivelled anchorites'. Instead they dwelt upon severities which the anchorites themselves could scarcely have bettered. Somewhere inside this defiant devotee of the ancient liberated gods there was a sadly unliberated Victorian schoolboy kneeling at the whipping block, his posture and his punishment both dictated by the Christian penitential requirements from which he had supposedly broken free. The god of the beasts danced to the schoolmaster's tune.

The point was made more dramatically in Sabine Baring-Gould's *Book of Werewolves*, which came out in 1865. Lycanthropy, the sacramental identification of man and wolf, was as old as Pan himself. At Mount Lycaeus in Arcadia, the wildest and most mysterious part of Greece, a festival had been held at which a man was transformed into a wolf and retained that shape for nine years. Like the centaurs and the horned gods he was the quintessence of unbridled paganism, a savage union of man and beast. Yet here too Christianity managed to put a sinner inside the god. From being a pagan sacrament lycanthropy became part of hell's armoury, one among the many torments the Devil could impose upon the damned. Baring-Gould spared his readers none of the details:

The loup-garou is sometimes a metamorphosis forced upon the body of a damned person who, after being tormented in his grave, has torn his way out of it. The first stage in the process consists in his devouring the cerecloth which enveloped his face; then his moans and muffled howls ring from the tomb through the gloom of the night, the earth of the grave begins to heave and at last, with a scream, surrounded by a phosphorescent glare and exhaling a foetid odour, he bursts away as a wolf.

Meanwhile the study of comparative religion had extended its horizons far beyond Greece and Rome. Frances Power Cobbe was surprised to find ideas of heaven and hell in eastern mythology, as well as stories which she had thought to be uniquely European. She discovered that the tale of Prince Llewelyn's faithful hound Gelert, unjustly slain for killing the child he had in fact protected, had been told in ancient India long before Llewelyn's time. And at the confluence of eastern and western thought, possibly the source of both, she saw the culture of ancient Egypt. 'Their embalmed forms stand beside us in our studies,' she wrote, commenting on the Victorian craze for Egyptian mummies which continued to grow until in 1890 mummified cats shipped to Liverpool as manure were sold at auction for several shillings each. The ancient Egyptians themselves certainly ran no risk of bursting away from the tomb in animal form: their preparations for the hereafter had been meticulous and they had taken care to placate all the gods, animal or otherwise. The fact that a belief in immortality had existed in Egypt many centuries before the promises made in Christ's name by St Paul seemed to Miss Cobbe the final proof of the unity of all religions. A century earlier Alexander Pope had invoked God as 'Father of all in every age, in every clime adored' and now mankind was recognizing this truth. The god of the pagans and the god of the Christians were at one and were to be worshipped, as Pope had said, 'by saint, by savage and by sage'. The animal manifestations would fall away into unimportance, neither gods nor sinners but mere delusions, and the one universal religion would be accepted throughout the world.

Benjamin Disraeli, Chancellor of the Exchequer in Lord Derby's administration of June 1866, brought together Christianity and other religions in a rather different way. 'Man, my Lord,' he told Bishop Wilberforce at a public meeting in 1864, 'is a being born to believe . . . the characteristic of the present age is a craving credulity.' He went on to say that in the debate over whether man was an ape or an angel he was 'on the side of the angels' because the contrary view was abhorrent and 'foreign to the conscience of humanity'. The bishop was impressed but shrewder and more cynical observers had their doubts. Disraeli was a Jew, they pointed out, and furthermore he was a Jew who in his published work had constantly spoken of the mystic power of the orient, of ancient Egypt, of the dark fertility rites which had held sway before Christ's birth and might yet hold sway again. *Punch* portrayed him as an Egyptian in two quite separate guises – as the sphinx, the symbol of the might and mystery of the Pharaohs, but also as a fairground conjuror, the sort of fortune-telling charlatan who was popularly dubbed 'gipsy', a corruption of 'Egyptian'. Sir John Skelton, who met him in Edinburgh towards the end of 1867, saw him as a mysterious and almost supernatural being:

The potent wizard himself, with his olive complexion and coal-black eyes, and the mighty dome of his forehead (no Christian temple, be sure), is unlike any living creature one has met. I had never seen him in the daylight before, and the daylight accentuates his strangeness. The face is more like a mask than ever, and the division between himself and mere mortals more marked. I would as soon have thought of sitting down at table with Hamlet, or Lear, or the Wandering Jew . . . England is the Israel of his imagination, and he will be the Imperial Minister before he dies – if he gets the chance.

Disraeli was to have his chance to be 'Imperial Minister' in 1874 and was to use it in ways more startling than anything Skelton could have anticipated.* When Skelton met him his government had just

* See below, pp. 106–109.

entertained the Sultan of Turkey and the Khedive of Egypt, an unprecedented gesture, and the soldiers who had stood guard over these eastern potentates with flaming brands had been hailed by the newspapers as 'human torches'. Although Disraeli's peculiar ability to inject pagan fantasy into Britain's humdrum politics was not to come to full flower until 1874 he was already a master of invention, having bombarded the Queen throughout the autumn of 1867 with stories of conspirators who were renting empty houses throughout London in order to set fire to them. He also conjured a ship out of thin air, a Danish brigantine which he said had left New York with a crew of thirty men sworn to assassinate Victoria and her ministers. Neither the arsonists nor the brigantine ever materialized.

Probably the most symbolically significant of the pagan gods who arrived in London in 1867 came in a large crate to a house in Maitland Park Road two days before Christmas. It was a statue of Zeus, more than life-size, and it was a Christmas present for Karl Marx, to whom it bore a striking physical resemblance. In his youth Marx had published poems celebrating the horned gods in their Christianized form as devils and demons and he also had a lively interest in the things they had originally stood for: his letters to Engels were peppered with erotic references and with descriptions of his own genitals. But it was appropriate that he should now see himself as Zeus rather than as Pan because he had recently returned from delivering the first volume of *Das Kapital* to his publishers in Hamburg. He had overthrown Christianity and its capitalist advocates not with bawdy or with devilry but by the use of reason and calculation. Starting as a rebel against a particular god he had ended by laying down iron laws which held captive both gods and men. Like Zeus, he looked down from Olympian heights on the whole of the universe.

William Winwood Reade was going through a somewhat similar experience. He had spent the early 1860s in West Africa collecting material for an ambitious work to be called *The Origin of Mind*, which was to do for the history of the human mind what *The Origin of Species* had done for the history of the human frame. His avowed aim was to record Africa's share in the spiritual evolution of mankind: he knew a lot about the varieties of African religious experience, the rituals which Bishop Heber had dismissed as heathens bowing down to wood and stone, and he wanted to give them as honourable a place in the history of religion as the Greeks and the Egyptians already had. But when his book appeared in 1872 under the title *The Martyrdom of Man* it contained surprisingly little about African beliefs and a great deal about Greece and Egypt. 'There is no problem in history as interesting as the unparalleled development of Greece,' he declared early in the book. Nearly three hundred pages later, as his argument moved towards its triumphant conclusion, he invoked Apollo, the Greek god of reason and enlightenment: 'Glorious Apollo is the parent of us all.' 'Where now is Isis the mother, with the child Horus on her lap?' he asked, 'They are dead; they have gone to the land of the shadows. Tomorrow, Jehovah, you and your son shall be with them. Men die, and the ideas which they call gods die too.'

But not apparently Apollo, who was the god of reason as well as the god of the sun. As science continued to explore and explain the universe, reason, which Apollo defended both against the old horned gods and against dark Christian superstitions, would be seen to be supreme in the moral sphere just as the sun was supreme in the physical sphere. 'Life is bottled sunshine,' Reade wrote, 'and Death the silent-footed butler who draws out the cork.' He had nothing but contempt for Marx and the Communists – 'every millionaire enriches the community,' he proclaimed defiantly – but his scientific determinism proved as dogmatic as Marx's economic determinism. Men must accept the conclusions of science and acknowledge 'the supreme and mysterious Power by whom the universe has been created, and by whom it has been appointed to run its course under fixed and invariable laws; that awful One to whom it is profanity to pray, of whom it is idle and irreverent to argue and debate.' Reade wore the mantle of Apollo as confidently as Marx wore the mantle of Zeus. Just as Miss Cobbe saw beliefs that did not fit into her universal religion as products of an unreal dream world, so Reade saw the Africans whose contributions to spiritual history he was supposed to have been celebrating as 'savages who have been led by indigestion and by dreams to believe in ghosts'. 'The savage lives in a strange world,' he explained a little condescendingly, 'He knows nothing about the laws of nature. Death itself is not a natural event. Sooner or later men make the gods angry and are killed.' Hence the reaction of one African chief who cried out furiously: 'If I could see God I would kill him at once, because he makes men die!'

Some indignant readers found Reade's own threats equally outrageous. As well as consigning God to the land of shadows along with Isis and Horus he dismissed the promise of personal immortality as 'a sweet and charming illusion'. If he killed the God who conquered death then the future would indeed be the season of mental anguish which he predicted, a sad and dark world from which youth and beauty would have vanished for ever. When he passed into the land of shadows himself in 1875 at the sadly early age of thirty-six his uncle, Charles Reade the novelist, felt constrained to write to the press saying that if he had lived longer he would no doubt have 'cured himself, as many thinking men have done, of certain obnoxious opinions which laid him open to reasonable censure'. Nor was he censured only by the orthodox: even those who welcomed the merging of Christianity and other religions still felt a desperate need to believe in a hereafter. During the 1860s they formed the Radical Club and the Free Religious Association in America while in London they found an effective vehicle for their ideas in the *Theological Review*. And it was precisely because they were becoming respectable that they were determined not to be thought atheistic, especially where immortality was concerned. Now that more and more people were drawn to their attractively multi-coloured religious umbrella it was vital that it should not let in the rain. Miss Cobbe in particular felt that belief in an afterlife was essential for the future of civilized society. 'It would probably need only that five per cent of the population should publish their conviction that there is no Future State,' she warned, 'to make the greater part of the remainder so far lose reliance upon it as to become quite insensible to its moral influences.'

This did not stop her being extremely angered by the startling success of Guillaume Figuier's *Le Lendemain de la Mort*, which was published in English in 1872 as *The Day after Death; or, Our Future Life according to Science* and ran through five editions. 'Simple readers ask for bread,' she cried indignantly, 'and the Frenchman drops into their mouths a bonbon.' Figuier certainly had produced an enticing confection. 'Of course you do not believe that your soul will be extinguished with your life on the day of your decease,' he wrote comfortingly at the beginning of his book. He then went on to assure his readers that life after death was a scientific fact and was made possible by the sun. Reade had made Apollo the parent of all mortal things and now Figuier made him the parent of immortality as well: eternal life, like life on earth, was bottled sunshine: 'solar radiation is maintained by the continuous unbroken succession of souls in the sun.' Science proved that sunbeams were the souls of the virtuous floating for ever through the interplanetary ether. Imperfect souls remained below on earth and were reincarnated again and again until they achieved perfection and were conveyed to the sun. The souls of animals might be reincarnated in human beings, which accounted for inborn talents and tendencies. 'A child who has a faculty for music may have received the soul of a nightingale, the sweet songster of our woods. A child who is an architect by vocation may have inherited the soul of a beaver.' Although Figuier claimed to be a scientist he was in fact a student of comparative religion, since most of what he said could be traced to Hindu and Buddhist beliefs. Miss Cobbe might find him infuriating but she had nevertheless played her part in creating the climate of opinion which helped to make him so astonishingly popular.

By the early 1870s this climate was coming to be taken for granted and the wrath of the orthodox was vented upon outright atheists rather than upon the Free Religious Association or the contributors to the *Theological Review*. Ten years of literary and intellectual excitement on both sides of the Atlantic had led not to the rebirth of the lascivious horned gods but merely to a polite accommodation between Christianity and the more rational of the pagan deities. There had been such accommodation before – after all it had been Virgil who had guided Dante on his journey through hell and purgatory and heaven – and theologians and philosophers had always known that Christian thought was based firmly on the Greek Socratic tradition. As long as Pan and Dionysus were kept out there was no harm in letting Apollo in, even though Reade and Figuier might make unwelcome use of him. And for every man or woman who read Reade or Figuier or any other of the innovators there were at least ten who read nothing on the subject but continued to believe what they had been brought up to believe. In spite of the ferocious things Jehovah had once said to Moses he could safely allow a few enthusiasts to play with some of his more respectable rivals.

One man who did vent his wrath upon innovators and intellectual games was Matthew Arnold, who said some extremely scathing things about Miss Cobbe and her like. For him the 1860s were desolate years. He saw anarchy ahead, both political and spiritual, and he despised those who prattled about new dawns and universal truths. Back in 1851 he had written 'Dover Beach' but had put it aside because its pessimism was out of tune with the times. Now he felt that the times were changed and in July 1867 he included it in his new volume of poems. Swinburne was delighted with it, saying that Arnold had finally abandoned 'the sad task of sweeping dead leaves fallen from the dying tree of belief'. It was a poem about the sea, the sea which ran down the beach at Dover and also the wider sea of faith which had once embraced mankind but was now retreating down the vast edges of the world. Arnold could hear no reassurance in the sound it made, no vibrant promise of universal truth, only a melancholy roar as the pebbles were sucked down and then flung up again. Men and women were in the same helpless state, pushed and pulled hither and thither in a world without meaning or purpose or certitude. 'We are here as on a darkling plain,' he concluded, 'Swept with confused alarms of struggle and flight, Where ignorant armies clash by night.'

Friedrich Nietzsche, appointed to the chair of classical philology in the University of Basle at the age of twenty-four, had a similar vision of the human condition but for him it led not to despair but to exultation. 'Our whole threadbare culture plunges at the frightful demon's breast,' he cried when the Franco-Prussian War broke out in July 1870, 'What things we shall see! We may be already at the beginning of the end!' He served with the Prussian army as a medical orderly on the plains of northern France, 'scattered all over with countless mournful remains and reeking with corpses', and saw at first hand the confusion and the clash of armies. He contracted dysentery and diphtheria and during his convalescence, in a strange delirious state which those about him described as 'a dream of carnival', he produced the most powerful invocation of the old gods that the Christian world had yet seen.

It was called *The Birth of Tragedy* and it was a hymn to Dionysus, the god of ecstasy and unreason who had ruled the Greeks before they had been beguiled into thinking that reason and logic, the two-dimensional propositions of Socrates and Plato and Aristotle, could describe the real world. Apollo deluded men into believing that their lonely thought processes had meaning, but Dionysus could break this spell and lead men back to the natural life they had lived before they had been so foolish as to enmesh themselves in a network of seemingly rational diagrams. Nietzsche had long ago rejected the solitary intellectual life – 'the hundred books on the table in front of me are so many tongs which pinch out the nerve of independent thought,' he wrote in 1867 – and now he exulted in a life shared with other men, with nature itself, and drawing its inspiration from the will rather than from the reason. 'Socratic man has run his course,' he told his readers, 'crown your heads with ivy, seize the thyrsus, and do not be surprised if tiger and panther lie down and caress your feet! It has fallen to your lot to lead the Dionysiac procession out of India into Greece.'

The Birth of Tragedy sold very few copies and it was many years before it made much impression on British or American readers. Nevertheless it was the most searching and in the end the most potent of the rediscoveries of the old gods. Mrs Browning's dallying with Pan, Thoreau's mystic identification with nature, Swinburne's worship of the lithe and lascivious goddess of pain, the universal religion recommended by Theodore Parker and Miss Cobbe – all these played their part in remoulding the Victorian imagination but with the possible exception of Swinburne's poetry they had little connection with events of the time. The hymn to Dionysus, on the other hand, related to reality in a way which none of the other invocations ever could. There was to be a Dionysiac procession out of India, even a Prince whose feet were caressed by tigers. Events were to wrap themselves so closely around Nietzsche's fantasies that fantasy itself came to rival intellectual analysis and religious belief as a way of coming to terms with a new world of violence and uncertainty.

5 THE COMING OF THE LORD

WHAT WAS NEEDED WAS ACTION. GOD MUST COME down to earth in order to show once and for all that he was real and his rivals mere phantoms projecting and personifying the delusions of misguided men. In the Bible he had done this in differing ways. He had made Mount Sinai quake in order to appear to Moses in the midst of thunder and lightning but some time later, on Mount Horeb, he had produced storm and fire and earthquake only to pass them by and speak to Elijah in a still small voice. The change suggested progress: perhaps on Sinai other gods had been present and had had to be outdone, while on Horeb God had been in sole charge and had been able to use his stage effects as a prologue rather than as a demonstration. It remained to be seen which course he would follow halfway through the increasingly faithless nineteenth century.

Dr Cumming was still announcing that the Lord would be accompanied by meteorological disturbances which would make those on Sinai and on Horeb look like spring sunshine. Harcourt Bland, a comedian at the Theatre Royal in Glasgow, took issue with Cumming in 1855 and the prophet's replies were not particularly convincing. *The End: or, the Proximate Signs of the close of this Dispensation*, published in the same year, was less successful than *Apocalyptic Sketches* and seemed confused on some points. Whereas earlier prophecies had cited the growth of popery as proof that the world was about to end, this one made the decline of popery serve precisely the same purpose. And it seemed that the bottom of the barrel was being scraped in search of signs: even phylloxera, the blight which had recently struck French vines, was dragged in to prove approaching apocalypse. More predictions followed, fixing on 1867 as the year in which the existing dispensation would come to an end. *The Times* reviewed Cumming's work respectfully and when the *Saturday Review* dared to ridicule him his

72

supporters dismissed it as 'a notoriously irreligious paper'. 'It is not uncommon for great Revelations, Discoveries and Warnings to be treated with scornful indifference or mirthful contempt,' wrote a Sheffield clergyman when audiences in that city laughed at Cumming's lectures.

The change of heart over popery highlighted a puzzling question about God's coming. Would it happen when men were at their worst or at their best? 'An evil and adulterous generation seeketh after a sign,' Christ had told the pharisees, 'and there shall be no sign given to it.' Originally Cumming had seemed to be saying the same thing: times were wicked, popery strong, and so the sign would come from Antichrist and not from God. Now he seemed more hopeful. 'Should we be about to enter very soon upon a new and nobler era, let us lift up our heads: our redemption draweth nigh,' he wrote in 1855. Now that Christians were less popish and more worthy it was perhaps God himself who was coming and not the Great Beast of the apocalypse.

It was hard to believe that he was coming to the British, who showed few signs of preparing themselves for a new and nobler era. There were riots in London in 1855 when Lord Robert Grosvenor tried to get Parliament to limit Sunday trading and he had to yield to the violence and withdraw his measure. There was more trouble when the authorities wanted to stop bands playing in the parks on Sundays. By the spring of 1856 it became necessary to fortify the Archbishop of Canterbury's London residence against attack from an infuriated mob. Lord Palmerston, Prime Minister since February 1855, had a reputation for caring little about religion and even Queen Victoria accused Grosvenor and his like of 'incomprehensible blindness and mistaken piety'. In September 1857, when she was asked to sanction a Day of National Prayer and Humiliation because of the mutiny in India, she replied that such things did more harm than good. Meanwhile the Archbishop of Canterbury and nine other prelates were supporting a new divorce law which working people said would make the country 'too wicked to live in'. The efforts of religious enthusiasts served only to push Britain farther away both from godliness itself and also from any agreement between different social classes as to what it was.

America seemed to have achieved both. It was said of the great religious revivals in New York State in 1855 that 'they all commenced and made their first progress among the higher classes of society.

This was very favorable to the general spread of the work and to the overcoming of opposition'. Philip Schaff of Pennsylvania declared in the same year that 'Providence has evidently prepared this country and nation for the greatest work and no power on earth can arrest its progress and prosperity if we are true to our calling, if we fear God and love righteousness.' He was sure that the 'unbridled radicalism and fanaticism' of which Americans had once been accused had died out and that the pursuit of material success had had 'a most salutary influence on the moral life of the nation'. Roman Catholicism would also die out because its 'mediaeval traditions, centralized priestly government and extreme conservatism' were at odds with liberty and republicanism. The Protestant Reformation would culminate in the United States, which would become 'the phoenix grave not only of European nationalities but also of all European churches and sects'. 'All is yet in a chaotic state,' he concluded, 'but organizing energies are already present and the spirit of God broods over them, to speak in time the almighty word: "Let there be light!" and to call forth from chaos a beautiful creation.'

Organizing energy and the spirit of God provided themes for Robert Baird's *Religion in America*, the New York edition of which came out in 1856. Because the United States allowed no established religion, because church revenues were neither provided nor sanctioned by the secular government, everything sprang from 'the mere unconstrained goodwill of the people, especially those among them who love the Saviour and profess His name'. Nor was it just a matter of the things that could be seen and heard on Sundays, the packed churches built by those who worshipped in them and the well loved ministers paid by those to whom they preached. On the other six days as well, at work and in the home, the voluntary principle harnessed organizing energies to the service of God. Workshops and factories were 'proverbial for ignorance and vice' in Britain but in America they were virtuous and well-ordered. 'Those may tremble for the result,' Baird wrote, 'who do not know what the human heart is capable of doing when left to its own energies, moved and sustained by the grace and love of God.' Americans who did know these things knew also that they were ideally placed to greet God when he came.

It was generally agreed that he arrived in America during the late summer of 1857. 'It is recognized as among the most noteworthy phenomena of the day,' wrote the English author Mrs Bishop early in 1859, 'that the influence of the Holy Spirit has been felt during the

74

past eighteen months in the United States to an extent unprecedented in any other country or period.' As early as January 1857 Dwight Moody, going to revivalist meetings in Chicago every evening, became convinced that God was present in the city; but it was not until the Ohio Life Insurance Trust Company collapsed on 24 August of that year, starting a disastrous financial panic, that the divine presence was universally felt. 'It would seem that the mighty crash was just what was wanted,' one evangelist wrote, 'to startle men from their golden dreams.' God made his appearance 'in our chief commercial centres, precisely where the credit of religion had been most impaired and the tide against it was the strongest,' and he showed that he could use even the uncaring world of finance for his own purposes. Within a few months nearly five thousand firms went bankrupt and as confidence in man-made prosperity crumbled confidence in God soared. 'This winter of 1857–58 will be remembered as the time when a great revival prevailed throughout all the Northern states,' wrote the preacher Charles G. Finney, 'It swept over the land with such power that for a time it was estimated that not less than fifty thousand conversions occurred in a single week.' One man arriving in Boston from distant Omaha reported that his journey had been one continuous prayer meeting as men and women came together to share their sense of God's presence.

Finney went on to say that 'a divine influence seemed to pervade the whole land', bringing with it at least half a million conversions, but his definition of the whole land was still limited to the Northern states. 'Slavery seemed to shut it out from the South,' he concluded, 'the Spirit of God seemed to be grieved away from them.' Philip Schaff, who could claim credit for predicting the revival, saw slavery as less of a problem. He was sure it was dying out and indeed would have died out already had it not been for the reaction produced by the abolitionists. He seemed to regard the campaign for abolition as part of that 'unbridled radicalism and fanaticism' whose passing he was so anxious to see. He was writing shortly after Theodore Parker had incited an illegal attempt to rescue Anthony Burns, an escaped slave whom the authorities were about to hand over to his Virginian master. Parker's view of the matter was clear: if the law sent men back into slavery the law must be defied. He had already given up his life's work, a history of world religion, in order to concentrate on the campaign against slavery. He was chairman of a secret committee to help Captain John Brown, a fanatical abolitionist who was believed to be planning a large-scale negro revolt throughout the Southern states. If such an uprising did take place Schaff would not be alone in condemning its instigators as unbridled radical fanatics. The social tensions which religious enthusiasm produced in Britain were mild compared with the holy war to which rival interpretations of the coming of the Lord might yet give rise in America.

Most of those who watched the American religious revival of 1857–58 from across the Atlantic thought of it as the prelude to the abolition of slavery. Mrs Bishop declared that America was 'rapidly assuming a prominence among empires to fulfil God's purposes towards the human race,' but she could not imagine this fulfilment taking place until the slaves were free. The British and Foreign Anti-Slavery Society had been campaigning against the slavers of the Southern states for many years and it had inspired the 1841 articles in *The Times* describing their cruelties. But in the wake of these articles an angry army officer had written to the paper saying that there was 'a conviction of immense superiority to the English deeply seated in the national mind and temper of the Americans' and that this would inevitably lead to war between Britain and the United States. In such a war Britain's strategy must be to turn them into the disunited states, to break up the Union by blockading the North and starving its industries, and it was therefore very unwise to alienate the South by inveighing against slavery and by hinting, as some sources in Britain did, that there might be British support for a slave revolt.

He had been by no means alone in his opinions even in the 1840s and now there were added reasons for the British – or at any rate for the English and the Scots – not to get involved in a crusade for the freeing of the slaves, however loudly people like Mrs Bishop might hail it as fulfilling God's purposes for the human race. In New York during the winter of 1857–58 John O'Mahony, an Irish rebel who had escaped arrest in 1848, formed the Fenian Brotherhood, a society dedicated to the overthrow of British rule in Ireland by violent means. 'Every Irishman in the United States is in favour of slavery,' Theodore Parker pointed out grimly. If the British backed the abolitionist crusade they might find its opponents seeking to free one of the many races they themselves held in subjection.

A British version of the threatened slave insurrection had already taken place in India during the summer of 1857. 'What a terrible time dear old England has in India,' wrote Theodore Parker to Miss Cobbe that December, 'but I suppose Father Bull will conquer, kill ten men and violate twenty women where the Indians did but one or two, and then celebrate thanksgivings in all his churches.' 'Of course you know what a sad commercial panic we are passing through in America, as in England,' he continued, 'I hope both nations will come out of it wiser than before.' London had been hard hit by the financial crisis – Palmerston told Queen Victoria on 12 November that the Bank of England's reserve funds were running out – and it might seem that God was giving the two countries the same treatment, shaking their complacency by means of financial uncertainty and assailing their consciences with the cries of oppressed peoples. In December 1858, when he felt that the American revival had enough impetus to be able to do without him, Charles Finney went to England 'to see if the same influence would not pervade that country.' He found his friends at the Borough Road chapel in London demoralized and depressed, but after he had preached 'it was soon very perceptible that the Spirit of God was poured out'. He had similarly gratifying experiences in the northern and eastern counties and soon there was talk of an English as well as an American revival. Finney had little doubt that God had crossed the Atlantic with him.

Meanwhile in February 1858 the Virgin Mary had appeared to Bernadette Subirous in a cave near Lourdes in southern France. Catholics were somewhat more cautious in welcoming her, somewhat more scrupulous in seeking her credentials, than Protestants had been when they had felt God moving among them. For this reason if for no other her visit was to be remembered and celebrated long after the revivals had been forgotten. In July 1858 the American Catholic editor Orestes Brownson published a crushing condemnation of Protestant hysteria, saying sternly that 'in the Catholic Church this excitement is judiciously directed and moderated.' Gradually, reluctantly, the fashion for detecting God's presence in every gathering, his hand behind every event, began to wane. In New York a start was made on building St Patrick's Cathedral, a sign that Catholicism in America was far from sinking into the decline that Schaff had predicted. Its phenomenal growth was to be the most spectacular feature of American religious life during the next quarter of a century. 'Mediaeval traditions, centralized priestly government and extreme conservatism' were to prove more durable than the God-intoxicated fervour of 1857–58.

There were still those who saw the powers of darkness and the forces of good forming up for a great cosmic confrontation. 'I hold Louis Napoleon in loathing and count him Beelzebub,' wrote Theodore

Parker to Miss Cobbe from Switzerland in July 1859, 'but he is now casting out other devils'. To the south of him Louis Napoleon, Emperor Napoleon III of the French, was helping the King of Sardinia to throw the Austrians out of Italy, a struggle which Parker described to his congregation back in Boston as 'the great battle of mankind against institutions which once helped but now hinder the progress of mankind.' 'The actual war is local,' he explained, 'confined to a small part of Italy. It may become general before you read this note.' The Rev. Richard Shimeall of New York identified Napoleon III as the Beast of the Apocalypse and Catholic intellectuals in America were worried about the hold he had over their priests. 'France not Rome governs the Catholic mind in this country,' wrote Orestes Brownson, 'There is the great difficulty.' And was France now to swallow up Rome, as she had nearly done in the time of the first Napoleon? If the French Emperor's Italian allies wanted to unite their country they would be ranged against the papacy as well as against the Austrians. It would indeed be ironic if the Great Beast, the incarnate Beelzebub, should cast out the Scarlet Woman and robe himself in her garments. Events might not yet be fulfilling Dr Cumming's predictions but at least they helped to explain his uncertainty as to the Papacy's place in the apocalyptic scenario.

It had been hoped that Parker's trip to Europe might restore his shattered health. Instead he grew worse and he was near to death when he got to Florence in May 1860. Miss Cobbe was there waiting for him and at last the two met. He asked her what day it was and she said it was Sunday, 'a blessed day.' 'True, it *is* a blessed day,' he replied, 'when one has got over the superstition of it.' He died four days later. At the end of his life his thoughts turned from fears of Armageddon to more hopeful things. He was unable to read *The Origin of Species* but he was sure it was 'one of the most important works the British have lately contributed to science.' He also conceded, in spite of his recent remarks about India, that the British had done much to deliver mankind from superstition and tyranny. In Britain itself there was less confidence. Wilberforce's campaign against Darwin's book opened shortly after Parker's death and the heavens provided portents in the shape of a spectacular comet and a winter that lasted until July. As death rates rose *The Times* published a leader on the ominous weather, calling it 'a strange season of menace and gloom.' There was menace from other quarters as well. Irish papists were kidnapping Protestant children and Napoleon III, 'the disturber of the world', was thought to be about to launch an attack. Two years earlier a pamphlet called *Invasion invited by the Defenceless State of England* had caused a great stir and now, as the report of a Royal Commission on Defence came out, fears were renewed. It was alleged in the press that the French could 'effect a landing in Sussex or the Isle of Wight and bombard Portsmouth and Spithead from a safe distance.'

During Parker's absence his friends looked after his congregation in Boston. Emerson preached there and in November 1859 Thoreau gave a lecture entitled 'A Plea for Captain Brown'. On 16 October John Brown with a force of five negroes and sixteen whites had seized the arsenal at Harper's Ferry in Virginia, an action reported in New York under such headlines as 'Negro Insurrection at Harper's Ferry' and 'Extensive Negro Conspiracy in Virginia and Maryland'. The insurrection had not materialized and Brown had had to surrender after he had been wounded and ten of his men killed. Thoreau told how even in prison, wounded and in the shadow of death, Brown was regarded as 'a supernatural being'. 'Sure enough, a hero in the midst of us cowards is always so dreaded,' he added. His plea was ignored and Brown was hanged. Thoreau gave two further lectures, 'The Martyrdom of John Brown' and 'The Last Days of John Brown', in which he completed his transformation of the man from abolitionist fanatic to Christian saint: 'What a transit was that of his horizontal body alone, but just cut down from the gallows-tree! Like a meteor it shot through the Union from the southern regions towards the north! It seemed to me that John Brown was the only man who *had not died*: he has earned immortality.' Emerson also described Brown as a saint and Longfellow in his diary marked the day of the execution as 'the date of a new revolution, quite as much needed as the old one.'

The revolution was not long delayed. In 1860 the Democratic party split and put up two opposing presidential candidates, one representing the party as a whole and the other the slave states, whose determination to stand firm against the abolitionists had been stiffened by the affair at Harper's Ferry. Between them they polled more of the popular vote than Abraham Lincoln, the Republican candidate, but their divisions and his strength in the electoral college secured his election. Since Lincoln had made his opposition to slavery clear in the strongest terms the slave states thought they had no choice but to secede from the Union. This they prepared to do. Queen Victoria's eldest son the Prince of Wales was touring Canada and the United

States in the autumn of 1860 and saw the crisis at first hand. In Philadelphia on 6 October he joined Republican crowds who were celebrating success in the Pennsylvania elections, the victory which finally made Lincoln's presidency certain. He then went to New York and was greeted with 'the enthusiasm of more than half a million people worked up almost to madness and yet self-restrained within the bounds of a most perfect courtesy'. The actress Fanny Kemble wrote that 'the whole land was alive with excitement and interest'. London newspapers were delighted to hear of the Prince's reception and could not believe that a people capable of restraining madness within the bounds of a most perfect courtesy could really be on the brink of civil war. 'For the safety of the Union itself we confess we have no fear,' said *The Times* when the news of Lincoln's election came through, 'Of course, it will take some time before men can cool down from the bluster which has been so profusely used.' Five months later the Confederacy of slave states ordered its forces to open fire on a Federal fort in Charleston harbour.

God's re-emergence was immediate and dramatic. Armies on both sides marched behind him and the Confederate commander Robert E. Lee habitually quoted him in his General Orders. In Boston a clergyman suggested that his congregation should think of the Stars and Stripes as nailed to the Cross, since Christ and the Union were inseparable, and a Cincinnati newspaper told its readers that Confederates killed in action were slain 'through the instrumentality of an avenging God' and sent straight to hell. Finally, in December 1861, Mrs Julia Ward Howe made the most famous of all declarations of the divine presence. She was attending a review of the troops encamped around Washington, the Federal capital, when news of enemy activity brought the review to a hasty end and the bugles sounded to call the men to action. As Mrs Howe and a clergyman called Mr Clarke tried to make their way back to the city their carriage was frequently held up by marching columns and to pass the time they joined in the soldiers' songs, the most popular of which was 'John Brown's body'. 'Mrs Howe,' said Mr Clarke, 'why do you not write some good words for that stirring tune?'

And so she did, telling how her eyes had seen the glory of the coming of the Lord, how she had seen him in the watchfires of a hundred circling camps, how she had heard him sound the trumpet that should never call retreat. At first it was just a poem, a poem which her friend James Fields published in the *Atlantic Monthly* under the title 'The Battle Hymn of the American Republic', but as the struggle grew more ferocious and more embittered the idea that it was God himself who watched over their camps and sounded their bugle calls became more than a literary exercise for the Federalists. This new and more glorious coming of the Lord far outshone his earlier visits during the revival. But there was a price to be paid. 'As he died to make men holy, let us die to make men free,' cried Mrs Howe, reminding Federalists that they had gone to war not just to preserve the Union but to end slavery. As Lincoln seemed to evade the issue, declaring in his inaugural address that he would not interfere with slavery, he lost support not only at home but across the Atlantic. Whatever the dangers from their own subject races the British would back a war against slavery but they would not back coercion for merely constitutional reasons. 'No distinction can in my eyes be broader,' wrote Gladstone, 'than the distinction between the question whether the Southern ideas of slavery are right and the question whether they can justifiably be put down by war from the North.'

Lincoln proclaimed emancipation at the beginning of 1863. Although the proclamation was so hedged round as to have little practical effect it did turn the war into a crusade to free the slaves. In Britain it even secured the support of the Lancashire textile workers, who were unemployed because of the Federal blockade of Confederate cotton exports. In America it brought about such a change of heart that James Fields, in an *Atlantic Monthly* editorial looking back on 1863, could speak of God's presence and aid:

Such was the year of the Proclamation, and its history is marvellous in our eyes. It stands in striking contrast to the other years of the war ... We have been saved 'by the mighty hand of God.' Whether we had the right to expect Heaven's aid, we cannot undertake to say; but we know that we should not have deserved it, had we continued to link the nation's cause to that of oppression, and had we shed blood and expended gold in order to restore the system of slavery and the sway of slaveholders.

The words 'In God We Trust' started to appear on American coins in 1864 and when Lincoln was re-elected for a second term his inaugural address declared that if God willed it the war would continue 'until every drop of blood drawn by the lash shall be paid by another drawn by the sword'. 'The judgments of the Lord are true and righteous altogether,' he concluded. On 4 April 1865, just a month after delivering the address, he walked through Richmond, the captured

Confederate capital, and was greeted with cries of 'The kingdom is come and the Lord is with us!'. 'I'd rather see him than Jesus!' cried one liberated slave. The Confederate commander surrendered five days later and on 14 April Lincoln was shot and mortally wounded. He died early the next morning. The struggle which had begun with one martyrdom ended with another. Thoreau had died in 1862 and there was nobody to speak of Lincoln as he had spoken of John Brown. Perhaps it was not needed: many felt that Lincoln had long walked with the immortals and waited upon his God. The years of conflict had brought President and nation immeasurably closer to the glory of the Lord.

A little of the glory spilled over into British life. The greatest of the American revival hymns, 'Stand up, stand up for Jesus, Ye soldiers of the cross!', crossed the Atlantic during the 1860s and the marching songs of the civil war took their place alongside equally bellicose British hymns written and published during the same period. *Hymns Ancient and Modern* appeared in 1861 and close on its heels came 'O happy band of pilgrims' and 'Christian, dost thou see them' in 1862, 'Fight the good fight' and 'Soldiers of the cross, arise' in 1863, 'For all the saints' and 'Onward, Christian soldiers' in 1864. Never in the history of hymnody had so much been written in so short a time on the military duties of Christians. Metaphorical soldiers of Christ marched steadfastly through the pages of the hymn books with their loins girded, urging on their counterparts in the real world to deeds of valour. There was no crusade against slavery to be undertaken in Britain but there was still a holy war to be waged. Its nature was made clear in the hymn with which Sabine Baring-Gould brought the Christian war cries to a climax in 1867: 'Through the night of doubt and sorrow'. It was 'the light of God's own presence,' wrote Baring-Gould, that would chase away the gloom and terror which the doubters had spread. The coming of the Lord would be at once the inspiration and the reward of those who made a stand against unbelief. If Christians in Britain wanted to share Mrs Howe's vision they must fight the sceptics and the materialists as manfully as the Americans had struggled against the slave owners.

The Times led the way in May 1864 with a leading article on the encroachment of science upon religious belief. Six months later Disraeli told Wilberforce's Society for Increasing Endowments of Small Livings in the Diocese of Oxford that he was 'on the side of the angels' against

Darwin and that man was 'a being born to believe'.* More than seven hundred scientists signed a formal declaration regretting that their investigations had cast doubt on the Bible, while a group of clergymen set up the Victoria Institute as a centre from which Christian thinkers could combat science and all its works. The Duke of Buccleuch brought the campaign to a triumphant conclusion by telling the British Association for the Advancement of Science that its activities must always be subordinated to religion: 'I cannot put discoverers of that which exists in a higher position than the Author of that which is discovered.' When James Bowling Mozley was invited to give the 1865 Bampton lectures in Oxford he chose to speak about miracles. There were two possible explanations of them: that of the scientists, that they were legends, and that of the Christians, that they did indeed happen. Of these it was the scientific account that was irrational because it failed to recognize 'the supremacy of a Personal Will in nature'. Christians on the other hand 'dare trust our reason and the evidence which it lays before us of a Personal Supreme Being'. The 1866 Bampton lecturer, Henry Parry Liddon, defended the miracle of the loaves and fishes and other supernatural happenings in the New Testament against those who wished to expunge them from allegedly 'scientific' lives of Christ. Such a life had just been published anonymously under the title *Ecce Homo* and Lord Ashley, now Earl of Shaftesbury and the most influential Christian layman in the country, called it 'the most pestilential book ever vomited from the jaws of hell'.

Meanwhile Dr Cumming was preparing for the ultimate miracle. *Behold, the Bridegroom Cometh*, *The Last Warning Cry* and *The Reasons for the Hope that is in me* appeared in 1865 and in the following year he settled down to his most urgent work, *The Sounding of the Last Trumpet, or, The Last Woe*. He quoted *The Times* as saying that 'public law in Europe, such as it is, is shaken to its foundations and the last seven years have brought about portentous changes'. He also pointed to a paralysis of transport, unprecedented shipwrecks, pestilence reminiscent of the plagues of Egypt, 'financial and monetary convulsions', extensive earthquakes. Finally there was a widespread desire for reunion with Rome which showed 'degeneracy in the hearts of many Anglicans'. As he wrote the night sky above him was lit up by showers of meteors which looked, said the newspapers, 'like sparks flying from an incandescent mass of iron under the blows of

* See above, p.65.

a Titanic hammer'. That was in the middle of November, a mere six weeks before the opening of the year which was to see the coming of the Lord. Torrential rains, terrible thunderstorms, disastrous floods, all bore witness to the cosmic drama which was about to unfold. The weather was one long succession of 'wonderful phenomena and antagonistic manifestations,' declared *The Times*. 'We are about to enter on the Last Woe,' Cumming told his readers, 'and to hear the nearly-spent reverberations of the Last Trumpet'.

To Arthur Munby, alone in his room in London as the bells rang in 1867, it seemed that the everyday world was unreal. 'Within the room there is warmth and light,' he wrote, 'and signs of comfort and culture; selfish comfort which may vanish, profitless culture which leads to nothing.' Twenty-four hours later the everyday world disappeared under deep snow, the beauty of which came as a revelation. 'Instead of the roar and rush of wheels, the selfish hurry, the dirt and cloudy fog,' marvelled Munby, 'we had the loveliness and utter purity of new-fallen snow.' Others fulminated against the halting of transport, the incompetence of the authorities, the idleness of labourers who failed to sweep away the snow. Matthew Arnold was horrified by London's 'state of helplessness' and even the *Annual Register*, usually a fairly level-headed publication, wrote ominously of approaching disaster. 'The signs, for those who can read, are present and can be plainly seen,' it said darkly, 'when the signs become clearly visible the catastrophe will perhaps have ceased to be avertible.' The root cause was 'unreasonable disagreement between class and class'.

Neither the Prime Minister Lord Derby nor his Chancellor of the Exchequer Benjamin Disraeli did much to dispel the gloom. There had been serious rioting in 1866 when a Reform Bill giving working men the vote had been thrown out by Parliament and now Disraeli, with much talk about dark horizons and impending storms, brought forward a second Bill. He foresaw anarchy if it was defeated and a spate of strikes running through the spring and into the summer gave point to his warning. Derby thought that reform was 'a leap in the dark' and others talked of 'Shooting Niagara'. The Bill became law in August but widespread anti-Catholic riots and Fenian outrages showed that the danger had not passed. Matthew Arnold wrote that the country was in 'a strange uneasy state, a loosening of all old prejudices, respects and habits'. The fears he had just made public in his poem 'Dover Beach', fears of a world robbed of stability and meaning, were now modulated from a religious into a secular key. And at this point, as the gullible listened for the trumpet calls promised by Cumming and saner men wondered whether their secure world was indeed coming to an end, the Anglican bishops met in conference at Lambeth Palace. They concluded by issuing an address which seemed to give official approval to Cumming's apocalyptic imaginings. 'Beloved brethren,' they said solemnly, 'with one voice we warn you; the time is short; the Lord cometh; watch and be sober.'

It was not only the conventionally devout who felt a sense of unease. John Addington Symonds, a brilliant young man who was later to be a scourge of the orthodox, wrote that he was 'in a strange state in which the unreality of everything tortures me hourly and I long for God or what of Truth abides behind these phantoms to burn in on me. The great fact of my life is that the spiritual cannot emerge from the material.' He was not alone in his aspirations or in his frustrations. Lord Derby resigned in February 1868 and Disraeli became Prime Minister, determined to winkle the spiritual life of the nation out of its material shell. He had already insisted that he stood for 'a philosophic system of politics' and this, as he later explained, meant that 'the spiritual nature of man is stronger than codes or constitutions ... He who has a due sense of his relations to God is best qualified to fulfil his duties to man.' 'Society has a soul,' he declared, 'as well as a body'. Under his guidance the British would follow the example of Tancred, the nobly born hero of his most recent novel, who spurned 'the fatal drollery called a representative government' in order to go to the mysterious orient and listen to the voice of God.

Queen Victoria's initial doubts about having such a visionary as her Prime Minister were dispelled when he heaped praise on her *Leaves from the Journal of Our Life in the Highlands*, which was published at the beginning of 1868. It was above all a book about her beloved Albert and its success convinced her that he was still alive in her people's hearts as well as in her own. When her second son the Duke of Edinburgh survived a Fenian assassination attempt in March 1868 she thought she saw the hand of God, Mozley's 'supremacy of a Personal Will', and the Prince of Wales publicly called his brother's escape a miracle. Then the Queen's youngest son Prince Leopold fell ill and was restored to her 'from the brink of the grave', so that she became even more convinced of the divine presence. Longfellow visited England that summer, a reminder not of the embittered postwar politics of the United States but of the white heat in which Americans had seen the coming of the Lord. The only discordant note was struck by Gladstone and the Liberal opposition, who set up a cry for the disestablishment of the Irish Church as a first step towards redressing Irish grievances. Disraeli accused them of wanting to 'dissolve for the first time the connection between government and religion' and when they forced disestablishment resolutions through Parliament he told the Queen that 'the time has gone by for ministries to be subverted by abstract resolutions'. He dismissed the Liberals as 'one of those bands of minstrels one encounters in the sauntering of a summer street'.

At the end of the year the band of minstrels defeated him in a General Election and formed a government which disestablished the Irish Church. In Dublin a Church Congress railed against 'a creedless and godless State' and for good measure it also condemned 'the influence of scientific investigations on the minds of those who conduct them'. John William Draper, a professor in the University of New York, had recently published *A History of the Intellectual Development of Europe*, a sustained attack on Christianity as the blinkered opponent of scientific progress, and the orthodox on both sides of the Atlantic saw all liberals and all scientists as enemies of religion. A further storm broke when Gladstone invited Frederick Temple to be Bishop of Exeter. As headmaster of Rugby school Temple had introduced science into the curriculum and he had also been a contributor to *Essays and Reviews*. Pusey said that the appointment 'surpassed in its frightful enormity anything which has been openly done by any Prime Minister' and suggested that if Gladstone was going to behave like this he might as well disestablish the Church of England as well. There were angry demonstrations when Temple's election was confirmed and there was also an attempt to condemn him formally in Convocation.

Gladstone described the anger of the orthodox as 'vehement but thin' and as his administration went from strength to strength, sweeping away abuses in almost every corner of the nation's life, the same seemed to be true of Disraeli's claim to be the guardian of society's soul. *The Times* published a remarkable leading article on the relation of religion to politics, saying that twenty or thirty years earlier 'men who leant towards Liberalism in secular politics were brought back to Conservatism by their religious sympathies. We now see just the reverse'. Gladstone had turned Liberalism from something godless and suspect into a philosophy in tune with the infinite, performing here on earth the things which all good men hoped to see performed in a better life to come. When set beside this progressive idealism

86

Disraeli's visions seemed like the gaudy illusions of a fairground conjuror. 'Conservatism is now felt to have in it a certain element of comedy or even of farce. The leaders of the party do not believe in it ... their accession to power would be but the accident of a day'. Party leaders held a secret meeting to consider replacing Disraeli with someone less given to exotic flights of religious fantasy. One of the whips told them that Disraeli's leadership could cost them forty or fifty seats at a General Election. The time had come to put aside heady talk of the coming of the Lord and fight the Liberals with their own less imaginative weapons.

But the outbreak of the Franco-Prussian War in July 1870 had already set in motion a chain of events that would totally change the political and religious climate, saving Disraeli and bringing the British into unexpected contact with their God. The defeat of the French Emperor turned France into a Republic and the King of Prussia into the Emperor of Germany. French troops withdrew from Rome and the Romans voted to become part of the new Kingdom of Italy, thus ending the temporal power of the papacy. Three weeks later there was an unparalleled display of the aurora borealis and terrified crowds knelt in the streets of Rome at this obvious sign of divine displeasure. Londoners also took to the streets, not to beg forgiveness but to watch 'what they imagined to be the progress of the largest fire that had ever occurred', and the engines of the city's Salvage Corps rushed hither and thither looking for the non-existent conflagration. Swinburne was so excited by the overthrow of Napoleon III and the discomfiture of the Pope that he wanted to kiss everybody he met and roll naked upon the ground. From her eldest daughter, who was married to the Crown Prince of Prussia, Queen Victoria learned that the Prussian victory meant the triumph of liberal principles over an unprincipled Napoleonic state which had constantly corrupted the morals of visiting Englishmen.

The Queen was not reassured. 'The bloody, sad, eventful year '70 has sunk in dark clouds,' she noted in her diary on New Year's Day, 'and '71 rises as sad and gloomy'. On the same day the *Fortnightly Review* proclaimed that the events of the past few months had 'shaken the monarchical principle itself among classes otherwise not easily accessible to theory and doctrine'. In Britain it was shaken further by fears of a German invasion and the consequent unpopularity of the Queen's German connections. 'From private sources I know that the military aristocratic caste in Prussia, the Junkers, already assert "the turn of England will come next",' wrote an army officer in the *Contemporary Review*. *The Times* printed a solemn warning that no proper steps had been taken to fortify London and that 'the utter collapse of the Empire' would follow when the capital fell. 'The Battle of Dorking', a fictitious account of such an event, was published in *Blackwood's Magazine* in May and was enormously successful. A German newspaper, the *Allgemeine Zeitung*, made matters a good deal worse by announcing that England was 'in her decay and decrepitude' and should agree to be ruled by Germany.

Atheists and republicans took the opportunity to read funeral orations over Christianity and monarchy. 'Communism is a not impossible future. Positivism is a not impossible future. The *status quo* is impossible,' declared Frederic Harrison. Positivists, of whom Harrison was one, believed that the science of society was more sacred than revealed religion and had sacraments and prayers of their own based on sociology instead of on the supernatural. Communists were already in control of Paris and the Queen was horrified to learn that 'they go on quite as in the days of the old Revolution in the last century'. On Whit Sunday Gerard Manley Hopkins and his fellow Jesuits prayed for those of their order who were held hostage by the Paris Commune. The Introit for the day was grimly appropriate: 'Let God arise and let his enemies be scattered'. The next day they learned that the hostages had been shot. The Communists in their turn were massacred as government troops recaptured the city.

Yet even Hopkins, a conventional English gentleman converted to Roman Catholicism, could find it in him to admire the Communists. 'I must tell you I am always thinking about the Communist future,' he wrote to Robert Bridges, 'Horrible to say, in a manner I am a Communist ... The more I look the more black and deservedly black the future looks'. The press openly discussed the possibility of a British republic, to Swinburne's huge delight. 'Shall we live after all to see the Hanover rats smoked out,' he asked Rossetti in June, 'and the old mother of the royal rabbit-warren stifled in her burrow?' When a son born to the Princess of Wales died soon after birth a radical newspaper attacked 'the miserable mockery of interring with royal funeral ceremony a piece of skin and bone, grandiloquently called "Prince", not twenty-four hours old ... to augment the folly of the entire proceedings the Court goes into mourning for the loss of the wretched abortion'. A few weeks later the Queen was faced with public demonstrations against her favourite son and when she insisted on leaving London for Balmoral Gladstone said that her conduct was 'the most sickening piece of experience which I have had during near forty years of public life'. 'Worse things may be easily imagined,' he continued, 'but smaller and meaner cause for the decay of Thrones cannot be conceived'. When the Queen's doctors hinted that her mental condition was such that she would probably retire more and more from public life they were told roundly by her secretary that this would mean abdication and 'an alteration in our form of government'.

On 6 November Sir Charles Dilke, MP for Chelsea and a close associate of French republicans, made an elaborate attack on the incompetence of the Prince of Wales during recent army manoeuvres. He then went on to advocate a British republic. His speech, in a crowded hall in Newcastle, was wildly cheered. 'The meeting was largely composed of the working classes,' *The Times* noted apprehensively, 'and there was great enthusiasm.' 'There is a widespread belief,' Dilke concluded amidst tremendous applause, 'that a Republic here is only a matter of education and time. I say, for my part – and I believe the middle classes in general will say – let it come!' Republicanism was now a political force and its champions, led by Dilke and George Odger, began a triumphant round of speech-making. The Queen tried to ignore the movement but when Gladstone failed to rebut it her anxieties came into the open and she told him coldly that she was dissatisfied with his lukewarm defence of monarchy. 'At present, and now for many days,' she added, 'these Revolutionary Theories are allowed to produce what effect they may in the minds of the Working Classes. Gross mis-statements and fabrications injurious to the credit of the Queen and injurious to the Monarchy remain unnoticed and uncontradicted.'

On 22 November, the tenth anniversary of the Prince Consort's fatal attack of typhoid, the Queen heard that the Prince of Wales was ill with the same disease. 'How all reminded me so vividly and sadly of my dearest Albert's illness,' she noted in her journal as the Prince's condition got rapidly worse. Sunday 10 December was a Day of National Prayer and Supplication, observed everywhere with extraordinary fervour, but the Prince continued to weaken and the next day the Queen was told he was beyond hope. Public entertainments were cancelled out of respect for his approaching death. But on 14 December, the day his father had died, he began to mend. 'Instead of this date dawning upon another deathbed, which I had felt almost certain of,' Victoria wrote, 'it brought the cheering news that dear

Bertie had slept quietly ... the respirations much easier and food taken well'. At the end of the year she issued a letter of thanks to her people for the prayers that had brought her son safely through the valley of the shadow of death. There was much talk of a miracle, of a Prince saved by the supplications of his people, and the Queen's cousin the Duke of Cambridge had no doubts on the matter. 'The republicans say their chances are up – thank God for that!' he wrote, 'Heaven has sent this dispensation to save us.'

It was not easy to see what had been dispensed and how. Had God sent the typhoid germs as part of a plan to scotch republicanism and carry out the obligations placed upon him by the words of the British national anthem? Or had he only been involved at a later stage, condescending to spare the Prince when the national volume of prayer was sufficient to satisfy him? Or was he responding to the invitation issued in the Whit Sunday Introit and appearing in person in order to scatter his enemies, who of course were also those of the British Royal Family? If so they were scattered in some unpleasant ways. George Odger was attacked by an infuriated crowd on Reading station and driven into the urinal. Francis Kilvert told how a republican who mocked one of the bulletins about the Prince's illness was stripped naked and kicked up and down the street like a football. He was near to death when the police finally rescued him. Dilke's meetings were broken up by massive monarchist demonstrations and he abandoned them, saying that he had been misreported and had never intended to attack the Royal Family. Whether or not the nation's cries had been heard, whether or not there was a God to take a hand in its affairs, the prayers had undoubtedly transformed the political situation. They might not have changed God's mind but they had certainly changed the hearts and minds of those who offered them up.

The drama of the Prince's return from death's threshold reached a suitably Tennysonian climax when he was conveyed to the healing valleys of the Isle of Wight to convalesce. Tennyson's King Arthur had been taken by black-robed queens in a barge to the island-valley of Avilion; the Prince of Wales went in a steam yacht from Portsmouth and in his case the black-robed queen was waiting for him on the island, but the moral was the same. 'More things are wrought by prayer,' Arthur had proclaimed from the deck of his barge, 'Than this world dreams of.' Even Gladstone expressed a Tennysonian hope that the Prince's recovery might be 'like Arthur's Round Table in its moral effect'. At the Thanksgiving Service the crowds greeted him with jeers whilst applauding Disraeli wildly. A few short weeks had turned a reasonably popular Prime Minister into a republican suspect and a discredited opposition leader into a seer. When he got back to the Carlton Club Disraeli stood for a long time gazing out of the window with an expression on his face which onlookers described as 'that of one who looks into another world'. It was a world which Gladstonian reforms and Gladstonian sound finance had come near to dispelling, a world in which nations could be uplifted by visions instead of being cushioned in material progress. It was a world of allegories and fantasies, a world inhabited by more gods than most Victorians cared to meet. 'The potent wizard', as Skelton had called Disraeli, now had it in his power to cast strange spells. Whether or not God came to his aid he was determined to rescue the British from the enervating grasp of reality.

6 THE USES OF FANTASY

In the summer of 1871, replying to the accusations of the *Allgemeine Zeitung*, *The Times* admitted, not without a certain pride, that Britain had a tradition of 'saturnalia of a political character'. At the same time Parliament instituted Bank Holidays and one of these was the occasion for a political saturnalia in Manchester to launch Disraeli's assault on the prosaic statesmanship of the Liberals. Arriving on Easter Monday 1872 he was greeted by huge holiday crowds who removed the horses from his carriage and drew it through the streets in triumph. Two days later, assisted by two bottles of a liquid which his audience thought was water but was in fact a conveniently colourless brandy, he roused a mass meeting to frenzy with his vision of a country regenerated by the loyalty and piety of its people. 'England is a domestic country,' he cried amidst tremendous cheering, 'Here the home is revered and the hearth is sacred. The nation is represented by a family – the Royal Family.' He rounded on Gladstone for supporting republicans and he told his audience that Britain's future greatness would spring from the twin institutions of throne and altar. Geography had intended her to be part of some European state but if she was true to her spiritual inheritance she would find a more glorious rôle. A few weeks later, in the appropriate setting of the Crystal Palace, the Bank Holiday dream world in the London suburbs, he declared that Britain must be 'an Imperial country, a country where your sons, when they rise, rise to paramount positions and command the respect of the world.'

Tennyson embarked upon a similar imaginative journey from personal piety through national regeneration to imperial greatness. 'If I ceased to believe in any chance of another life, and of a Great Personality somewhere in the Universe, I should not care a pin for anything,' he told his friends in the summer of 1872. He remodelled his Arthurian poems yet again, adding to them an epilogue addressed to the Queen in which he reminded her how 'London roll'd one tide of joy through all her trebled millions' at the time of the Thanksgiving Service. This moment of inspiration would lead 'the mightiest of all peoples under heaven' to be true to its 'ocean-empire'. The shameful demand to give away Canada, voiced recently by some Liberals, would be dropped and the dangers he had pinpointed in his Arthurian allegory – 'softness, breeding scorn of simple life', 'cowardice, the child of lust for gold', 'art with poisonous honey stol'n from France' – would be met and mastered.

Others still saw science as the real enemy and with the miracle of the Prince's recovery to reassure them they took up the struggle anew. 'Let science set herself to reform man's belief in his own immortality,' wrote Thomas Fowle angrily in the *Contemporary Review*, 'instead of engaging in the unnatural and hopeless task of destroying it.' *The Times* had already attacked Darwin for the 'disintegrating speculations' of his new book, *The Descent of Man*, and the *Family Herald* declared that 'society must fall to pieces if Darwinism be true'. When Charles Bastian published *The Beginnings of Life* in July 1872, claiming that organic life had evolved from the inorganic world without a divine creator, he was told sternly that 'when science, passing beyond its own limits, assumes to take the place of theology ... it is invading a province of thought to which it has no claim.' There was a warm welcome for the pious pseudo-science of St George Jackson Mivart's *Genesis of Species*, which seemed to show that natural selection was 'perfectly compatible with the creative and guiding power of God'. It was 'a most interesting and satisfactory book', noted Charles Dodgson.

Mrs Lynn Linton's novel *The True History of Joshua Davidson, Christian and Communist* hinted that God might have been involved in the events of the previous year in a very different way from that envisaged by the orthodox. Her hero Joshua Davidson, a Christ-like figure who championed the oppressed in England and in France, was denounced as an atheist on his return from the Paris Commune. The denunciation, made at a public meeting by a clergyman who should have been his friend, resulted in Joshua being beaten to death by an angry mob shouting 'You insulted God and religion'. The parallel with the crowds who had been incited to demand Christ's crucifixion was too obvious to be missed. Meanwhile in August 1872 Darwin's cousin Francis Galton, a distinguished scientist and explorer, had dealt the miraculous interpretation of the Prince's recovery a shrewd blow. His article in the *Fortnightly Review*, 'A Statistical Inquiry into the Efficacy of Prayer', showed that among social groups having 'the advantages of affluence' the shortest lived were members of the Royal Family, even though they were prayed for regularly in every church in the land. 'The prayer has therefore no efficacy,' he concluded coldly, 'unless the very questionable hypothesis be raised, that the conditions of royal life may naturally be yet more fatal, and that their influence is partly, though incompletely, neutralized by the effect of public prayers.'

Floods in Cheshire that summer swept away four bridges, prompting the county surveyor to bring an action against the lady whose ornamental lakes had overflowed and caused the damage. He lost his case because the courts decided it had been an Act of God. The lawyers, like the Duke of Cambridge, could infer divine action even if they could not see it. A terrible storm later in the year convinced Francis Kilvert that 'the Almighty was making the clouds His chariot and walking upon the wings of the wind', but he did not claim to have seen God with his own eyes. Only foolish papists did that. For Bernadette Subirous in France to say she had seen the Virgin Mary was superstitious nonsense but for dukes and men of law in England to detect God's hand in the recovery of princes or in the overflowing of lakes was sound religion. In July 1872 the *Westminster Review* set out to explode this sort of humbug. Christians must make up their minds whether or not God could override natural law. If he could the so-called superstition of the Roman Catholics was simple recognition of truth. If he couldn't all forms of Christianity were suspect. There was no halfway house between superstition and open disbelief, even though Protestants might think they had built one. Their religion had provided 'a resting place which has sheltered man on his way from bondage to freedom,' rather than 'a permanent dwelling place for the mind'. 'We deem not only its eclipse but its disappearance to be merely a question of time: the ultimate contest must take place over the admission of the Supernatural, in any form, into the observed phenomena of the universe'.

Frederick George Lee, ritualist vicar of All Saints Lambeth, took up the challenge gleefully and cited the phrase about the ultimate contest in the introduction to *The Other World, or Glimpses of the Supernatural*, a two-volume work based on the proposition that Christianity was meaningless without belief in miracles and visions. His convictions were soon to lead him to accept consecration as an Anglican bishop at the hands of some rather dubious Roman Catholics at a secret meeting in Italy, but for the time being he contented himself with recording all the instances of ghosts and witches and visitations he could find. *The Times* was furious. 'The worst enemies of the Church of England or of Religion,' it thundered, 'could hardly seek a better ally than a clergyman who drags into the light of day these relics or survivals of heathenism and who claims our belief in the name of religion for every lying legend'. It was a point of view with which most Anglicans agreed: in spite of the *Westminster's* strictures they jealously guarded their right to tread the tightrope which Protestantism had stretched between popish gullibility and scientific scepticism.

In the United States the rope was harder to tread because there was no established church, no divinely ordained monarchy, to keep it taut and to regulate the performance. There were certain parallels between Julia Ward Howe and Queen Victoria – they had been born within three days of each other and their respective visions, the coming of the Lord and the spiritual presence of Prince Albert, had both been vouchsafed in December 1861 – but 'The Battle Hymn of the Republic' could hardly be said to have the same standing as 'God Save the Queen' where divine aid was concerned. God was well used to being asked to save Victoria and his recent intervention on her behalf was more specific and more dramatic than anything he had done on the other side of the Atlantic. It had also been endorsed and promulgated by the Church of which she was Supreme Head, a process which could not be duplicated in the United States.

The forces which American religion could field in the fight against unbelief had plenty of enthusiasm but they had no figure-head to follow and no army to join. If the *Westminster Review* was right, if Protestantism was being crushed between Roman Catholic superstition and scientific scepticism, then the pressure was worse in America than in Britain. On the one hand Irish immigration was daily swelling Catholic ranks and on the other the influence of scientific and materialist thought was growing as never before. Whitelaw Reid, editor of the *New York Tribune*, declared in 1873 that American students no longer read English poetry and English novels in their spare time, as they had done in earlier years, but English science and English philosophy. 'Herbert Spencer, John Stuart Mill, Huxley, Darwin, Tyndall, have usurped the places of Tennyson and Browning and Matthew Arnold and Dickens,' he concluded. Henry Ward Beecher, one of the most influential preachers in America, told teachers and students at

Yale in 1872 that if Christianity resisted scientific progress it would shrivel and die. 'The providence of God is rolling forward in a spirit of investigation that Christian ministers must meet and join,' he warned.

But the common ground which devout scientists and progressive Christians sought to occupy was already being raked by atheist fire. Robert Green Ingersoll, Republican politican and former attorney general of Illinois, embarked in the early 1870s on a series of nationwide lecture tours. They were enormously successful – Ingersoll's manager said they brought in more money than any others in the history of lecturing – and their chosen target was the Christian religion. For more than twenty years 'the notorious infidel', as he came to be called, held huge audiences spellbound as he reduced conventional beliefs to an unsightly rubble of delusions. And there was no potent wizard, no charismatic politician of Disraeli's standing, to overcome Ingersoll's spells and lead pious processions into fantasy of the sort witnessed in Manchester.

The only active and self-confessed wizard in American politics was General Nathan Bedford Forrest, Grand Imperial Wizard of the Ku Klux Klan, and his message was not divine love but human hate. Originally founded for sport, so that its members could scare superstitious negroes by riding at night through the Southern countryside dressed as the sheeted dead, the Klan soon developed into a sinister secret society. Klansmen's fantasies ran to imagined orders of chivalry – Knights of the Black Cross, Knights of the Rising Sun, Knights of the White Carnation – whose avowed purpose was to defend their vision of Christianity against decadent latter-day liberalism. Jefferson Davis, president of the Confederacy during the Civil War, had declared that the emancipation of the slaves was an offence against God and would mean that 'several millions of human beings of an inferior race, peaceful and contented labourers in their sphere, are doomed to extermination, while at the same time they are encouraged to a general assassination of their masters'. Now, in the name of the God who had been offended, the Ku Klux Klan set about righting the wrong and asserting white supremacy by means of terror and intimidation. In North Carolina a teacher who dared to bring a crippled negro boy to church was expelled by his congregation and then taken to nearby woods at night to be ritually whipped and disfigured by a posse of Klansmen. The *Westminster Review* had seen the coming struggle as one between superstition and materialism but in the

Southern states the superstition had turned into a nightmarish fanaticism.

This was largely because materialism had turned into the worst kind of corruption. Enlightened liberals of the kind envisaged by Whitelaw Reid and Henry Ward Beecher, trying to combine Christian values with an awareness of intellectual and scientific progress, soon found their ideals used to cover squalid self-seeking. Unscrupulous Republican politicians from the North moved into the Southern states and used the Reconstruction Acts, passed by Congress to rebuild the areas devastated by war, as a means of establishing their own suprem-acy. They made the liberated slaves pawns in their political game and this helped to provoke the excesses of the Klan. Dishonest electoral practices became so common that in Louisiana, after a particularly notorious rigged election, there were two rival governors and two rival state legislatures.

In Texas bitterness was laced with hope because the war had left unscathed vast herds of cattle whose value increased tenfold when they were taken a thousand miles north to the railheads in Kansas. The cowboys who drove them rode a trail into fantasy as well as into Kansas. In 1872, only five years after Joseph McCoy set up the first Kansas cattleyard at Abilene, Buffalo Bill Cody starred in Edward Zane Judson's play *The Scouts of the Prairie* and then began to tour the country with a Wild West show which included Wild Bill Hickok, who had just completed a stint as marshal of Abilene. Hickok claimed to have killed over a hundred men and Cody had certainly killed over four thousand buffalo. Writing under the name of Ned Buntline, Judson went on to produce more than four hundred dime novels about the Wild West, most of them with Buffalo Bill as hero. Prentiss Ingraham, also a friend of Buffalo Bill, contributed a further six hundred. The legend-ary world of the Wild West, where lawless cowboys emptied their six-shooters into whisky bottles and into one another, was destined to play a vital part in the imaginative life of the English-speaking peoples.

Britain too had its images of lawlessness. After the serious rioting which accompanied the General Election of February 1874, there was once again talk of the danger of revolution. In the Birmingham area there were fears that 'the whole population would be up in arms' and *The Times* compared the sinister advance of the working classes to an encroaching ocean. 'The better class public watches the swelling tide and the rising breakers till they come to its very feet,' it said anxiously, 'and knows not the laws which will compel them to ebb in due time, or at least prevent an inundation.' During the ensuing months William Rathbone Greg, once an industrialist and now a writer both on religion and on class conflict, published a series of articles in the *Contemporary Review* under the title 'Rocks Ahead, or the Warnings of Cassandra'. Like many other writers of the time he was worried about possible industrial decline and about what he called 'the political supremacy of the lower classes', but he was even more concerned with the gulf between conventional Christianity and contemporary thought. If politicians and other leading men were keeping up a mere pretence, trying to hold the lower classes off by brandishing spiritual and moral precepts in which they had themselves lost faith, then how could social breakdown and revolution be avoided? He concluded with an eloquent but despairing appeal for a change of heart before the country finally ran on the rocks:

Is there no other way of escape? Is it hopeless to avert and preclude the danger instead of meeting and mitigating it when it comes? Is it idle to dream that in the course of years the Religion of the nation may be modified in the direction and under the guidance of its best Intelligence, since that Intelligence can no longer accept the common Creed? The thing is possible, but not likely. I seem to see how it might be done, but I have no hope that it will be done. The divergence is too wide; the sources of the alienation lie too deep.

In the 1840s writing of this kind would have been the province of the prophets of apocalypse. Self-appointed seers like Marsh and Elliott and Cumming would have used the approach of anarchy and revolution on both sides of the Atlantic as proof that God had finally lost patience with the turbulence and infidelity of mankind. But now Marsh was dead, Elliott was dying and Cumming had fallen silent after publishing one last book to show that the events of 1870 had proved him right. It had made very little impact. In his day he had been enormously influential and the public had shown an insatiable appetite for his successive prognostications. But now his day was done and the business of prediction had passed into other hands. The disaster which Greg foresaw would not be divine retribution for loss of faith but quite the reverse: it would happen in spite of God rather than because of him and it would result from a failure to abandon conventional religion. The contrast between the two kinds of prophecy showed how much attitudes had changed in the space of thirty years. It was hard to imagine that thousands of ordinary people would ever again flock to hear men like Cumming tell them what God was up

98

to and how the threats and promises he had made in the Bible were being fulfilled.

But there was still an appetite for fantasy, a hunger for signs and portents. It was not gullibility that was dying but merely the readiness to clothe it in conventional biblical forms. The public wanted something more exciting, more occult, than pious expositions of the Book of Revelation. In 1862 Charles Hindley of Brighton had published a prophecy by Mother Shipton, a fifteenth-century witch from Yorkshire, which included the lines:

> The world to an end shall come
> In eighteen hundred and eighty one.

Hindley had subsequently admitted that he had written the prediction himself but this made little difference to its popularity. It was constantly re-issued, selling many thousands of copies, and it had a particular appeal to those who had recently been bereaved and did not want their loved ones to wait too long for their resurrection. Moses Hickman, an undertaker who had premises in the Commercial Road in London, was quick to see the value of such concern. He put a prominent advertisement in the 1872 edition of the pamphlet offering a lead-lined coffin, the ultimate in sepulchral security, for as little as £20 – a price which included a hearse and four horses, two mourning coaches, ostrich plumes, black velvets and a suitable number of funeral mutes. The publishers declared that the lines about 1881 had become 'the talk of the whole civilized globe' and offered to sell the page containing them separately, 'believing that many of our readers would prefer it in this shape for Albums, Scrap Books, etc.'

Mother Shipton received support from an unexpectedly authoritative quarter. Professor Charles Piazzi Smyth, Astronomer Royal for Scotland, had spent many years examining the Great Pyramid and was sure that it was a divinely inspired calendar in stone. Having noted that 985 years had elapsed between the building of the Tower of Babel and the Exodus of the Jews, followed by a further 1,542 between the Exodus and the birth of Christ, he had then found these figures were reproduced in inches as principal dimensions of the Grand Gallery of the pyramid. And the other main dimension, from the end to the great wall, was precisely 1,881.4 inches. This proved that the rule of Christ would last for 1,881.4 years, just as the 'Mosaic dispensation' had lasted for 1,542. Because of inaccuracies as to the accepted date of Christ's birth the moment of destiny would arrive not in 1882 but in the spring of 1881. Smyth's book *Our Inheritance in the Great Pyramid* was illustrated with photographs taken during a royal tour of Egypt and when he gave the Royal Society a first report on his findings in 1864 he was assured that 'if they are facts they form the most remarkable discovery of the age.'

But when in 1874 he announced that his definitive account was now ready he found that the officials of the Society had changed their minds. They refused to give his paper a hearing and after a furious row he resigned from the Society – though not from his position as Astronomer Royal – and turned from his fellow scientists to the general public. He brought out three successive revised and enlarged editions of his book, lacing his calculations with predictions as lurid as any that Cumming had produced. 'Badly as the last 1250 years of the Christian dispensation have distinguished themselves by their numerous wars and over-abundant bloodshed,' he warned, 'the last few years still remaining to it threaten to be more terrible than ever.' And the event to which these remaining seven years would lead was no longer seen merely as the end of the Christian era but as Christ's Second Coming. 'And meanwhile the Great Pyramid will assist in witnessing to the supernatural preparations for the universal earthly kingdom of the returned Lord Christ.' Even though Smyth's starting point in the dark tombs of ancient pharaohs had all the fascination of the occult his conclusions were the same as those reached by conventional pedlars of biblical apocalypse.

It was by no means certain that the returned Lord Christ would be prepared to rule over all who claimed to be Christians, for the book made it clear that the inheritance was that of the English-speaking peoples only. They had been especially favoured with the divinely ordained measurements of yards and feet and inches, the language in which God spoke to mankind, and they must be sure to remain true to them if they wished to come into their inheritance. 'National apathy, if not apostasy, has brought some Englishmen so low that they have begun to talk about abolishing their own hereditary measures,' Smyth wrote angrily. The proposed alternative, 'the Communistic French metric system', was 'part of the general drifting of the European nations into infidelity.'

On the day Smyth resigned from the Royal Society, 7 February 1874, Gladstone decided to concede defeat in the General Election and make way for Disraeli. Smyth's career as a popular prophet and

100

Disraeli's period of office as Prime Minister had begun together and might well end together, either triumphantly or otherwise, for under the Septennial Act the new Parliament could not last longer than 1881. Disraeli's fantasy of Britain's imperial destiny, that spiritual inheritance of which he had spoken in his Crystal Palace speech, must unfold alongside the predictions of the Astronomer Royal for Scotland. Both men had staked their reputations on a conviction that visions would become realities within seven years. The two visions had much in common – both rejected all things European and both drew inspiration from the mysterious orient, especially from ancient Egypt – but more significant was the mere fact that both were dreams. There were precedents for allowing dreamers to decide the fate of peoples. The Book of Genesis told how it had happened in ancient Egypt after Joseph had interpreted Pharaoh's dream about the seven fat years and the seven lean. However, it would be strange if such things were allowed to mould national policies and popular culture in the last quarter of the nineteenth century.

In the realm of popular culture successive accretions of occult wisdom quickly built up around the prophecies of Mother Shipton and Professor Smyth. Vast crowds gathered at Ham Hill in Somerset on Good Friday 1879 to watch the local stone quarries disappear into the earth on the stroke of noon, an event which Mother Shipton was said to have foretold but which failed to take place. She was back in the news the following year when a Yorkshire village slid into the Leeds Corporation reservoir. It was widely claimed that she had predicted this disaster as one of the things which would herald the end of the world. Indeed it seemed that no natural phenomenon could escape being woven into her remarkable foresight. 'Should the spring be late, the summer cold, or snow fall earlier than usual,' one sceptic wrote angrily, 'we are at once told that Mother Shipton prophesied that we should not know winter from summer, except by the leaves on the trees, before the world was at an end.' In 1880 Houlton and Sons of Paternoster Square in London brought out *The End of the World in 1881–2, according to Mother Shipton, the Great Pyramid of Ghizeh and other Ancient Prophecies related to Russia and Turkey*, a curious compilation which hovered between simulated disapproval and unashamed sensationalism. It told how an eminent professor had declared that the 1881 census would show that England had 33,950,000 inhabitants, a figure pregnant with meaning for those who knew that Smyth had put the length of the Grand Gallery at precisely 339.5 inches. It pointed

101

out that the contract for carrying mail between London and Bombay ran out at the beginning of 1881, as did the Protectorate set up in Syria and the tenure of certain emoluments in Britain. Even the completion of the new Law Courts in the Strand, scheduled for New Year's Day 1881, was cited as evidence that this would inaugurate the year of destiny.

There were also suggestions that 1881 might not be an end but a beginning. It seemed that the height of a certain step in the Great Pyramid indicated that 'the period of tribulation' would last until 1887. Professor C.A. Grimmer, 'an American astrologer of some repute', was quoted as saying that the years from 1880 to 1887 would witness 'one universal carnival of death'. In fact Professor Grimmer had used a less frivolous word. His book *The Voice of the Stars, or the coming Perihelia of Jupiter, Uranus, Neptune and Saturn with attendant Plagues, Storms and Fires from 1880 to 1887 supported by Historical Facts* predicted 'one universal carnage of death'. Ships would rot upon the ocean, 'their dead human freight drifting where the winds and waves might take them', and the sun would be as red as blood. The poor would rise against the rich, bringing fanaticism and anarchy, and the face of the earth would be changed by volcanic action. It would be impossible to eat either fish or meat and God would show his rejection of the human race by producing 'remarkable displays of electricity, frightful to witness'.

While Smyth's dream gathered adherents Disraeli's ran into trouble. 'You were very right in saying that the only obvious difficulties might be religious ones,' he told his colleague Lord Salisbury shortly after forming his administration. Before he could propose any other measures Victoria made it clear that priority must be given to a law to stop 'all these Ritualistic practices, dressings, bowings, etc., and everything of that kind'. Salisbury, who had only agreed to join the government if no steps were taken against the High Church, began to talk not just of resignation but of 'civil war in the Church of England'. The Queen admitted that such a measure would cause 'inconvenience and difficulty' but insisted that it could not be put off. Disraeli gritted his teeth and prepared to trim his vision of Britain's destiny to fit the convictions of his sovereign.

The first step was to suggest that the proposed Public Worship Regulation Act would defend the Church of England against insidious pseudo-Catholicism, against what Disraeli called 'the Mass in masquerade'. 'I have never addressed any body of my countrymen for the last three years,' he told the House of Commons, 'without having taken the opportunity of intimating to them that a great change was occurring in the politics of the world, that the great struggle between the temporal and the spiritual power, which had stamped such indelible features upon the history of the past, was reviving in our own time.' Having thus preserved the British from papal tyranny he would turn his attention to his avowed policy of lifting them from base materialism to true spirituality and imperial greatness. But in September 1874, when the Bill became law and he went to Balmoral as the honoured guest of a grateful sovereign, he fell seriously ill. 'I am a sort of prisoner of state in the tower of a castle,' he wrote to Lady Bradford, 'a royal physician comes two or three times a day to feel my pulse, etc., and see whether I can possibly endure the tortures that await me.' While he languished in his tower the religious strife predicted by Lord Salisbury became increasingly bitter. High Churchmen proclaimed that they would not obey the new courts set up by the Act and Gladstone said that the country now resembled 'the field and the eve of the Battle of Armageddon'.

Several London clergymen defied the Act and went on with their ritualistic practices. The most notorious was the Rev. Arthur Tooth of Hatcham near New Cross. By the beginning of 1877 special trains were arriving at New Cross station on Sundays, packed with men and boys who had allegedly been hired to break up Tooth's services. One of his outraged parishioners claimed that the men had been paid a pound each and the boys a shilling. Even *The Rock*, a periodical hostile to the High Church, reported that 'forty dockyard "lambs" or labourers received ten shillings each together with seats in the church and the whole body, police and lambs included, were fed at one shilling and sixpence a head by Mr Page of New Cross.' There were ugly brawls, involving up to eight thousand people, and the police had to send for reinforcements. Even when Tooth gave himself up and was gaoled the troubles did not end. Fighting in his church was worse than ever and further violence erupted in Folkestone, where another turbulent priest persisted in the dressings and bowings that had so angered the Queen. Worst of all, it seemed that the Act had increased rather than reduced the Catholic danger: 'It is to Rome that individuals are silently migrating,' wrote the Bishop of Gloucester anxiously.

Meanwhile another and very different threat to established belief was opening an even wider gulf between Anglican clergymen and their flocks. Shortly before Disraeli became Prime Minister the *Contemporary Review* published an article by Sir Henry Thompson, an eminent surgeon, advocating cremation. Most of his arguments were practical ones – graveyards were getting crowded, pollution from cemeteries was a cause of disease – but his real target was belief in bodily resurrection and in the grave as a place of eternal rest. 'Could I paint in its true colours,' he wrote grimly, 'the ghastly picture of that which happens to the mortal remains of the dearest we have lost, the page would be too deeply stained for publication.' It was inconceivable that what the writhing maggots left behind could ever walk the walls of heaven.

There was worse to come. Bishop Fraser of Manchester, consecrating new burial land at Bolton in March 1874, took occasion to refer to the cremation controversy because 'he wished his hearers to dissociate the resurrection from physical conditions'. If God so wished he could raise up a body 'out of elementary particles which had been liberated by the burning' as easily as from 'the elements of bodies which had passed into the structure of worms'. But he might well do neither, for the words of the burial service did not constitute a guarantee. When the priest at the graveside said that Jesus Christ would 'change our vile body, that it may be like unto his glorious body' he was merely stating a personal belief, not making promises to the corpse at his feet. Some bodies might prove too vile to be changed and their owners might never inherit eternal life.

Some bodies might even be too vile to be buried. When Frederick Merrett of Cowley near Oxford died in January 1875 his vicar, the Rev. J. Coley, refused to bury him because of his 'notorious life'. Eight days later, with the corpse still above ground, Merrett's relatives tried to get Coley to let somebody else officiate. He refused to see them and locked himself in his church while several hundred of Merrett's supporters rioted outside. Three days later, when another clergyman finally arrived to bury the body, he found the church locked. The crowd of mourners and sympathizers, numbering well over a thousand even though it was a working day, forced its way into the church after a dozen men had climbed in through the belfry and ripped off the lock from the inside with crowbars. Merrett was given a proper funeral and a fortnight later an enormous crowd paraded Coley's effigy round Oxford with a placard on its chest proclaiming 'Cremation of Rev. J. Coley'. The figure was then publicly burned.

Perhaps the most significant feature of this extraordinary affair was the placard on the effigy. In the thirteen months since Thompson's article cremation had come to be regarded with horror and revulsion. It was an insult to the dead, an obscenity, and so it was appropriate that it should be visited on one who had tried to obstruct the progress to eternal life which burial was thought to guarantee. Those who voluntarily burned their dead were viewed with disgust. When Sir Charles Dilke's wife died in September 1874 he had her cremated in Dresden, 'in a furnace recently invented by Herr Siemens, with large numbers of scientific men attending'. The English press gave a horrific timed account of the proceedings: the coffin burst after six minutes, the flesh began to melt after another five and the skeleton was laid bare after another ten. Later the *Annual Register* recorded the 'intense horror and amazement' of the people of Woking in Surrey when they discovered that a certain Professor Gorini was constructing 'a cremating apparatus right in their very midst'.

There were other attacks on traditional interment and on the hopes which went with it. Francis Seymour Haden, a surgeon and a noted artist, argued that while ordinary burial was certainly insanitary cremation had even greater dangers, being a positive incentive to poisoners. What was needed was a wicker or *papier-maché* coffin so that the worms could obtain easier entry and complete their work more quickly. Swift decomposition was the best guarantee of public hygiene. His proposed perforated and perishable coffins, looking like overgrown wastepaper baskets according to *The Times*, were put on public display in London in the summer of 1875. The exhibition was open daily 'on presentation of an ordinary visiting card' but few undertakers bothered to go. They knew that their customers wanted security, with lead linings if they could afford them, rather than swift decomposition. The resurrection of the body might be an unhygienic fantasy for Haden but it was a profitable one for undertakers.

The authorities were worried about the impact the American revivalists Dwight Moody and Ira Sankey might have on a Britain torn apart by ritualism and beset by doubts about the dead. After a successful mission in Scotland in 1873 and 1874 Moody and Sankey held their first London meeting in March 1875. At first it was noted with some relief that their congregations 'appeared for the most part to consist of the middle class', but later *The Times* had to admit that they had brought in 'not less than 335,000 of every class of society'. The Prince of Wales attended a meeting but the Queen declined on the grounds that this was sensationalism and not true religion. 'The

105

attraction is a love for religious excitement,' *The Times* explained loftily, 'apt at times to run riot in ordinarily sober races'. The Marquis of Bath brought the business of the House of Lords to a standstill in June by demanding parliamentary action to stop the Americans holding a meeting at Eton. *The Times* published a letter of protest against the meeting signed by seventy-four members of Parliament, all Etonians or parents of Etonians. Edward Hugessen Knatchbull-Hugessen, who orchestrated the campaign against Moody and Sankey, had written a book called *Whispers of Fairyland* and this led to a certain amount of mockery; but he stood his ground and insisted that as a writer of children's books he knew that 'spasmodic and sensationalist religion' did harm to boys of an impressionable age. In the end the battle on the playing fields of Eton between fairyland and the kingdom of God resulted in a draw: Moody and Sankey were prevented from using the marquee which had been prepared for them but they drew a crowd of 500 to an impromptu meeting which they held in the back garden of a draper's shop.

Meanwhile the Prime Minister who had proclaimed the importance of society's soul was having to concern himself with its body. A deepening trade depression led to wage reductions and strikes. The government put forward a programme of reform but this had little effect on the immediate situation. Disraeli spoke of 'much fright and confusion' but he still had faith in his own visionary powers. 'I see, as from a tower, the end of all,' he wrote calmly when things were at their worst. In the autumn of 1875, as the Prince of Wales set off on a tour of India, the vision began to unfold. *The Times* had already said, in connection with a ball at which the Prince's brother had appeared in a leopard skin with gold claws, that 'The pride of our people requires that there should be a well-ordered magnificence in the lives of their Princes'. Now the accounts of the oriental splendours with which the Prince was received in India ministered both to the nation's pride and to Disraeli's politics of fantasy.

In the midst of the splendours, just after he had shot his first tiger, the Prince learned that one of his companions, the loose-living Lord Aylesford, was being paid in his own coin: his wife was running off with Lord Blandford. And when the party reached Egypt on its way home the Prince heard that Blandford's brother, Lord Randolph Churchill, had shown the Princess of Wales some letters from the Prince which were allegedly so compromising that if they were to be published the Prince would never succeed to the throne. The Prince sent Lord

Charles Beresford off across Europe with a curt letter challenging Churchill to a duel. The royal procession out of India appeared to have little respect for conventional morality and the satirists began to talk of 'Prince Pagan'. Pagan or not the Prince certainly had that strange power over animals which Nietzsche had promised to the followers of Dionysus. Lord Lytton, who went aboard the royal yacht *Serapis* in the Suez Canal, was astounded by the vessel's barbaric splendours and by the tigers and other beasts who roamed its decks. 'The Prince really seems to have won the hearts not only of the Rajahs and Maharajahs but also of the wild beasts in India,' he told the Queen.

During the Prince's absence in India the British government had acquired the Khedive of Egypt's shares in the Suez Canal. Disraeli described his achievement in typically colourful terms: 'We have had all the gamblers, capitalists, financiers of the world, organized and platooned in bands of plunderers, arrayed against us, and secret emissaries in every corner, and have baffled them all'. The route to the riches of the east was secure and the land of the pharaohs was locked as firmly into the popular mind as even Professor Smyth could have wished. *Punch* published a cartoon showing Disraeli in the sands of Egypt brandishing his acquisition in the form of a key – 'The Key of India' – while the Great Pyramid looked on and the immemorial sphinx winked. At a ball given by the Lord Lieutenant of Ireland a lady came dressed as the Suez Canal:

A head-dress of Egyptian fashion, formed of pearl and turquoise beads, with a tiara of diamonds; and a long flowing robe of rich cloth of gold, to represent the Desert, traversed by wavy bands of azure satin, embroidered with pearls, to typify the blue waves of the Mediterranean passing through the sands of the Desert and bearing the wealth of the Indies; a red satin under-skirt embroidered with Egyptian designs, to represent the Red Sea; the corsage of blue satin, to represent the Mediterranean Sea, girdled with roses and lilies for England and France; the neck and arms covered with Egyptian jewels; and a long flowing veil, enveloping the whole figure, of tissue of gold, like a cloud of gold-dust. At her girdle was a golden key, with a label attached, 'Suez Canal, four millions'.

But the lady had not come alone. She was part of a quadrille entitled 'The Eastern Question' and her three companions represented the Mediterranean, the Neva and Constantinople – reminders that Russia and Turkey, now moving steadily towards war, were also interested

107

in Egypt. In 1876 the Turks put down with barbaric cruelty a revolt in Bulgaria and many people felt that Disraeli – now Earl of Beaconsfield – should join with Russia in a crusade against Turkish power in the Balkans. Instead the Queen and her ministers supported the Turks. The Queen was convinced that Russia had incited the revolt in order to push through the Balkans and cut Britain's route to India. 'It *ought* to be brought home to Russia,' she wrote angrily, 'and the world *ought* to know that on *their* shoulders and *not* on *ours* rests the *blood* of the murdered Bulgarians!' And in any case the Bulgarians were not true Christians at all but ritualists, idolaters, kissers of icons, 'far worse than the Mussulmans'. The Low Church journal *The Rock* told its readers that the Whore of Babylon, the Roman Catholic Church, was leading a conspiracy of all forms of superstition, Russian, Bulgarian and ritualist, against the British Empire, the only true citadel of the only true faith. When Beaconsfield said publicly that there was a network of secret societies trying to undermine Turkey and Britain the exasperated Russian ambassador in London told his government that British foreign policy was now 'a conspiracy of a half-mad woman with a minister who once had genius but has degenerated into a political clown'.

The Queen and her Prime Minister did not have a monopoly of fantasy. Gladstone told his colleagues in the Liberal party that Beaconsfield, as a Jew, was working deliberately against Christianity. W. T. Stead, editor of the *Northern Echo* and a violent critic of the government, proclaimed that God was behind Gladstone and Antichrist behind Beaconsfield. As both sides prepared for Armageddon, each totally convinced of its own rectitude, charges of madness and diabolic possession began to accompany the other insults. An article in the *Contemporary Review* on 'Working Men and the Eastern Question' declared that both leaders had taken leave of their senses, Beaconsfield because of his fantasies about secret societies and the hidden destiny of nations and Gladstone because he seriously thought that Britain could drive the Turks from Bulgaria. Nevertheless Gladstone's impassioned speeches, together with his pamphlet *The Bulgarian Horrors and the Questions of the East*, did much to mobilize public opinion against the government. Then in the autumn of 1877 the Turks caught the popular imagination by their defence of Plevna, a fortress in Bulgaria, against the Russians. By the time Plevna fell in December 1877 its defenders had become heroes in Britain and a popular music-hall song, based appropriately enough on the conjuror's cry of 'Hey

Jingo!',* served to project Beaconsfield's wizardry onto a wider stage than ever before:

> We don't want to fight, but by jingo if we do
> We've got the ships, we've got the men, we've got the money too.

By the end of January 1878 the song's impact was so overwhelming that Liberals in the House of Commons accused the government of encouraging its mindless belligerence. In February Gladstone's house was attacked by a Jingo mob and the opposition press began to speak of 'the Jingoes – the music hall patriots who sing the Jingo song' with an indignation that was tinged with apprehension. A few months earlier the Queen had been ready to abdicate rather than 'remain the sovereign of a country that is letting itself down to kiss the feet of the great barbarian', but now she took heart as Beaconsfield went from strength to strength, halting the Russians with naval threats and then wringing from them concessions of dubious significance at an international conference in Berlin. When he returned in July 1878, claiming that he had brought back 'Peace with Honour', the London streets were filled with rapturous crowds uplifted by his vision of Britain's imperial destiny. Even more remarkable was the reaction of Londoners a few weeks later when 'Cleopatra's Needle' was erected on the Thames Embankment. There had been many complaints about the expense of bringing this obelisk from Egypt and when it was put in place there were last-minute delays and the crowd was expected to be hostile. Instead there was a strange atmosphere of awe and excitement. 'So far from displaying any chagrin or disappointment,' reported *The Times* in some surprise, 'the enthusiasm of the crowd burst forth in ringing cheers'. The aura of Egypt had become so pervasive that even an inanimate object could cast its spell.

More familiar and more domestic visions seemed tame by comparison. To Francis Kilvert, walking in his Herefordshire churchyard and gazing at a host of tombstones facing the morning sun, 'it seemed as if the morning of the Resurrection had come and the sleepers had arisen from their graves and were standing upon their feet silent and solemn, all looking toward the East to meet the Rising of the Sun'. Such moments had comforted countless generations but now they paled before the great cosmic drama projected by Professor Smyth

---

* 'Hey Jingo' is the counterpart of 'Hey Presto': the first is used to make things appear and the second to make them disappear.

and Lord Beaconsfield. Country life itself, the rhythm of seed-time and harvest which had seemed changeless and divinely ordained, was being transformed by the vision of empire and by its economic results. There were terrible storms and floods throughout the summer of 1878 but in spite of the bad weather wheat prices fell, causing widespread rural distress, because of imports of cheap grain from the colonies. British agriculture was being sacrificed on the altar of imperial greatness and there was little that Beaconsfield could do about it. 'Starvation has no answer', he wrote grimly. Even his most admiring biographer admitted that his proposals for dealing with the agrarian depression were 'somewhat fanciful'.

The American stockbroker poet E.C. Stedman visited England in 1879 and was appalled by the contrast between the richness of her imaginative life and the poverty of her economy. She would soon be 'more of a Museum, Park, Picture Gallery, for the world at large to visit than anything else.' An Egyptian obelisk similar to the one in London was on its way to New York, where it was to be set up in Central Park, but there was to be no need for a miraculous change of public mood because the costs were borne by the railroad millionaire William Henry Vanderbilt. The rough edges of public controversy, spiritual as well as secular, were smoothed away by America's growing wealth just as they were sharpened by Britain's deepening recession. 'Everybody finds his income reduced,' reported the American consul in Birmingham, 'and everybody blames America for the reduction.'

Gladstone saw a dreadful consistency in everything that had happened since the Prince's illness. At every turn common sense and sound religion had been pushed aside by overblown imaginings. So far from defending God against the sceptics and the materialists these fantasies were playing into their hands. True Christians must assert the supremacy of reason before it was too late. 'Thought,' he exclaimed passionately, 'thought is the citadel'. The politics of fantasy had been tried and found wanting. 'The government have done and said many strange things,' remarked one critic, 'The public mind, which at first responded adequately to the surprises prepared for it, has latterly become jaded and insensitive. It has supped too full of marvels. Lord Beaconsfield and his colleagues have in fact debauched the national faculty of wonder.'

Nevertheless in March 1880, after a run of government by-election victories, Beaconsfield advised Victoria to dissolve Parliament early. She did so with a will: 'The Queen believes the time has been well chosen,' she wrote, 'and that the Government will be more successful even than they would have been later.' She was outraged and horrified when the General Election gave the Liberals a majority. 'If the Opposition force themselves upon her it will make her quite ill,' she told her Private Secretary. She fought off Gladstone as long as she could but in the end she had to accept a ministry which even included the objectionable Sir Charles Dilke. All that had been achieved since her son's miraculous recovery seemed now in jeopardy. Gladstone for his part saw his return to office as the triumph of thought over fantasy. 'The downfall of Beaconsfieldism is like the vanishing of some magnificent castle in an Italian romance' he wrote. The simile was appropriate but over-confident. The castle of fantasy might no longer be manned by politicians but it could still boast many thousands of defenders. Its battlements stretched halfway round the world and those who stood upon them were already proclaiming a new dawn.

7 WATCHERS UPON THE HIGH TOWERS

BEHIND THE TALK OF THOUGHT AND FANTASY, BEHIND the metaphorical citadel of the one and the insubstantial castle of the other, lay the oldest and most difficult question of all. Was the outward appearance of things a guide to their real nature? Could the universe be understood simply by observing and cataloguing the elements of which it was made up or was there a more reliable way of interpreting it? Plato had long ago suggested that outward appearances might be mere shadows cast by a reality men could not see, while eastern sages taught that existence was a veil which concealed rather than revealed creation's true glory. Christians had inherited these doubts about the physical world and some had seen it as nothing but a facade devised by the Devil for the deception and damnation of anyone foolish enough to take it at its face value. By the 1870s even the most pious were reluctant to dismiss scientists as mere dupes of Satan but the churches still taught that the 'scientific method', the drawing of conclusions and the framing of laws from the observation of physical phenomena, could never explain God's creation unless it was based on an understanding of God himself. The scientists were like men visiting a craftsman's workshop with the craftsman absent and the bits of his masterpiece spread out on the floor: they might learn something of the masterpiece by examining the bits but they would learn far more by looking for evidence of the craftsman's intentions.

God had provided such evidence in the Bible and also – if Roman Catholics were to be believed – in divinely authorized statements from St Peter's successors in Rome. Observation by itself could describe things but it could not define them. It was as if beings from outer space, aliens with no buttocks and no concept of sitting, were to imagine they had understood a chair once they had catalogued its

112

dimensions. They would know everything about it except the one thing that mattered – its purpose. The unaided scientific observer would know everything about what he observed except the one thing that mattered – its part in God's plan. So where was the line between thought and fantasy to be drawn? Those whom Gladstone saw as denizens of some imaginary castle in an Italian romance were at least working the right way round: they were putting divine revelation before the deceptions of outward appearance, even if the revelations in which they dealt were a little bizarre. They did not mistake mere observation for thought. They had behind them not just eighteen centuries of Christian teaching but many thousands of years of other creeds and other philosophies. The distrust of outward appearance, the search for deeper meaning, pervaded both eastern and western thought. It was science's battering ram, not fantasy's castle, that was new and unorthodox. Christians who heard its blows hurried to the ramparts without stopping to think which fortress they were defending. When the Evangelical Alliance met in New York in 1873 many Protestants expected it to come out against the recent declaration of Papal Infallibility. Instead it ranged itself alongside the Roman Catholic Church in the struggle against science.

Professor Draper of the University of New York, author of *A History of the Intellectual Development of Europe*,* determined to take over the citadel of thought in the name of science. His new book, *A History of the Conflict between Religion and Science*, published in 1873, insisted that Protestantism and science must be allies in the war against superstition. There was 'a great and rapidly increasing departure from public religious faith' on both sides of the Atlantic because established Christianity, especially Roman Catholicism, rested on 'fiction and fraud' and was 'steeped in blood'. Intelligent men and women must decide not just between scientific method and the search for God's intentions but between scientific laws and the acceptance of God's caprices: 'We are now in the midst of a controversy respecting the mode of government of the world, whether it be by incessant divine intervention or by the operation of primordial and unchangeable laws'. In Belfast, arguably the most religious city in the British Isles, Professor Tyndall told the British Association for the Advancement of Science that questions about the meaning of the universe or about the origin of life could no longer be left to theologians: 'We claim

* See above, p. 86.

113

the freedom to discuss them. The ground which they cover is scientific ground'. Creation's ultimate secrets must yield not to revelation but to observation. Outraged clergymen denounced Tyndall from their pulpits and the Belfast newspapers orchestrated a campaign of hate against him. Even after the initial fury had cooled the London *Annual Register* still felt that he had given 'serious alarm to the religious world, as seeming to betoken the atheistic leanings of modern science'.

While men like Draper and Tyndall stormed the citadels of Christian thought the defenders of the castles of Christian fantasy sallied forth to claim the whole field of battle for their own. In 1876 the Countess of Caithness brought out a book called *Old Truths in a new light, or, An Earnest Endeavour to Reconcile Material Science with Spiritual Science and with Scripture*. 'The further I read and the deeper I go into the spirit of this admirable address,' she wrote, 'the more I see that, so far from being opposed to each other, Professor Tyndall and I can shake hands over it ... To those who can read the signs of the times the present seems to presage a greater and more important change than any that has preceded it'. When this change came, when the new light dawned, the workings of God's universe would at last be clear. There would be no need to argue about measuring the pieces or reading the craftsman's notes because the craftsman himself would be once more in his workshop and would reveal all. In the following year, in a work on the Eastern Question entitled *England and Islam*, the Countess's admirer Edward Maitland suggested that Tyndall knew there were more things in heaven and earth than mere scientific observation: 'To this ingenious scientist are due the thanks of the intuitionalist for the recognition he has accorded to the imagination as an instrument of scientific research.' There was some indication of what an intuitionalist might be in Maitland's account of how the book had been written:

The first physical manifestation received by me consisted in my wrist being grasped by some invisible agency, while I was using my typewriter, and forcibly guided over the keys, the words being presented simultaneously to my mind, but only as they were being written ... The presence I had felt bending over me darted itself into me just below the cerebral bulb at the back of my neck, the sensation being that of a slight tap, as of a finger-touch; and then in a voice full, rich, firm, measured and so strong that it resounded through the room, exclaimed in a tone indicative of high satisfaction, 'At last I have found a man through whom I can speak!'

114

There were greater marvels to come. It seemed that intuition, as well as putting one in touch with would-be authors from other worlds, could also carry out summary executions in this one. In February 1878, sitting on the steps of the *Ecole de Médecine* in Paris, Maitland learned from his friend Anna Kingsford that her thought waves had just killed Claude Bernard, a French scientist notorious for his experiments on animals. 'If it prove that I really possess such a glorious power, woe be to the torturers!' she exulted, 'I will make it dangerous, nay deadly, to be a vivisectionist.' She had been in touch with the spirit world since childhood and she had long ago left her husband, a pious clergyman in Shropshire, in order to study the occult and develop supernatural powers. When she and Maitland returned to London they realized that if they were to cast other and more potent spells they would need a manual of magic arts. They asked Lady Caithness, who was still in Paris, to get them the works of the French sorcerer Eliphas Lévi. She did so willingly, remarking that the miraculous extermination of vivisectionists was a sign of the cosmic change which was coming. There would be, she assured them, 'a New Dispensation whose light is already dawning upon the humanity of the earth, at least upon the minds of those who are, as it were, the watchers upon the high towers'.

Once they had received their compendium of necromancy Edward Maitland and Anna Kingsford quickly built their own high tower. 'The revelations came in rapid succession,' Maitland recorded excitedly. In *England and Islam* he had inveighed against 'the materialistic rule in politics', by which he had meant Gladstone's rejection of the destiny prepared for the English-speaking peoples in ancient Egypt. Professor Smyth and Lord Beaconsfield had told of it and now Edward Maitland saw it with his own eyes. He found himself, 'between waking and sleeping', in a tomb hewn from the rock in the ancient Egyptian city of Thebes. He realized that this was the place of his initiation into the divine mysteries in a previous incarnation, since Thebes was the birthplace of the god Osiris who had been hacked to pieces and then restored to life by Isis. All was confirmed when Maitland visited a friend who painted Egyptian scenes. 'Several of his paintings of that country were then in the studio and in one of them, a view of Thebes, I instantly recognized the scene of my vision'.

Meanwhile Anna Kingsford left her physical body and visited the planets one by one, each with its own attendant angel. She had visions of a future in which France had become a battlefield for British and

German armies, with the Germans in occupation of Belgium, and this led her to seek out Joan of Arc, 'who hated women's clothes and loved fighting against oppression just as I do'. Having discussed transvestite pleasures with Joan of Arc she went on to speak with Winowa, a Red Indian girl acquainted with Osiris and Jesus Christ. The presence of Jesus was especially welcome since Anna knew that in an earlier life she had been Mary Magdalene. Clearly the change which the watchers upon the high towers could now glimpse would bring together both these gods who had died for their people and would thus reconcile science not only with Christianity but also with the older revelations from which both had sprung. When they went to the British Museum to check up on the prophetic measurements of the Great Pyramid they were referred to shelf number 1881 for books on the subject. 'The officials to whom we pointed out the coincidence were greatly amused thereat,' Edward wrote later, 'We refrained from telling them that the prophecy was actually in course of fulfilment and that the world was really coming to an end in that year in the sense intended'. From New Year's Day 1882 Lady Caithness dated her letters 'Anno Lucis 1' – Year One of the Enlightenment.

The three of them no longer watched from lonely towers. They had joined the Theosophical Society, a corps of international observers walking the battlements of fantasy from New York to Madras. It sprang from a meeting in New York in September 1875 at which George Felt lectured on 'The Lost Canon of Proportion of the Egyptians, Greeks and Romans'. As well as elucidating Professor Smyth's predictions he also suggested that the Dwellers of the Threshold might be persuaded to materialize. These mysterious beings, who controlled the destiny of mankind from another world, had been described in some detail in Edward Bulwer-Lytton's novel *Zanoni*, which had been enormously successful in America as well as in Britain. Helena Petrovna Blavatsky, a Russian lady who heard the lecture, maintained that under the guise of fiction Lytton had revealed the greatest of all truths, for she and her friend Colonel Olcott, a New York newspaper correspondent and author of *People from the Other World*, had been favoured with a supernatural message from a similarly elemental being called Tuiti Bey of the Brotherhood of Luxor in Egypt. It was decided to form a society to 'collect and diffuse a knowledge of the laws which govern the universe'. At first it was to be called the Egyptological Society but it soon became clear that its business was theosophy, the quest for divine wisdom. Edward Maitland and Anna Kingsford joined the London lodge of the Society and Lady Caithness was soon presiding over a branch in Paris.

Madame Blavatsky set to work on *Isis Unveiled*, an enormous compilation of occult learning which linked the Dwellers of the Threshold with Serapis, a god who had combined the attributes of Osiris and Dionysus and had been popular in Greece when Alexander the Great had taken his armies to India and re-enacted the legendary Dionysiac procession. As Blavatsky delved into these matters the Prince of Wales brought his Dionysiac entourage back from India in the yacht *Serapis* and Lord Lytton, son of the man who had told of the Dwellers, marvelled at the tigers who caressed the Prince's feet. Coincidences like this, mere converging symbols, helped to prepare theosophists for the greater convergence which would come when Christianity rediscovered the wisdom of the ancients. By the time *Isis Unveiled* was published in September 1877 public opinion in the United States as well as in Britain was falling into line behind Beaconsfield's vision, just as Maitland had predicted in *England and Islam*. 'We have a sort of truce in our home politics while we watch politics abroad,' wrote the American correspondent of *The Times*. The hatred which Americans had felt towards Britain in the 1860s was turning to sympathy. The unenlightened attributed the change to Sir Edward Thornton, British ambassador in Washington since 1867, but the watchers knew that more profound forces were at work.

While politicians looked beyond the Balkans and the Suez Canal to the riches of India, the theosophists gazed over the heads of Greek and Egyptian gods to the Buddha and the Hindu Vedanta. In May 1878 the society was renamed 'The Theosophical Society of the Arya Samaj' after Blavatsky and Olcott met Swami Dayananda Saraswati, leader of a Hindu revivalist movement of that name. One of the Masters of Wisdom, Indian Dwellers of the Threshold, projected his astral body several thousand miles from his mountain fastness in the Himalayas in order to appear to Olcott, who set out for India with Blavatsky. After a brief visit to the London Theosophical Society they landed at Bombay in February 1879 and set up their headquarters at Adyar near Madras. They did not entirely please the Masters of Wisdom, who sent a magical message to Alfred Sinnett, a theosophist in Bombay, instructing him to write a book without telling Olcott or Blavatsky. He sailed for England forthwith and on the voyage he wrote *The Occult World*, which was published in London in June 1881.

It was not very well received. Reviews of *Isis Unveiled* had been mixed – the *New York Herald* hailed it as 'one of the most remarkable productions of the century' while the *New York Sun* called it 'discarded rubbish' – but few critics had a good word to say for Sinnett. The *Saturday Review* treated him as a lone eccentric, describing him ironically as 'the torch-bearer of the new light from the East' and insisting that the ancient soothsayers he cited 'made a mystery of their knowledge because they knew very little'. But there were other and more reputable torch-bearers. 'The study of Indian wisdom, conducting by another path to conclusions entirely in harmony with the results of natural science, is destined to affect, and is affecting, the European mind in a degree not inferior to the modification accomplished by the renaissance of Hellenic philosophy,' wrote Helen Zimmern in a book on Arthur Schopenhauer which she published in February 1876. Schopenhauer had been a masterly interpreter of Indian thought, 'a European Buddhist', and when Lord Lytton first read him he found that it was 'like visiting the house of a stranger and finding it full of my oldest and most intimate acquaintances'. The Bishop of Madras published an article suggesting that the exorcising of evil spirits by Indian holy men might be a continuation of the same miraculous process which had been seen in Galilee eighteen centuries earlier. If Europeans dismissed such things as the delusions of unwashed fakirs were they not also dismissing that first fakir who had healed the sick and raised Lazarus from the tomb?

The American faith-healer Phineas Parkhurst Quimby had already bridged the gap between Christ and the fakirs. One of those he helped, Mary Baker Eddy, coined the term Spiritual Science to describe what he did. Whereas ordinary table-rapping spiritualism was of little importance, Spiritual Science was nothing less than a rediscovery of the principles of healing known in Christianity's early days. Her book *Science and Health and a Key to the Scriptures*, published in 1875 after Quimby's death, became the basis for a new religion, Christian Science, which had apparently been foretold in the Book of Revelation. The title echoed Lady Caithness's 'Earnest Endeavour to Reconcile Material Science with Spiritual Science and with Scripture' and anticipated Madame Blavatsky's book, the full title of which was *Isis Unveiled: a master key to the mysteries of ancient and modern science and theology*. All three ladies claimed that the coming dawn would unite the revelations of God and the observations of men instead of setting them against one another.

In London James Knowles, editor of the *Contemporary Review*, decided that the time had come to debate the credibility of these two approaches in public and see if a convergence could be achieved. For some years past such matters had been the concern of the Metaphysical Society, which he ran from his house on Clapham Common. Protestants and Catholics, scientists and laymen, freethinkers and traditionalists, had all given papers to the Society, many of which had subsequently been published. Now he founded a new journal, *The Nineteenth Century*, to bring such things to the attention of a wider public. It began publication in March 1877 and its first number opened with a poem by Tennyson which indicated the aims, as well as the agonies, of its varied contributors:

> For some, descending from the sacred peak
> Of hoar high-templed Faith, have leagued again
> Their lot with ours to rove the world about;
> And some are wilder comrades, sworn to seek
> If any golden harbour be for men
> In seas of death and sunless gulf of Doubt.

Once Tennyson had been the most trusted of navigators on the waters of death and doubt. He was to regain his mastery of this most compelling of images with the publication of 'Crossing the Bar', but in 1877 things were different. Lewis Carroll had recently brought out *The Hunting of the Snark*, a strange and disturbing epic about a Bellman who took a shipload of assorted characters to hunt for a Snark. One of them, a Baker, had been warned by his uncle that if his Snark turned out to be a Boojum he would softly and suddenly vanish away and never be met with again. In the end this fate had overtaken him, leaving the Bellman discomfited and discredited. Henry Holiday, the poem's illustrator, made the Bellman into an unmistakeable likeness of Tennyson. Suddenly the Poet Laureate's solemnity seemed outlandish and a little portentous, closer to that of the controlled fanatic who led the Baker to his doom than to the needs of the real world. When John Bright met him at Gladstone's house he thought him 'a weird-looking tall old man', while Lord Houghton began to refer to him as 'His Poetic Majesty'. London society was more amused than over-awed when this monarch of the pen took a town house for three months in March 1877 and announced grandly that he would only accept dinner invitations if they were for his chosen time of seven o'clock.

The deep dark sea, the sunless gulf of doubt, dominated the first few issues of *The Nineteenth Century*. The Bellman was able to keep the members of his crew from getting wet by 'supporting each man on the top of the tide, By a finger entwined in his hair', but Tennyson had no such power. Some contributors were confessedly engulfed by the tide of unbelief and saw Christianity only as wreckage floating on its surface. 'No drowning sailor ever clutched a hencoop more tenaciously than mankind will hold by such dogma, whatever it may be,' wrote Professor Huxley. William Mallock, an Anglican who lived in a state of recurring spiritual crisis and ended up a Roman Catholic, produced a piece called 'Is Life Worth Living?' He concluded that without God, without belief in life after death, it most certainly was not: 'For unless, let our Atheists remember, we can find such an end in life as that which we have been demanding, we shall be like dismasted ships, without sail and without rudder, left to welter on a sluggish sea of small and weary impulses, with no escape from the shoreless accursed surface, till at last, and one by one, we sink for ever under it.'

What Mallock feared and what Lewis Carroll portrayed had much in common, for there were few seas as shoreless as that sailed by the Bellman and his crew. The Bellman's chart of it was 'A perfect and absolute blank ... Without the least vestige of land'. The only relief from the empty unending ocean was a nightmare landscape of chasms and crags and when the Baker fell into a chasm he was sucked down into nothingness. It was a vision not merely of death but of total annihilation. For the Baker, as for all whose Snarks were Boojums, there was no future, perhaps no past, certainly no eternity. In his other incarnation as Charles Dodgson, Oxford mathematics don, Lewis Carroll told how the final line, 'For the Snark *was* a Boojum, you see', came into his head unbidden as he tramped alone over the Surrey hills. 'I knew not what it meant then,' he said, 'I know not what it means now; but I wrote it down: and sometime afterwards the rest of the stanza occurred to me, that being its last line: and so by degrees, at odd moments during the next year or two, the rest of the poem pieced itself together, that being the last stanza'. He would never admit that it might be prophetic, that at the end men and women might fall not into the everlasting arms but into the emptiness of a Snark that was a Boojum.

Even stranger things came into the head of another solitary walker in high places during the fateful year 1881. There were earthquakes and cyclones all across Europe that summer and the Alps themselves seemed to be on the move. Across them strode Nietzsche, laughing and shouting with exultation in the mountain silence. 'On my horizon,' he cried, 'thoughts have arisen such as I have never seen before. I sang and talked nonsense, filled with a glimpse of things which put me in advance of all other men'. The previous year, in Marienbad, he had stumbled on the imagery in which his revelation was now to be clothed: there had been a mysterious crime in the hotel in which he had been staying, with strange agonized cries and digging in the forest at dead of night. The dark memories came flooding back as he put into words his vision of a world without meaning, a world which had seen the most terrible of all crimes:

Whither is God? I shall tell you. *We have killed him* – you and I. All of us are his murderers ... Whither are we moving now? Away from all suns? Are we not plunging continually? Backward, sideward, forward, in all directions? Is there any up or down left? Are we not straying as through an infinite nothing? Do we not feel the breath of empty space? Has it not become colder? Is not night and more night coming on all the while? Must not lanterns be lit in the morning? Do we not hear anything yet of the noise of the gravediggers who are burying God? Do we not smell anything yet of God's decomposition? Gods too decompose. God is dead. God remains dead. And we have killed him.

It was ironic that the year which was supposed to have seen God giving a new message to the world should see instead this image of the world killing God. This was, wrote Maitland, 'The year announced in so many prophecies as the pivot upon which the world's destinies hinged, the turning point between that old and that new dispensation, the former of which had been divinely condemned as "evil and adulterous" and the latter indicated as introducing the kingdom of heaven on earth.' Nietzsche stood such hopes on their heads. Instead of a future in which religion became as certain as science he saw one in which the scientists were as impotent as the pious. And the ultimate irony was that this vision came just as the world's existing scientific framework was indeed crumbling. The first to feel the breath of empty space was the American physicist Albert Abraham Michelson who was carrying out experiments in 1881 to find the speed of the earth's movement through space. He devised an instrument which split a beam of light in two, sending one half in the direction of the earth's movement and the other in the opposite direction. The halves were then brought together again so that the fringe of interference where they met could show the difference between the speed of the one which had ridden with the earth and the speed of the one which had gone against it. He found no interference at all, suggesting that whatever the light was travelling through – the framework of the universe, God's firmament on high – was not itself still.

Perhaps there was no framework, no firmament. Perhaps there was no up and no down, only a purely relative difference between one direction and another, one movement and another, one dimension and another. Michelson's conclusions, confirmed and extended as a result of more experiments undertaken with Edward Morley in 1887, were to provide the basis for Albert Einstein's revelation of a universe in which traditional scientific absolutes had no more place than the spiritual absolutes of the Christian religion. Edmond Schérer's prediction had come true: the absolute was dead in men's souls. For centuries they had thought they were slowly discovering and deciphering the meaning of the universe. Now they found that they had conjured that meaning from their own heads and imposed it upon a universe which knew nothing of absolutes, which was in the final analysis a question and not a statement.

There were still those who waited for the world's destinies to hinge on the 1881 pivot. As the year began Gerard Manley Hopkins greeted the return of the age of miracles when a boy dying of typhus recovered after being anointed. 'It was no doubt due to the sacrament,' he noted. Certainly there were portents for those who sought them. There was ominously cold weather early in the year, with harbours icebound along the Atlantic coast of America and enormous ice floes in the Thames which halted shipping and carried away piers. All over Europe the cold brought wolves out of the forests and into towns and villages. Snow blocked railways on both sides of the Atlantic and when it thawed floods rendered thousands homeless. In Lancashire hussars were called out to break up riots and at Windsor men were heard plotting to blow up the Queen. Gladstone cut his head open, causing great public concern, and his colleague John Bright, 'wearied with the disorder which it seemed impossible to suppress', felt that 'we must be approaching some crisis or catastrophe.' But when Beaconsfield died in April, the supposed month of destiny, the climax of his visions had still not arrived. Then came the death of Dr Cumming, who had also 'debauched the national faculty of wonder', but his predictions remained equally unfulfilled.

As Fenian and Nihilist atrocities became commonplace, as the assassination of the Tsar of Russia was followed by that of the President of the United States, Maitland's hopes of heaven on earth seemed increasingly inappropriate. Some thought hell more likely and Bright wrote that the crimes and cruelties were 'rather the doings of fiends than men'. But the year had one last surprise in store for optimists and pessimists alike. It came, like Christianity, from an empty tomb. In early December, as devotees of Mother Shipton noted the unseasonable fruiting of the strawberry plants, the dead Earl of Crawford was found to be missing. Nobody knew the size of the stone which had been taken from Christ's sepulchre but the granite slabs covering the Crawford family vault at Dunecht in Scotland were six feet square and several inches thick. They might have been moved by an angel but certainly not by an unaided human being. Crawford had died in Florence a year earlier and after elaborate embalming he had been brought home in a wooden coffin sealed inside a soldered lead shell. This had then been placed in another coffin of carved oak ornamented with silver. Now all three stood empty in the vault and the body was gone.

Queen Victoria was appalled. The Home Secretary was instructed to drop everything else and give Dunecht his undivided attention. The affair aroused great interest in America, where a millionaire's body had recently been held to ransom. Scores of policemen came up to Dunecht, bringing the sleuth-hound Morgan, 'the same sagacious animal that was the means of discovering the fragments of the body of the child killed at Blackburn'. When the sagacious animal found nothing spiritualists were called in. They had a vision of three men taking the body to a field which sloped down to a little copse. The press pointed out that a man whose dream had been published a short time before had seen the same thing. The police dug in the spot indicated but found nothing. Then they took up Charles Soutar, a poacher who told them he had disturbed four masked men burying a body at night several months before. They had terrified him into silence but now he led police to the spot and they dug up the body. The Queen sent a congratulatory telegram to Lady Crawford and everyone waited for the body snatchers to be apprehended.

But the finding of the body had contradicted rather than confirmed the assumptions on which the police had been working. Hypotheses crumbled, reputations were put in jeopardy. And so the police turned on the only culprit they had: they committed Soutar for trial, not for concealing evidence but for stealing the body. This raised awkward questions. If he was guilty, why did he not denounce his accomplices and claim the reward and free pardon which had been offered to anyone who turned Queen's evidence? And if there were no accomplices what had happened to police insistence that no man could have committed the crime alone? These considerations were worrying but the press said a conviction was unlikely and in any case the penalty would be light. *The Times* assured its readers that body snatching had never been punished with more than two years in prison. At Soutar's trial there were no witnesses for the defence and nobody cross-examined witnesses for the prosecution. There was amazement in court when he was found guilty in spite of the flaws in the police case and there was even greater amazement when the judge brushed aside the precedents of the past: 'What was adequate punishment in those offences is not, in my opinion, adequate punishment on this occasion. The sentence of this Court is that you be subjected to penal servitude for a period of five years.'

For the watchers upon the high towers prospects were good. The Dunecht affair made the occult popular and in the summer of 1882 a group of men who had been members of a Ghost Society as Cambridge undergraduates formed the Society for Psychical Research. Edward Maitland was an associate member and his books were to be found in the Society's library along with those of Lady Caithness and other theosophists. Arthur Balfour, future Prime Minister and author of *A Defence of Philosophic Doubt*, was a vice-president of the Society and with a splendid sense of timing went straight from its inaugural meeting to the House of Commons in order to prevent an atheist member, Charles Bradlaugh, from taking his seat. Bradlaugh had Gladstone's support but it availed him nothing; the castles of fantasy were more respectable than the citadels of thought. And hopes that Year One of the Enlightenment would bring Christianity closer to ancient Egypt were certainly not disappointed. Progressive Victorian society, the society that had condemned the excesses of Frederick Merrett's friends at Cowley, the society that had been told by its church leaders to dissociate hopes of resurrection from physical conditions, had defended the hallowed dead as fiercely as any curse inscribed on a pharaoh's sarcophagus. Charles Soutar's fate, the mockery of his trial and the savagery of his sentence, showed that the funeral chambers of the pyramids had indeed cast a shadow over the English-speaking world, even if not quite the one forecast by Professor Smyth.

A few weeks after Soutar's conviction Gladstone chose Bishop

124

Benson of Truro as Archbishop of Canterbury. Benson had founded the Cambridge Ghost Society and was still deeply interested in psychic phenomena. 'Our illustrious premier,' wrote Swinburne to Edward Burne-Jones, 'has been mercifully guided in the election of a substitute who will (I cannot doubt) fill the highest seat in our Church more worthily than myself.' In more serious vein Dr Hort, Professor of Divinity at Cambridge, wrote to warn Benson that the Church must put fact before fantasy if it was to win back ordinary people: 'The convulsions of our English Church itself, grievous as they are, seem to be as nothing beside the danger of its calm and unobtrusive alienation in thought and spirit from the great silent multitude of Englishmen, and again of alienation from fact and love of fact: mutual alienations both.' He described the country's religious state as 'self-glorifying chaos'. The alienation of ordinary people from established religion was shown some months later when the authorities prosecuted G.W. Foote, editor of *The Freethinker*, for blasphemy. The judge told him that he had 'prostituted his talents to the work of the Devil' – even though the Privy Council had already relegated the Devil to the realm of fantasy – and gave him twelve months hard labour. 'The sentence was followed by a scene such as has seldom been witnessed within the walls of the Court,' reported *The Times* in horror, 'a perfect storm of hissing'.

Meanwhile Edward Maitland was hard at work on his book *How the World came to an End in 1881*. It might seem odd to be writing an epilogue to apocalypse but he did not doubt that the prophecies had been fulfilled 'in the sense intended'. Like Nietzsche he was 'filled with a glimpse of things which put me in advance of all other men'. He could not see the death of God but he could see the passing away of the dogmas and rituals and half-truths by which God had so far been sought. The old dispensation had gone and old intimations of the divine were dying. They would be replaced by something brighter, more direct, more potent. Josiah Strong, Ohio representative of the American Home Missionary Society, had similar hopes. His nation-wide lectures, delivered in the early 1880s and published in 1885 under the title *Our Country*, looked forward to the transformation of the world within a decade as a result of the efforts of Americans. 'It is fully in the hands of the Christians of the United States, during the next ten or fifteen years,' he cried, 'to hasten or retard the coming of Christ's kingdom in the world by hundreds, and perhaps thousands of years.' But first they must stop letting members of inferior races into America,

125

since only the Anglo-Saxons were 'exponents of a pure *spiritual* Christianity'. Then they must steer clear of idleness, atheism, popery, alcohol and above all socialism, 'which attempts to solve the problem of suffering without eliminating the factor of sin'. Labouring men could be heard quoting 'the infidel ribaldry of Robert Ingersoll, the socialistic theories of Karl Marx' and many were idlers who had no right to live: 'If loafers had any appreciation of the eternal fitness of things they would die.' The Librarian of Congress later said the book had an impact second only to *Uncle Tom's Cabin*.

Predictions about the destinies of nations came from men of science as well as from men of God. 'Looking to the world at no very distant date,' wrote Charles Darwin in July 1881, 'what an endless number of the lower races will have been eliminated by the higher civilized races throughout the world!' He did not say how the elimination would be achieved. Would there have to be genocide or would the lower races, like the American loafers, appreciate the eternal fitness of things and die? Six weeks after this forecast Lord Hartington, Secretary for India, answering routine questions in the House of Commons, revealed that in one gaol in Bengal the death rate had risen from 282 per thousand in 1879 to 612 per thousand in the first quarter of 1881. He could not be sure whether prisoners had been starved to death or whipped to death: there had been more than thirteen thousand floggings during this period and in most cases men had been flogged for non-performance of hard labour when their diet was already below starvation level. In their modest way the Indian authorities were helping to hasten the day to which Darwin looked forward.

Hartington's calm revelations, like the sentencing of Soutar and Foote, left doubts as to which aspects of God had died with the old dispensation and which were the glory of the new. The watchers upon the high towers had seen a great light, a fiery dawn in which the true God had arisen phoenix-like from the ashes of ancient error. It had been hoped that this revelation would shame the mere observers, the weighers and measurers of the world's constituent parts, into admitting that there were more things in heaven and earth than their scientific method could fathom. Instead it had made them more contumacious than ever and it had alienated ordinary men and women from spiritual and secular leaders whose values seemed to have little in common with those of Jesus Christ. Being a fabulous creature the phoenix was in any case more likely to appeal to lovers of fantasy than to lovers of fact; now it looked as though its appeal was even more limited. It seemed to be an Anglo-Saxon bird, or at any rate a bird of 'the higher civilized races', and it hovered more happily over thrones and dominions and powers than over the humble and the oppressed. It was a poor substitute for the dove, the earlier and gentler Christian symbol of God's love. Now that the year of destiny had come and gone it was easier to believe in the death of the old dispensation than in the birth of a new one.

8 THE TRIUMPH OF FICTION

ONE OF THE BENEFICIARIES OF THE DUNECHT AFFAIR was Robert Louis Stevenson. He was staying at Pitlochry, some sixty miles from Dunecht, and writing stories about the dead. One, 'Thrawn Janet', concerned a woman whose soul belonged to the Devil and whose body, neck awry because of hanging, walked the earth long after death until it was finally exorcised by a godly minister. The other, 'The Body Snatcher', was about a dismembered corpse which found a grisly way of terrifying those who had handed it over to the anatomist's knife. It was so gruesome that it shocked even its author, who said it had been 'laid aside in a justifiable disgust, the tale being horrid'. The disgust was not to last long. 'Thrawn Janet' was published shortly after the theft of Crawford's body had generated renewed interest in the vengeful dead. Stevenson was then able to take 'The Body Snatcher' from its shelf and offer it to the editor of the *Pall Mall Gazette*, who greeted it with enthusiasm and advertised it all over London with placards so horrific that they were seized by the police, thus ensuring the story's notoriety. Meanwhile the enormous success of *Treasure Island*, which its author described as 'quite silly and horrid fun', led the *Saturday Review* to hail Stevenson as a writer who would lift fiction above 'the mere annals of the boudoir and the tennis lawn'.

Stevenson was more ambitious than the *Saturday Review* realized. For most of his adult life he had agonized over the conflict between his literary aspirations and the conventional piety of his parents. 'I have a pistol at my throat,' he told his friend Charles Baxter, 'If all that I hold true and most desire to spread is to be such death, and worse than death, in the eyes of my father and mother, what the *devil* am I to do?' He knew that there was more to life than outward appearances and animal appetites yet he could not bring himself to mumble conventional prayers and seek a conventional heaven. 'I feel every day as if religion had a greater interest for me,' he told his father, 'but that interest is still centred on the little rough-and-tumble world in which our fortunes are cast for the moment. I cannot transfer my interests, not even my religious interest, to any different sphere'. Now that he was an authority and an oracle he would reconcile art and religion. By transforming fiction he would transfigure everyday life. He would bring God into the rough-and-tumble world. 'A stately music. Enter God!' he wrote to W. E. Henley in 1883, 'Ay, but you know, until a man can write that "Enter God" he has made no art!' In November 1884 he asserted publicly the right of the creative artist to hold back the curtain, to thrust aside the veil of existence, to herald God's entry upon the world's stage. As a means of interpreting reality fiction was just as respectable, just as reliable, as the sciences:

Man's one method, whether he reasons or creates, is to half-shut his eyes against the dazzle and confusion of reality. The arts, like arithmetic and geometry, turn away their eyes from the gross, coloured and mobile nature at our feet and regard instead a certain figmentary abstraction. Geometry will tell us of a circle, a thing never seen in nature; asked about a green circle or an iron circle, it lays its hand upon its mouth. So with the arts ... Life is monstrous, infinite, illogical, abrupt and poignant; a work of art, in comparison, is neat, finite, self-contained, rational, flowing and emasculated.

The scientists and the philosophers were indeed laying hands upon their mouths. Ernst Mach's *Science of Mechanics*, published in 1883, declared that it was no longer possible to believe in absolute space, in absolute time or even in the concept of cause and effect. The Oxford philosopher Thomas Hill Green had long argued that observation and scientific method were fallible because when human beings tried to perceive the external world they only achieved an understanding of their own thought processes. By the time he died in 1882 he had gathered around him a school of thought dedicated to the proposition that any order or coherence observable in the universe could only have been put there by the observers themselves. Mankind hung like a spider, suspended by a thread spun from its own guts. Must it spin God in the same way? Stevenson shared with Nietzsche the ability to sniff and savour prevailing winds of thought without clogging his lungs with their every particle. His vision of man bringing God on stage was the counterpart of Nietzsche's image of man doing God to death. Dead or alive, skeleton or marionette, the deity danced to

129

man's tune. The respectful perspectives of conventional religion were gone.

Where Stevenson led others were quick to follow. Herbert George Wells, who was soon to make his name by putting science to the service of fiction, did a piece for the *Fortnightly Review* called 'The Rediscovery of the Unique'. 'When we teach a child to count,' he proclaimed, 'we poison its mind almost irrevocably.' How could men think that number had meaning, that ten score separate entities could lose their unique qualities simply by being paraded as two hundred allegedly identical objects? Just as geometry was about imagined and unreal circles, so arithmetic and the statistical sciences based upon it were about imagined and unreal quantities. Individuality would triumph, no two peas in a pod would ever be alike, science would find its generalizations bouncing helplessly back from the surrounding darkness:

Science is a match that man has just got alight. He thought he was in a room – in moments of devotion a temple – and that his light would be reflected in pillars carved with philosophical systems and wrought into harmony. It is a curious sensation, now that the preliminary sputter is over and the flame burns up clear, to see his hands lit and just a glimpse of himself and the patch he stands on visible, and around him, in place of all that human comfort and beauty he anticipated – darkness still.

Man must stand resolute on his own patch and know the flame for what it was – his own imagination. Fantasy and fiction kindled it, fantasy and fiction kept it alight, fantasy and fiction reached out into the dark and brought back such comfort and beauty as could be found. And that was all. If you wanted pillars carved with philosophical systems you must carve them for yourself. Even members of the government seemed to prefer imagining to calculating. George Goschen, Chancellor of the Exchequer, told students at Edinburgh University that the human imagination was the source of all knowledge as well as 'your most faithful guide on all the problems which a governing people such as ours has to solve.' A week later Arthur Balfour, First Lord of the Treasury, reminded Glasgow students of the limitations of mathematical and scientific thought: 'The future of the race is encompassed with darkness; no faculty of calculation that we possess, no instrument that we are likely to invent, will enable us to map out its course, or penetrate the secret of its destiny'.

Meanwhile the worshippers of fiction grew more devout. George

Saintsbury in the *Fortnightly* declared that mankind was sick, dulled and enfeebled by intellectualism and solemn analysis. Things would not improve until 'the aspect of society is quite changed and we have bathed once more long and well in the romance of adventure and passion'. The *Westminster Review* burst out in praise of Hall Caine, a young novelist who would 'transmute the ordinary into the marvellous'. Caine said he was proud to believe in fiction as 'a beautiful lie, a lie that is at once false and true – false to fact, true to faith'. 'It satisfies our inborn sense of right;' proclaimed Amelia Edwards, 'it transports us into a purer atmosphere; it vindicates the ways of God to Man.' 'If the battle between the crocodile of Realism and the catawampus of Romance is to be fought out to the bitter end,' wrote Andrew Lang, 'I am on the side of the catawampus.' When Lord Randolph Churchill visited Eton in the summer of 1883 he found everyone there reading Stevenson's *Treasure Island* and he drew Arthur Balfour aside in the House of Commons to urge him to get a copy. Gladstone glanced through it at Lord Rosebery's house and then scoured London for a copy of his own. *King Solomon's Mines* had an equally overwhelming success in 1885 and its author, Rider Haggard, was hailed in his turn as a high priest of the new cult. 'More and more, as what we call culture spreads,' he wrote, 'do men and women crave to be taken out of themselves. More and more do they long to be brought face to face with Beauty and stretch out their arms towards that vision of the Perfect, which we only see in books and dreams.'

The new religion had its shrines as well as its scriptures. The rich could afford to buy novels but most people who wanted to stretch out their arms towards a fictional vision of the perfect had first to visit their local public library. The early nineteenth century had been a great age of church building but now, on both sides of the Atlantic, new churches were outnumbered by new public libraries. The American Library Association was formed in 1876 and public funding was supplemented by private benefaction. Andrew Carnegie, the steel millionaire, endowed nearly three thousand libraries in the United States as well as many in Britain. And it was works of fiction, not religious or educational books, which were in demand at these multiplying centres of mass culture. Even the *Westminster Review*, a friend to public libraries, had to confess that three out of every four books borrowed was a novel. It hoped that 'the time is not far distant when we shall have a good free library in every town in the kingdom', but it feared that 'these libraries are chiefly frequented by idlers, and such as seek

131

amusement in novel reading'. Mr J.Taylor Kay of the Manchester Free Library declared that 'schoolboys or students who took to novel reading never made much progress in after life. They neglected real practical life for a sensually imaginative one'. William James, America's leading philosopher and psychologist, proclaimed that there was no more contemptible human character than the 'nerveless sentimentalist and dreamer' produced by excessive novel reading. The fact that his younger brother Henry was a successful novelist did little to reconcile him to fiction's onward march.

Diatribes against the effect of fiction on the young were not new. In 1867 *The Bookseller* had launched a bitter attack on penny dreadfuls such as *Tyburn Dick, the Boy King of the Highwaymen* and *Admiral Tom, the King of the Boy Buccaneers*, which sold a quarter of a million copies a year in London alone while more wholesome publications, tales about God-fearing lads who fought and tamed natives in the outposts of the British Empire, had to be discontinued for lack of support. Ten years later the anonymous author of *Five Years Penal Servitude by One who has Endured it* told how he had shared a cell with a boy of thirteen who had battered in an old woman's head with a hammer and stolen £70 from her. 'I found from a few questions I asked that his head had been stuffed with the rubbish he had read of gentlemen pirates, highwaymen and bandit captains.' Opponents of public libraries said they were full of 'loafing office boys or clerks, who were using their masters' time for devouring all the most trivial literary trash they could get', while supporters insisted that on the contrary libraries converted youth from penny dreadfuls to better things.

By the 1880s the rearguard action against fiction was losing heart. It was no longer possible, argued Professor Jevons in the *Contemporary Review*, to prevent the masses from reading fiction and being influenced by it. All that the educated classes could do was to ensure that as far as possible it was good fiction. George Alfred Henty, editor of a boys' magazine called *The Union Jack*, set to work to undo the damage which *The Bookseller* had earlier lamented. Sales of his books about boys who helped to win the British Empire mounted steadily from 1884, when *With Clive in India* came out, until his death in 1902. The Religious Tract Society started *The Boy's Own Paper* in 1879, concentrating at first on tales of overseas adventure. R.M. Ballantyne's 'The Red Man's Revenge' was followed by Ascott Hope's 'Adventures of a Boston Boy Amongst Savages', both set in America and both showing white lads winning the respect of natives. They were followed by a

132

school story, *The Fifth Form at St Dominic's*, by Talbot Baines Reed. It was in some ways more adult than its famous predecessor *Tom Brown's Schooldays*: there was comparatively little beating and bullying and the plot hinged upon cheating in an examination rather than upon rivalry on the games field. Yet there was an extraordinary obsession with fighting: it seemed that if Reed's young heroes did not have a fight a day they were not getting full value from public-school life. In this way they proved their superiority over the lower classes. The only villains in the story were working-class idlers, great gangs of whom were easily vanquished by 'a pair of well-trained athletic schoolboys'.

The Boy's Own Paper was only one of the Religious Tract Society's many ventures into fiction. By the end of the century its publication of religious tracts had been far outstripped by the twenty million books and magazines which it put out from its home depot alone. The Society for Promoting Christian Knowledge, a more venerable institution, was issuing three times as many works of fiction as tracts, while similar changes were taking place in nonconformist and Roman Catholic publishing houses. With remarkable docility the devout and the orthodox were heeding Stevenson's stage direction. God was entering upon the stage – or at any rate entering into the consciousness of the young – through fiction rather than through conventional homilies and scriptural readings.

God's stage appearance posed problems. The Christian religion was firmly anchored in history and the curtain had come down on its earthly adventure more than eighteen centuries ago. It had been spectacular while it lasted, with vast crowd scenes and supernatural happenings and an impressive climax, but it had not been intended as drama and there was no room for a repeat performance. God had suffered an agonizing death not for man's entertainment but for his salvation: the sequel would take place in heaven and it would be a spiritual transformation scene, not another display of divine derring-do. It was not easy to turn the God of the Christians into the God of the adventure story. Thomas Hughes, the author of *Tom Brown's Schooldays*, did his best in a series of lectures published under the title *The Manliness of Christ*. He stressed not so much the humility and the purity of Christianity's founder as his physical courage and his ability to endure pain bravely – qualities that had already endeared the fictitious Tom Brown to admiring schoolboys. Stevenson talked about 'a theory of living in the Gospels which is curiously indefinable

133

and leans towards asceticism on the one side, although it leans away from it on the other'. 'I have never been in a revolution yet,' he told his cousin Katharine, 'I pray God I may be in one at the end, if I am to make a mucker. The best way to make a mucker is to have your back set against a wall and a few lead pellets whiffed into you in a moment.' The heroism of the Christian martyr still had its links with that of the contemporary idealist.

Stevenson soon found his latter-day hero and martyr. Although 1881 did not see the Second Coming predicted by Professor Smyth it did see the rise of a self-styled Messiah, the Mahdi, who led a revolt in Upper Egypt and the Sudan. The British government decided to evacuate the garrisons in the area and put General Gordon in charge of the operation. Brave and chaste, deeply religious and a natural leader of men, Gordon was a living story-book hero. He was also a great believer in Smyth's impending apocalypse. When he got to the Sudan he determined on defence rather than evacuation and before long he was besieged in Khartoum by rebel forces. As he had disobeyed orders Gladstone's government was reluctant to send a relief expedition. When a British force did arrive, on 28 January 1885, it found that Gordon had already been killed. The outcry against Gladstone was immediate and impassioned. Stevenson was appalled by the disaster but he knew in his heart that he and his fellow writers must share responsibility for it. They had raised men's sights but they had given them nothing to aim at. Why sing of the glory and the beauty and the nobility of life, he asked John Addington Symonds, if you had no idea what it was for?

My own conscience is badly seared. What a picture this is of a nation! No man that I can see, on any side or party, seems to have the least sense of our ineffable shame: the desertion of the garrisons. Millais (I hear) was painting Gladstone when the news came of Gordon's death; Millais was much affected and Gladstone said 'Why? It is the man's own temerity!' *Voilà le Bourgeois! le voilà nu!* But why should I blame Gladstone when I too am a Bourgeois? When I have held my peace? Why did I hold my peace? Because I am a sceptic: i.e., a Bourgeois. We believe in nothing, Symonds: you don't and I don't; and these are two reasons, out of a handful of millions, why England stands before the world dripping with blood and daubed with dishonour.

So there was more to be done. It was not enough to make fiction the equal and even the master of scientific thought. It was not enough

134

to bring God into the world and trace the magnificent shadow he cast upon the human mind. Mankind must be given a purpose, an aim in life, sufficiently noble to justify the visions which fiction had conjured up. In 1886 Stevenson read Dostoevsky's *Crime and Punishment*, an experience which he found totally overwhelming, more like having an illness than reading a novel. It was the greatest book he had read for many years and it made him see that 'fundamental errors in human nature stand on the skyline of all this modern world'. Men and women should not pursue mere happiness in the real world any more than in the world of the adventure story. They would only find their true selves if they lived for 'rivalry, effort, success – the elements our friends wish to eliminate . . . As for those crockery chimney-piece ornaments the bourgeois and their cowardly dislike of dying and killing, it is merely one symptom of a thousand how utterly they have got out of touch of life'.

In the spring of 1887, Queen Victoria's Golden Jubilee Year, when most journals were full of smug articles about the wonderful things achieved during her reign, Stevenson struck a discordant note with a piece in the *Contemporary Review* called 'The Day After Tomorrow'. 'Liberty has served us a long while,' he wrote, 'and it may be time to seek new altars.' Democracy was dying and Parliament in London was as decadent as Congress in Washington. On both sides of the Atlantic man had been deceived into pursuing false aims and dreaming false dreams. 'He is supposed to love comfort; it is not a love, at least, that he is faithful to. He is supposed to love happiness; it is my contention that he rather loves excitement.' Danger and adversity, not comfort and happiness, were 'the true elixir for all vital spirits'. Stevenson's own sharpest experience of such things had been in America a few years earlier, when he had journeyed in extreme discomfort from Scotland to California to seek out and wed Fanny Osbourne. From San Francisco he had written to Edmund Gosse confessing that for six weeks he had been unable to decide whether to live or to die: 'I felt unable to go on farther with that rough horseplay of human life'. Now, in the summer of 1887, he crossed the Atlantic again, this time as the advocate of the horseplay, of mankind's delight in danger and adversity.

He had certainly come to a land where the horseplay of human life was achieving a kind of glory. In December 1881, shortly after the famous gunfight at the O.K. Corral in Tombstone Arizona, President Arthur told Congress that armed desperadoes menaced the peace of the western territories. A few months later, as the President threatened to put Arizona under martial law, the young English writer Oscar Wilde arrived in St Joseph, Missouri to find the whole town mourning the notorious train-robber Jesse James, who had just been murdered. 'Two speculators absolutely came to pistol-shots as to who was to have his hearth-brush, the unsuccessful one being, however, consoled by being allowed to purchase the water-butt for the income of an English bishop ... The Americans, if not hero-worshippers, are villain-worshippers.' The immense popularity of the dime novels meant that the Wild West, though never as wild in reality as in fiction, was rapidly becoming the most significant single source of the elixir which Stevenson wished to dispense to vital spirits.

Rider Haggard, writing angrily about American fiction in February 1887, refused to take Wild West stories into account. He reckoned there were forty million novel readers in the United States, all of them subsisting on a diet of stories pirated from England. 'Most of the books patronized by this enormous population are stolen from English authors ... The Americans are destroying their own literature, that cannot live in the face of the unfair competition to which it is subjected'. Instead of red-blooded tales of adventure American writers produced effete romances which had about them 'an atmosphere like that of the boudoir of a luxurious woman'. It sounded like a description of the kind of fiction the *Saturday Review* had said Stevenson would transcend. It might almost have been a description of the work of Henry James, whom Stevenson had already dismissed as a man incapable of appreciating Dostoevsky. The American novel which did suit the new cult was Mark Twain's *Huckleberry Finn*, which came out in 1884. Stevenson said it was 'incredibly well done' and its reputation continued to grow. T.S. Eliot was to compare Huck Finn to Ulysses, Faust, Don Quixote, Don Juan, Hamlet 'and other great discoveries that man has made about himself ... His is not the independence of the typical or symbolic American but the independence of the vagabond'. And the vagabond, like the vital spirits beloved of Robert Louis Stevenson, despised mere comfort and happiness. 'I reckon I got to light out for the Territory ahead of the rest,' said Huck at the end of the book, 'because Aunt Sally she's going to adopt me and sivilize me and I can't stand it. I been there before.'

British authors could only produce part-time boy vagabonds. When Richard Jefferies put his pagan vision of the natural world into *Wood Magic* in 1881 it met with considerable hostility but in the following year, when he laced it with boyhood adventure in *Bevis, the Story of a Boy*, it proved far more popular. Bevis and his friend Mark left civilization behind and lived for a time close to nature. 'In those days of running, racing, leaping, exploring, swimming,' wrote Jefferies, 'the skin nude to the sun and wind and water, they built themselves up of steel, steel that would bear the hardest wear of the world. Had they been put in an open boat and thrust forth to sea like the Vikings of old, it would not have hurt them.' Two years later the survivors from the shipwrecked yacht *Mignonette* were landed at Falmouth and admitted that after three weeks in an open boat they had killed and eaten their companion, a boy of seventeen named Richard Parker. He too had been in good physical condition when he was first 'thrust forth to sea like the Vikings of old', but it had not saved him. He did not have Jefferies or Stevenson to write a happy ending for him. Nor were the imagined benefits of a harsh life confined to boys. Maurice Hewlett, whose romantic tales were set in a shadowy mediaeval world, had a heroine who dressed as a boy and fell in with some charcoal-burners who starved her and thrashed her and over-worked her. Mediaeval graveyards had been well stocked with children who had succumbed to such treatment but in the case of Hewlett's Lady Isoult it proved therapeutic: 'Her hair curled and wove about her neck, her eyes shone and were limpid, her roses bloomed unawares; she grew sinewy and healthy in the kind forest air. She worked very hard, ate very little, was as often beaten as not. All this made for health.'

In real life cruelty killed and the cruel survived. Actual conflicts and excitements, unlike adventure stories, tended to result in the triumph of the 'crockery chimney-piece ornaments' and the salvation of their world. In America the years that saw the cowboy trails blazed from Texas to Kansas in the West also saw the rise of rich and powerful industrialists in the East who were determined to bring down the cost of labour. Dominant in the money markets, buttressed by widespread political corruption, they enforced wage reductions and when workers protested the militia fired point-blank into crowds, killing and wounding hundreds of men in Baltimore, Pittsburgh, Chicago and other cities. Churchmen urged the authorities to continue the slaughter. 'If the club of the policeman, knocking out the brains of the rioters, will answer, well and good,' wrote one, 'but if it does not promptly meet the exigency, then bullet and bayonet, canister and grape, constitute the one remedy and the one duty of the hour.' 'There are times when mercy is a mistake,'

137

added the periodical *Christian Union*.

The climax came in May 1886 in Chicago, where police fired indiscriminately into an anarchist demonstration after a bomb had been thrown. Eight anarchist leaders were arrested and seven were condemned to death though there was no evidence to connect them with the bomb. In November 1887, as Stevenson told the Americans of the importance of danger and excitement, the President of Cornell University told the British of the importance of these convictions. In a piece for the *Contemporary Review* on 'Contemporary Life and Thought in the United States' he remarked that 'the decision of the Supreme Court of Illinois, that the condemned anarchists of Chicago have no legal cause for complaint over their sentences, has exerted a wholesome influence ... some of our best political thinkers are firm in the belief that the wage-worker has no real grievance'.

In Britain too the violence of the real world vied with fiction. A man shot at Queen Victoria in March 1882 and a few weeks later another was given ten years penal servitude for threatening to murder her. Meanwhile the Secretary and Under-Secretary for Ireland had been set upon and hacked to death with surgical knives in Phoenix Park in Dublin. 'The Queen must call on her Government to protect her subjects from murder and outrage,' Victoria wrote furiously to Gladstone. 'The mischief Mr Gladstone does is *incalculable*,' she told the Prince of Wales, 'instead of *stemming* the current and downward course of Radicalism, which he could do *perfectly*, he *heads and encourages it*'. Her anxieties had an American dimension, for many in Britain thought that it was the cult of violence in the United States that lay behind the terrorism in Ireland. The *New York Tribune* strenuously denied that Americans would 'support inflammatory orators or arm malcontents', but this did not deter a gang of dynamiters in New York from announcing publicly that they would kill the Prince of Wales if he set foot in Ireland.

The Queen sought reassurance from the man whose magical island-valley of Avilion had brought comfort to her subjects. She summoned Tennyson to her own island-valley on the Isle of Wight and together they agreed to reject 'unbelievers and philosophers, who would try to make one believe there was no other world, no immortality, who tried to explain everything away in a miserable manner.' Tennyson was hopeful about eternity but not about things temporal. 'I am afraid I think the world is darkened,' he told the Queen. In London strange things happened in the darkness. Early in February 1886, in thick fog, a terrible panic gripped the city. There were said to be armies of revolutionaries pouring in from every side. To the south of the Thames, *The Times* reported, 'all shops closed and the people stood at their doors straining their eyes through the fog for the sounds of ten thousand men who were said to be marching'. A telegram was received at the paper's offices saying: 'Fearful state all round here in South London. Thirty thousand men at Spa Road moving to Trafalgar Square. Roughs in thousands trooping to West. Send special messenger to Home Office to have police in fullest force, with fullest military force also, to save London'. Detachments of mounted police galloped down the Old Kent Road to scatter the legions of revolt. Not until the fog began to clear was it apparent that the marching men had never existed. They were as insubstantial as the fog which had engendered them. The human imagination, the faculty which was supposed to bring God into the world and solve a governing people's problems, had given other and stranger proof of its power.

The gathering darkness which weighed upon Tennyson was the counterpart of the dazzling exhilaration of the adventure story. Each in its different way bore witness to the gap between man's aspirations and his understanding, between the vivid reality of the God within and the apparent indifference of the God who presided over the workings of history. In the year of the Queen's accession Tennyson had written 'Locksley Hall', a poem in which he had looked forward to a better and happier society brought about by technical achievement and religious zeal, by science harnessed to the service of democracy and Christianity. 'Forward, forward let us range,' he had cried, moving into the confident metallic metaphors of the railway age, 'Let the great world spin for ever down the ringing grooves of change'. As Jubilee Year approached he determined to take stock and see whether his earlier hopes had been fulfilled.

It seemed they had not. 'Locksley Hall Sixty Years After', published at the end of 1886, was among the bleakest of his poems. It was about darkness, the darkness of man's deeds, the darkness of his imaginings, the darkness of his despair now that high hopes of progress had withered. The cry of 'Forward, forward' was now 'lost within a growing gloom'. Democracy, instead of working for the good of all, had 'slaked the light with blood' and mankind was slipping into a new Dark Age without faith and without hope. Writers were concerned only to 'Rip your brother's vices open, strip your foul passions bare', while politicians bowed either to the bombs of the terrorist or

139

to the feckless votes of the uneducated. Many reviewers thought the poem 'unnecessarily melancholy' and Gladstone was furious. It should never have been published, he declared roundly in an angry article in *The Nineteenth Century* in January 1887: 'Justice does not require, nay rather she forbids, that the Jubilee of the Queen be marred by tragic tones.' In view of all the reforms that had been achieved during the Queen's reign pessimism such as Tennyson's was quite inadmissible. Gladstone came close to suggesting that those who did not believe in the inevitability of progress and in the efficacy of liberal reforms were as dangerous, as heretical, as religious unbelievers had been in an earlier age.

Across the Atlantic reactions were less indignant but equally dismissive. 'I think I should like to write a bit about Tennyson and the new Locksley Hall,' Walt Whitman told the editor of the *Critic*, 'intended for your first page if you wish.' The piece duly appeared on the front page of the journal on 1 January 1887. 'The course of progressive politics (democracy) is so certain and resistless, not only in America but in Europe,' Whitman wrote, 'that we can well afford the warning calls of such deep-sounding and high-soaring voices as Carlyle's and Tennyson's'. His article made reference not to the poem itself but to 'an apparently authentic summary' which said that 'a cynical vein of denunciation of democratic opinions and aspirations runs throughout the poem'. 'I should call it a signal instance of democratic humanity's luck that it has such enemies to contend with – so candid, so fervid, so heroic,' Whitman continued. 'We have a beautiful singer in Tennyson,' commented Robert Buchanan in London, 'and some day it will be among Tennyson's highest honours that he was once named kindly and appreciated by Whitman'.

Both Gladstone's indignation and Whitman's condescension overlooked the most important lines in the poem:

> Ay, for doubtless I am old, and think gray thoughts, for I am gray:
> After all the stormy changes shall we find a changeless May?

> After madness, after massacre, Jacobinism and Jacquerie,
> Some diviner force to guide us through the days I shall not see? . . .

> All the full-brain, half-brain races, led by Justice, Love, and Truth;
> All the millions one at length with all the visions of my youth? . . .

> Ere she gain her Heavenly-best, a God must mingle with the game:

Nay, there may be those about us whom we neither see nor name,

Felt within us as ourselves, the Powers of Good, the Powers of Ill,
Strowing balm, or shedding poison in the Fountains of the Will.

Clearly Tennyson did not rule out the possibility of progress towards higher things. What he doubted was man's ability to make that progress without 'some diviner force to guide us'. The summary that Walt Whitman had seen, with its talk of cynical denunciation, was a travesty of the poem's true intentions. There was nothing cynical about Tennyson's desperate concern for the future of mankind. The darkness of his despair about unaided human beings was relieved by the brightness of his hopes for them if they had a God to guide them. But the God whom theologians called 'God transcendent', the God out there, the all-powerful being who was supposed to hold the universe in the palm of his hand, seemed to grow more shadowy with every passing year. 'Locksley Hall Sixty Years After' was about his demise, about his desertion of mankind, just as much as it was about human fallibility. But there was still the God imminent, the God who was 'felt within us as ourselves'. This was the God for whom Robert Louis Stevenson had sounded his fanfare, the God who had been saved from extinction as the pundits of the 1880s hailed the new-found power of fiction. Men of science and men of orthodoxy shared the same darkness, straining their eyes as the match flared up and the pillars carved with philosophy failed to appear. Only vital spirits fortified by the elixir of adventure and unreality could still dream dreams and see visions. The rise and recognition of fiction had not changed the nature of God but it had changed man's perception of him.

As darkness closed in on him the God transcendent suffered the ultimate ignominy: he was snubbed by *The Times*. Early on 23 February 1887 an earthquake shook the French Riviera coast. It was Ash Wednesday, the first day of the lenten season of fasting and penitence, and exhausted Shrove Tuesday revellers were rudely awakened. One was the Prince of Wales, in Cannes for the festivities. 'If everybody had behaved like the Prince,' remarked *The Times*, 'the panic would not have been so great. Apprised by his suite of the fright caused by the earthquake, he declined to go down into the garden and, having tranquillized everybody, remained in bed.' Another was Nietzsche, who had long said the absurdities of the age could only end in a carnival of chaos. Now, as masked merry-makers fled in terror through streets littered with debris, he saw himself justified. 'We are living,

141

in fact, in the interesting expectation *that we shall perish*,' he wrote, 'thanks to a well-intentioned earthquake'.

But the days had gone when earthquakes could be thought to have intentions. *The Times* pointed out that the disaster had missed what surely should have been its prime target, 'the reprobate but fascinating Monte Carlo', 'We can imagine the sensation that would have been caused throughout the world,' it continued, 'had the Casino fallen a victim to the shock. What so appropriate as that on the first morning of Lent that home of wickedness should have been suddenly destroyed by the forces of outraged nature! Piety would have regarded the ruin as a judgment on a place that had so long tempted Providence and scepticism would have remarked that it was a singular coincidence'. The tone of the article was bantering, flippant, even contemptuous. It implied not just that God had missed his aim but that it was a delusion to think of him aiming at all. In its own inimitable way *The Times* was bidding farewell to the universe which had once been thought to be 'governed by incessant divine intervention'. But even *The Times* had no power over that other universe which Stevenson had had in mind when he wrote his 'Enter God!'. There, on the spacious stage of fiction, there were still some spectacular results to be achieved.

9 ALL TRUTH IS CHANGE

In Jubilee Year British readers were bombarded with prophecies of a new and nobler kind of religion. The *Fortnightly Review* was particularly insistent. 'The narrow thoughts, the petty sympathies, the anthropocentric creeds, the anthropomorphic gods that once sufficed us will no longer satisfy the yearnings of our enlarged natures. New beliefs and new impulses gather strength and head within us', declared the anonymous author of a piece called 'Our Noble Selves'. He was sure that for all its scientific scepticism the human race was still profoundly religious and would 'pour forth its full heart in profuse strains of unpremeditated cosmical music'. John Addington Symonds spoke of 'the restoration of spirituality to our thoughts about the universe' and of 'the destiny of the scientific spirit to bring God, Law, Christian morals, into a new and vital combination which will contribute to the growth of rational religion'. Richard Jefferies pictured mankind fortified by science and standing on 'huge mounds of facts' to glimpse the starry horizon of infinity. Professor Huxley said that although science was a drudge, a Cinderella who did all the hard work while religion and philosophy behaved like the ugly sisters, she had the clearest insight into the ultimate mystery: 'She lights the fire, sweeps the house and provides the dinner; and is rewarded by being told that she is a base creature devoted to low and material interests. But in her garret she has fairy visions out of the ken of the pair of shrews who are quarrelling downstairs. She sees the order which pervades the seeming disorder of the world'.

As long as this glimpse of underlying order was a genuine insight, not just a airy vision, Nietzsche's image of chaos following upon God's death could be discounted together with Tennyson's dark forebodings. Instead of leaving man 'straying through an infinite nothing' and 'lost within a growing gloom' the demise of the old God would allow him at last to see the creator as he or she or it really was, not just as a projection of man. The years of error would be over and the age of true religion, natural religion, could begin. The atheist poet James Thomson pointed out that there was a sense in which those who had talked of the death of Christ and the rebirth of Pan had been proved right: 'Now it is full time to proclaim the death of the great god Christ. Fate, in the form of Science, has decreed the extinction of the gods ... Pan lives, not as a God, but as the All, Nature, now that the oppression of the Supernatural is removed.' If Huxley was right the oppression of the irrational would also be removed. Instead of a sleep of reason bringing forth monsters there would just be rational human beings understanding and accepting the rational universe which had begotten them.

It was a pleasantly reassuring prospect but not one that all could share. Thomson himself in his darker moments felt the terrible oppression of the supernatural, of a universe ruled by cruel and monstrous and irrational forces, and his poems contained some of the ugliest nightmares brought forth by this age of dying gods and doubting humans. Huxley said that even Christianity at its worst, belief in the supremacy of evil and in man's innate depravity, chimed better with scientific truth than did 'the "liberal" popular illusions and other optimistic figments'. Whatever he might say in public his private convictions were closer to Tennyson's fears than to Gladstone's hopes. He told Tyndall in 1892 that Tennyson was 'the first poet since Lucretius who has understood the drift of science'; and this drift was clearly not towards a neat picture of a fixed and stable universe. Tennyson had foreseen this nearly sixty years ago. 'All truth is change' he had proclaimed in an early poem on the Greek philosopher Heraclitus. Whereas Socrates and Plato had taught that there were unchanging realities behind the shifting world of appearances, Heraclitus had argued that change was the reality and fixity the passing illusion. Just as Nietzsche rejected 'Socratic man' in favour of the older and fiercer dispensation represented by Dionysus, so Tennyson saw that if Heraclitus was right mankind would have to jettison moral absolutes along with scientific certainties: 'All thoughts, all creeds, all dreams are true.'

In the 1830s Tennyson had been alone but now he was part of a chorus. 'Men are beginning to look to Heraclitus not Socrates as the exponent of the true Greek spirit,' wrote Havelock Ellis in 1890. In 1889 Professor Patrick of the State University of Iowa published a new edition of Heraclitus and used Tennyson's poem to introduce

144

it. The rediscovery of Heraclitus was a recent thing, Professor Patrick explained: it had taken place within the past few decades, largely in Germany, and it was linked with Schopenhauer's rejection of the Socratic tradition. The link with Nietzsche was equally apparent and a few years later Patrick and his wife were to translate a history of contemporary German philosophy in which more space was given to Nietzsche than to any other thinker. Although only fragments of Heraclitus's works survived they were enough to show the vast gap between his dynamic vision of creation and the tidy world of Socrates. 'All things are exchanged for fire and fire for all things,' proclaimed Heraclitus, 'Good and evil are the same'. There was no such thing as a state of being, calm and complete and defined: there was only a state of becoming, mercurial and restless and unresolved. Violence and conflict were the only creators: 'War is the father and king of all and has produced some as gods and some as men, and has made some slaves and some free'.

'The world will be standing on its head for the next few years,' wrote Nietzsche in December 1888 as the new edition of Heraclitus went to press, 'since the old God has abdicated I shall rule the world from now on.' His title to the succession came not from Heraclitus but from Dionysus, in whose name he now began to sign his letters. Within a month he was declared insane. He had parted company not just with Socratic thinking but with reason itself. Others found reason and even faith compatible with a world standing on its head. Gerard Manley Hopkins wrote a sonnet called 'That Nature is a Heraclitean Fire and of the comfort of the Resurrection', the only poem he completed in 1888. It spoke of a universe without rest and without apparent meaning, an unfathomable dark in which the dead dross of matter and the brief fire of life were both overwhelmed. Yet they had met, the fire that was God had entered into the dross that was man. Christ's resurrection had made possible man's immortality just as surely as the meeting of fire and carbon inside the earth had made possible the dazzling and indestructible beauty of the diamond.

Hopkins was able to reconcile Christian and Heraclitean thinking, giving new intensity to both, because of his own sense of the God within him, the God imminent. The God transcendent, pavilioned for more than two hundred years in Sir Isaac Newton's stable universe, could not be so sure of surviving the baptism of Heraclitean fire. Nor for that matter could science, which in the hands of Newton's successors had turned from revealing God's glory to usurping it. Newton

145

had shown the lovers of system and order that the God of the Bible was the right god for them. Other scientists, equally tidy-minded, had laid down universal laws in order to contrast them with the vagaries of biblical revelation. But pious and impious alike wanted universal laws. They all needed to be sure there was a heavenly throne even though some knelt on its steps while others sat in it. How else could thought be objective? How could either God or man make sense of the whirling infinities without observing them from some fixed point where motion and direction were absolute and not relative?

Heraclitus could offer no such refuge and it was to be nearly twenty years before Einstein taught physicists to turn relativity itself into an observation platform. In the meantime it was the literary men rather than the scientists who made confident generalizations. The same Jubilee issue of the *Fortnightly Review* in which Symonds insisted that the scientific spirit would foster rational religion also contained a complacent account of Victorian scientific progress by Grant Allen, a Canadian-born philosopher who was making a name for himself in London literary circles. 'In marvellous contrast to the fragmentary and disjunctive science of fifty years ago,' he wrote, 'modern science offers us the spectacle of a simple, unified and comprehensible cosmos.' Like Symonds he saw this as the key not just to the physical world but to spiritual life as well. It was a sublime cosmic synthesis, 'one and the same throughout, in sun and star and world and atom, in light and heat and life and mechanism, in body, soul and spirit, mind and matter.' But he too sensed the shift from Socrates to Heraclitus and a few months later he substituted a dynamic Heraclitean theory of the universe for the comfortably comprehensible cosmos which he had praised so extravagently. When he published his new ideas in 1888 he felt constrained to apologize for being a heretic and rejecting current scientific orthodoxy.

It seemed that only scientific heresies, not religious ones, needed apologies. In an article in the *Fortnightly Review* in January 1890 Grant Allen dismissed God as a lump of rock: 'Jahveh, the God of the Hebrews, the God of Abraham and of Isaac and of Jacob, the God who later became sublimated and etherealized into the God of Christianity, was in his origin nothing more nor less than the ancestral fetish stone of the people of the Israel'. He then went on to publish *The Evolution of the Idea of God*, saying that all religions had originated in the worship of the deified dead. Winwood Reade had put forward a similar theory a quarter of a century earlier and had contrasted the imagined gods of the gullible with the real god of the scientists, 'the supreme and mysterious Power by whom the universe has been created and by whom it has been appointed to run its course under fixed and invariable laws; that awful One of whom we should never presume to think save with humility and awe'. Allen observed Reade's commandments as well as using his ideas. Pulling the old God to pieces, ferreting out the fetishes and detailing the stages of deification, was a legitimate activity of which nobody need feel ashamed; doubting the fixed and invariable laws of the awful One was matter for contrition.

In August 1894 the British Association for the Advancement of Science met in Oxford for the first time since the notorious 1860 meeting which had seen the confrontation between Huxley and Wilberforce over the rival claims of Darwin and God. Lord Salisbury, a past and future Conservative Prime Minister, was both Chancellor of Oxford University and President of the Association. His opening address ended by quoting the eminent scientist Lord Kelvin: 'Overpoweringly strong proofs of intelligent and benevolent design lie around us, teaching us that all things depend on one everlasting Creator and Ruler'. It sounded like a defence of the old God against the scientific doubters but it could also have been a vindication of Reade's awful One. Huxley, thanking Salisbury for his address, passed over the remarks about the Creator and Ruler and contented himself with pointing out that the orthodox biblical account of the immutability of species was now totally discredited. *The Times*, predicting confidently that Salisbury's address would have 'a beneficial influence on all serious-minded scientific workers', noted with approval the contrast between these civilized exchanges and the dreadful events of 1860. The passage of time might have softened the grim watchdogs of the God of the Book of Genesis but it remained to be seen whether it would do the same for those who defended the awful One and his invariable laws.

Some of the old watchdogs still had teeth. *Lux Mundi*, a collection of essays which appeared in 1889, contained a piece which suggested that some biblical stories might be dramatic narratives, 'true myths', rather than reliable history. Liddon, preaching in St Paul's, attacked this notion as fiercely as he had denounced the heresies of the 1860s. There was no half-way house, he told his congregation uncompromisingly: unless they believed everything in the Bible they would finish up believing nothing. Two years later Dr Alfred Williams Momerie, Professor of Logic and Mental Philosophy at King's College London, was ousted after accusations of unorthodox teaching. Things might have changed at the British Association since the slanging match of 1860 but they had not changed much at King's College since the enforced resignation of F.D. Maurice in 1853. Many Anglicans still felt that they were ringed round with atheism. In 1888 a bishop declared indignantly that you found unbelief everywhere, lurking in newspapers and novels, airing its views in your club or your drawing-room. You might even hear it from the lady who sat next to you at dinner.

Nevertheless the orthodox were reasonably cheerful, certainly more cheerful than agonized intellectuals trying to fit new trends in science and philosophy into a coherent whole. In 1886 churchmen were claiming that their influence had grown spectacularly during the past twenty years. It suffered something of a set-back in 1888 and 1889 in Wales, where there was a ferocious and determined campaign against the payment of tithes. Farmers threatened to shoot anyone who tried to collect them and vicars who demanded payment were burned in effigy. Hundreds of policemen were involved in hand-to-hand fighting with angry labourers. Finally Mr Stevens, the agent of the Ecclesiastical Commissioners, refused to make any further attempts at collection after large crowds armed with heavy sticks had forced him and his bodyguard to retreat. However, Archbishop Benson remained confident that he was healing the rift of which Dr Hort had warned him. He was sure that the masses were coming back to God in spite of tithe riots and in spite of the fashionable scepticism of the club and the dinner table. 'It is well known,' he said in 1891, 'that throughout the country the number of those who attend church has largely increased and is still increasing'. It looks now as though he was quite wrong: 1886 seems to have been the year in which the churches first fell behind and failed to keep pace with population increase. Attendances began to fall, especially in towns where the population was still rising. But such trends were not apparent at the time and so the optimism of the devout was undented.

There was optimism of another kind in America. In 1890 Congress decided to hold a World's Columbian Exposition to mark the four hundredth anniversary of the discovery of America. Charles Carroll Bonney, President of the Exposition's Congress Auxiliary, determined to make this the occasion for a World's Parliament of Religions, where representatives from every religion on earth would meet to proclaim the one over-riding divine truth. After many delays the Exposition finally opened in Chicago in May 1893, four hundred and one years after Columbus's voyage, and the Parliament of Religions opened on 11 September. Cardinal Gibbons of Baltimore led the delegates in the Lord's Prayer while Hindus and Muslims and Buddhists beamed approvingly at his side. Archbishop Benson had refused to have anything to do with the enterprise and so the Church of England was represented on the platform by Dr Momerie. At home he was now in deep disgrace, unable to preach without special permission from his bishop, but in Chicago he gave a confident address on 'The Philosophic and Moral Evidence for the Existence of God'. It was a strange piece of work which combined out-dated Newtonian arguments about the universe with some remarkably harsh remarks about the need for children to suffer for the sins of their fathers in accordance with the wishes of the God of the Old Testament. Nor was Momerie alone in rooting for his own God. The Chairman of the Parliament quoted with approval a bishop who said that 'civilization, which is making the whole world one, is preparing the way for the reunion of all the world's religions in their true centre, Jesus Christ'. It would be a difficult convergence if each religion saw itself as the only true centre.

Zenshiro Noguchi, a Buddhist from Japan, was not dismayed. 'Is there a hope of decreasing the number of religions?' he asked, 'Yes. How far? To one. Why? Because the truth is only one.' Laura Ormiston Chant of London was welcomed 'with more than the usual demonstrations of interest and applause' when she said that God himself was about to reveal the nature of this ultimate truth: 'Today, for the first time in the world's history, we are certain that God's duty to us will be performed'. She had just listened to a paper on comparative theology and she was not impressed. 'What marvellous intellectual jugglers these theologians are!' she observed tartly. She had had hopes of a new Day of Pentecost when the Holy Spirit would descend in tongues of Heraclitean fire not just on Christians but on the whole of mankind. Instead she found that many delegates regarded the whole affair as just another academic conference. Julia Ward Howe was even more contemptuous of theological subtleties, dismissing them as the tricks and charms of mischievous priests. Contributions like those of Mrs Chant and Mrs Howe, visions of a new heaven and a new earth, contrasted sharply with the cautious and scholarly papers of the intellectuals. Nevertheless the Parliament closed in an atmosphere of excitement and satisfaction and hope. 'What men deemed impossible, God has finally wrought,' said the chairman. Momerie, thanking his American hosts on behalf of all the foreign delegates, declared that 'It is

149

the greatest event so far in the history of the world and it has been held on American soil.'

Perhaps it was the event that Tennyson had been waiting for, the moment at which God 'mingled with the game' and led mankind away from the horrors into which it had been straying. Tennyson had welcomed the World Parliament and had agreed to serve on its Advisory Council for Great Britain, though by the time it opened he was dead. While Archbishop Benson raged at the very idea of the Parliament because it put Christianity on a par with other religions Tennyson and other eminent laymen gave it their support. As well as being the possible realization of their hopes it could also be seen as fulfilling the predictions of the watchers on the high towers, who had always said that divine truth would soon reconcile conventional thinking and occult inspiration, science and scriptural revelation, eastern mysteries and western observances. But the obstinate fact remained that the traditional God of the English-speaking peoples, the robed and bearded figure presiding over a stable Newtonian universe, was in no position to make such a breakthrough. He was in full retreat, pursued by the whirling furies of relativist and Heraclitean thought. When many of the buildings put up for the Columbian Exposition were destroyed by fire in January 1894 it did not occur to *The Times* to make play with the disaster as it had made play with the earthquake of 1887. It was no longer even amusing, let alone instructive, to consider whether the power that ruled the galaxies could indicate approval or disapproval of what had been going on in Chicago. It might seem a sad irony of the late Victorian age that an upsurge of questing spirituality should have coincided with the undermining of the foundations upon which spirituality was popularly supposed to rest.

In fact there was no irony and no coincidence. The search for God was as old as mankind and the desire for his presence had usually been in direct proportion to the fear of his absence. The deepest spiritual yearnings had always sprung from a sense of loss. What was new was that the yearnings and the loss had become separated. Instead of the same saints and mystics passing from the dark night of God's absence to the ecstatic knowledge of his presence, instead of the same congregations being led from a sense of sin through worship and contrition to a sacramental union, there was a number of people agonizing and theorizing in public as to whether or not God was in charge of the universe while another and far larger number agonized in private

150

over the gap between their aspiring fantasies and their circumscribed lives. In previous ages the very existence of this gap had been proof of God's presence. Browning had set it in a religious context only thirty years ago: 'A man's reach should exceed his grasp, Or what's a heaven for?' But now, as Rider Haggard had already pointed out, 'men and women stretch out their arms towards that vision of the Perfect which we only see in books and dreams'. The manuals of devotion had been replaced by novels, the collective fantasies of the pious had given way to the individual fantasies of the impressionable. Mystics had spoken of self-transcendence while Haggard spoke of men and women 'craving to be taken out of themselves'. The language differed but the yearning was the same. Could God rebuild his shattered image, could he pass through fiction as well as fire in order to bring his imminence and his transcendence together again?

This was perhaps the only way in which the hopes of 'Locksley Hall Sixty Years After' could be fulfilled. Characters from fiction might be better than real people at 'strowing balm or shedding poison in the Fountains of the Will'. Anna Kingsford was one of the few in the real world who attempted such things: her imperious will sought to bring balm to animals in laboratories and poison to those who tortured them. On 11 November 1886, as Tennyson's lines were going to press, she learned that she had 'smitten another vivisectionist', the scientist Paul Bert. But it was not a very convincing smiting: it had taken her several years to do it and the likelihood of it being a coincidence was even greater than in the case of Claude Bernard. The drugs which had helped to heighten her ecstasies had taken their toll and she had only fifteen months to live. The fountains of the will were not hers to command. As she celebrated her triumph over Paul Bert a struggling doctor in Southsea called Arthur Conan Doyle was celebrating the sale of his book *A Study in Scarlet*, a story about a private detective named Sherlock Holmes. The watchers upon the high towers had sought strange powers by moving from reality into a world of fantasy: Sherlock Holmes was to do precisely the opposite. No other character in fiction has been so successful in convincing readers of his reality. As men combed Baker Street to find the exact location of his lodgings, as they argued passionately about which university he had attended, he was able to mingle with the game of human life in a way which exceeded even Tennyson's expectations.

A Study in Scarlet was ruthlessly pirated in the United States, where it proved so popular that the Philadelphia publisher Joseph Marshall

Stoddart came to London to commission a second Holmes story. The result, *The Sign of Four*, was serialized in an American magazine in 1890. The story opened in the summer of Jubilee Year, when 22b Baker Street – unlike the non-fictional world – was swathed in a thick yellow fog. It was this unseasonable pea-souper, swirling down the street and drifting across dun-coloured houses, that drew from Holmes his cry of despair about the unprofitable world and its commonplace values.* It soon became clear that he was a devotee of Jean-Paul Richter, who had long proclaimed God dead, as well as a convert to Winwood Reade's impersonal supreme being. If men and women stretched out their arms to Holmes for 'a vision of the Perfect which we only see in books and dreams' they would find themselves clutching at something far from orthodox.

Sherlock Holmes began to cast his extraordinary spell over British readers in July 1891, when short stories about him started to appear in *The Strand Magazine*. Circulation soared and the public clamoured for more stories. Conan Doyle obliged, though with an increasingly bad grace because he felt that Holmes was keeping him from more worthwhile writing. At last in December 1893, after twenty-two stories, he decided the time had come to get rid of him. And so in the twenty-third story, 'The Final Problem', the great detective fell to his death over the Reichenbach Falls, locked in mortal combat with his arch-enemy Moriarty. It was supposed to be the end but it was not. Readers saw Holmes as a character too real to be a mere figment subject to the whims of an author and they also saw him, consciously or unconsciously, as a mythical figure who could never die. Conan Doyle was like a conjuror who tires of his tricks only to find them hailed as miracles. He found himself cast as a heretic against the divinity he had created, a doubting Thomas who refused to countenance the resurrection in which others so desperately wanted to believe. In the end he gave in and decided that Holmes had survived and had deliberately allowed himself to be presumed dead. The great detective had then plunged into a typically Holmesian mixture of scientific research and occult investigation, travelling for two years in Tibet and spending several days with the Dalai Lama – something which no non-fictional character could have done and which was closer to Colonel Olcott's dealings with the Dwellers of the Threshold than to the doings of ordinary mortals.

* See above, p.4.

The resurrection of Sherlock Holmes anticipated the scene in *Peter Pan* in which Tinkerbell was restored to life by the concerted acclaim of the audience. Like her he conquered death because those who believed in him were united in their determination that he should do so. He took on God's mantle, coming back to life by dint of the faith of his worshippers, but he was far from being a god himself. On the contrary, he seemed concerned to teach people to do without gods. In spite of his occasional perfunctory expressions of piety it was clear that he had little time for established religion or conventional morality. He made no apologies for his addiction to cocaine and he expected Watson to join him unhesitatingly in breaking the law when he thought it necessary. He said that his life was 'spent in one long effort to escape from the commonplaces of existence,' yet the end product of that life was the defence of the commonplace, the familiar and reassuring world of hansom cabs and Mrs Hudson's cooking, against all manner of strange and outlandish evils. His astonishing powers of deduction seemed like witchcraft – 'You would certainly have been burned had you lived a few centuries ago,' Watson told him – but he was always careful to show how they were based purely on observation and reason. He might be superhuman but he was not supernatural.

Nor was there anything supernatural about the threats he faced. The first of them, in *A Study in Scarlet*, originated in America, in Mormon fanaticism, and it was no accident that President Arthur was engaged in a campaign against the Mormons at the time the book was being written. Later Conan Doyle widened his net, calling forth horrors from Asia and Africa and Australia, but he still seemed fascinated by the United States as a breeding ground of hatred and violence. In the fifth short story, 'The Five Orange Pips', it was emissaries of the Ku Klux Klan who infuriated Holmes by killing his client. 'That hurts my pride, Watson,' he remarked when he saw the body, 'It is a petty feeling, no doubt, but it hurts my pride.' It was a typically Holmesian reaction, nicely poised between arrogance and apology. Rather similar had been his response in the first short story of all, 'A Scandal in Bohemia'. Then, when he had been outwitted by Irene Adler, he had asked his client for her photograph as the only reward for his services. He had no affection for her, no time for thoughts of love – 'for the trained reasoner to admit such intrusions was to introduce a distracting factor' – but he treasured her photograph and always spoke of her as *the* woman,

153

one who rivalled his own super-human powers.

To be superhuman without being supernatural was an enviable state and one to which many in the real world were beginning to aspire. George Saintsbury had said in Jubilee Year that society could be regenerated if it 'bathed long and well in the romance of adventure and passion'. Now Sherlock Holmes had added deduction and observation to the bathwater and the resulting heady mixture must surely refresh those souls whom religion could not reach. 'A wave of unrest is passing over the world,' wrote Hugh Stutfield in *Blackwood's Magazine* in 1895, 'Humanity is beginning to sicken at the daily round, the common task, of ordinary humdrum existence and is eagerly seeking for new forms of excitement. Revolt is the order of the day'. 'A new renaissance lies ahead of us,' cried Alfred Hake a few months later, 'and we are all struggling to reach it'. The philosophers of an earlier renaissance had proclaimed that man could make of himself whatever he wished. Now at last he would do so. The drive towards self-transcendence must be shifted not just from religious into secular terms, not just from Christian mystics to ordinary men and women seeking inspiration in fiction, but also from the one to the many, from the individual to the group. 'Christ made no attempt to reconstruct society and consequently the individualism that he preached to man could be realized only through pain or in solitude,' wrote Oscar Wilde. Once society was regenerated and the Christian ideals of pain and solitude rejected 'a larger, fuller, lovelier individualism' would spring from the realities of social co-operation.

One of the most uncompromising prophets of social regeneration was Edward Carpenter, an English disciple of Walt Whitman who had relinquished holy orders at the age of thirty. After visiting Whitman in New Jersey and finding in him 'a certain radiant power' he had made his home among labouring people and had tried to share their life. He was appalled by the blindness with which respectable guardians of society – clergymen, politicians, financiers, men of property – destroyed themselves as well as others. Unquiet, unresting, uncomprehending, they spun cobwebs over 'the calm miraculous beauty of the world' and fed their children on 'the refuse of dinner parties and the insides of committee rooms'. If there was a god at all it was not the one set up by these cardboard figures; it was 'the goat-legged God peering over the tops of clouds, shameless, lusty, unpresentable'. Havelock Ellis's *The New Spirit*, which began by proclaiming the return to Heraclitean thought, went on to hail Carpenter

154

as one who had found 'the perennial fountain which springs up within and which the measuring rod of science has never meted'. Ellis himself in his student days had been likened both to Jesus Christ and to Pan. His mistress found his naked body essentially Christlike but his wife insisted that he was 'a mixture of satyr and Christ'. She even took him to the National Gallery to show him, in a picture by Rubens, which satyr he was.

Ellis took such comparisons in his stride. He had already decided, during three lonely years of meditation in the Australian outback, that his mission in life was to bring together knowledge and belief by demonstrating the supremacy of sex in human affairs. Born into an age in which the collective fantasies of religion jarred against the seemingly unfantastic discoveries of science and materialism, he would restore unity to human thought by showing how all these things converged in the individual fantasies which governed the reproductive urge. For him 'the perennial fountain which springs up within' was a description of physical desire as well as a metaphor for true wisdom. Hence the picture by Rubens was of more interest than the scores of religious pictures in which he might have identified the Christlike part of his nature. Man's regeneration would come from within himself, by understanding and harnessing his urges instead of denying them, and if a god presided over the process it would be Pan and not Christ. Christianity turned away from the physical realities of human life while paganism accepted them and gloried in them. 'The free Greek was not ashamed of sex,' wrote Grant Allen, 'not ashamed of his own body and its component members. He despised the barbarian who shamed to show himself in the palaestra as the gods had fashioned him.' Having revised his ideas about Greek thought, having rejected Apollo in favour of Dionysus, Socrates in favour of Heraclitus, modern man must now come to terms with Greek life as well. Like all real life it was centred not on asceticism and the search for heaven but on sexuality.

The neo-paganism of the 1890s was more thoroughgoing than earlier dalliances with Pan. In the first place the phenomenal rise of fiction had given new life to the ancient concept of the hero, the archetypal figure who saved society not because he was supernatural but because he was superhuman. Already thinkers in Germany were hailing Nietzsche as prophet of the age of the superman: man had reached a dead end and could only survive by transcending himself. Philosophies of this kind were seen as blasphemies by many people in Britain

155

and America. How could men seek to become supermen without seeking to becomes gods? One possible answer was given in the first volume of Sir James Frazer's *The Golden Bough*, the publication of which in 1890 gave fresh impetus to the neo-pagan movement. It took its title from a priest who gained his office by plucking a golden bough in the sacred grove of Nemi. To do so he had to kill the priest who was there already, so that every priest was a murderer and would in due course become a victim. It was, as *The Times* pointed out, a ritual of life: the divine man in the grove never grew old, his strength and his virility were constantly renewed as they passed from one priest to the next.

Needless to say it was also a ritual of death. 'They shall grow not old, as we that are left grow old', words soon to be inscribed on countless war memorials, could equally well have been written of the priests of the sacred grove. It was to become clear in 1914, when the young heroes set off on their high adventure, that the demand for the ultimate sacrifice was as implicit in paganism as it was in Christianity. But in the 1890s 'the new paganism' seemed to be a life-enhancing force which would sweep away old inhibitions and prohibitions. In August 1892, when William Sharp brought out *The Pagan Review*, he put on its title page the motto *Sic Transit Gloria Grundi*: the long rule of Mrs Grundy, of Victorian prudery, was at last over. In a controversial article on 'The New Hedonism' in 1894 Grant Allen proclaimed that 'everything high and ennobling in our nature springs directly out of the sexual instinct'. Society would only be regenerated when it substituted this truth, the truth which lay at the root of the ancient Greek ideal of self-development, for the deluded Christian ideals of asceticism and penitence and self-sacrifice. Clearly the new hedonism was the new paganism under another name.

Grant Allen's piece was exceptional in that it presented a case rather than telling a tale. For the most part the neo-pagan movement of the early 1890s found expression in fiction rather than in disputation. Kenneth Grahame's *Pagan Papers* told of an approaching cataclysm which would sweep away the grey cohorts of respectability and leave the pagan hunter to 'string his bow once more and once more loose the whistling shaft'; but the prophecy was contained not in a philosophical or theological argument but in a series of stories. The new paganism, like Sherlock Holmes, sought to change the real world by invading it from the realms of fantasy. But where were the red-blooded pagans of fiction? There had been many influential fictitious characters

156

in the years since Saintsbury had recommended the bath of adventure and passion, but how many of them acted as though everything high and ennobling in their natures sprang directly out of the sexual instinct? There had been plenty of adventure but precious little passion. There was certainly none in Sherlock Holmes, cold and aloof with his photograph of Irene Adler filed away. 'They seem happier in their dealings with men than with women, and with war than with love,' remarked Andrew Lang of Rider Haggard and Robert Louis Stevenson, 'Mr Haggard's savage ladies are better than his civilized fair ones, while there is not a petticoat in *Kidnapped* or *Treasure Island*.' Contemporary fiction did not seem to be a very good medium for demonstrating the supremacy of sex in human affairs.

Rider Haggard was unrepentant. 'Sexual passion is the most powerful lever with which to stir the mind of man,' he wrote in 1887, 'for it lies at the root of all things human; and it is impossible to over-estimate the damage that could be worked by a single English or American writer of genius if he grasped it with a will.' Then, in one revealing question, he betrayed the reason for his reluctance to seize the sexual lever. 'Why do *men* hardly ever read a novel?' he asked plaintively. The young lions of neo-paganism might discuss sex as men of the world but novelists could not mention it as long as most of their readers were women and children. With Stevenson and Haggard and Conan Doyle pulling in the adult male readers it might be thought things were changing. But in 1891, when the Bristol public librarians divided their readers into categories, they found that 'females of no occupation' had taken out over ten thousand books, four times as many as clerks and nearly ten times the number taken out by professional men. The number of books read by schoolboys, errand boys and apprentices, either at home or in the library, was over fifteen thousand.

Boys in the upper classes were also at risk even though they might not frequent public libraries. In 1885 Dr Clement Dukes published a treatise on masturbation, which he said was practised by 'ninety to ninety-five per cent of all boys at boarding schools.' With a somewhat injudicious choice of idiom he declared that this terrible situation must be remedied 'if we, as a nation, are to hold our own'. The cure lay in what he called 'the elevation of women', though he admitted this was difficult when 'the demand for them for base purposes is so great.' It was entirely appropriate that boys should have fantasies about killing and fighting and torments and injuries but it was quite

157

undesirable that they should know how men and women made love or even that they felt the need to do so. Books given to schoolboys must encourage them to think of themselves as brave knights performing deeds of valour for chaste and elevated ladies. Companionship in arms and pure love between man and man had been ideals both of the ancient Greek world and of the knightly tradition – had not Tennyson's King Arthur spoken of the knights of the Round Table as 'the men I loved'? – and 'the new chivalry' became another name for 'the new paganism'. 'For one pleasure of life and physical delight in each other's presence, touch and voice which man and woman ordinarily share, it is not too much to say that the new chivalry has ten,' declared *The Artist and Journal of Home Culture*, after rhapsodizing about men sharing 'the evening tent-pitching of campers out and the exhilaration of the early morning swim'.

In 1891 a sensationally successful novel of schoolboy love was published. It was called *Tim* and it was by Howard Overing Sturgis, an American who had been at Eton under William Johnson Cory, a master who had to leave the school because of his affairs with boys. The book was very well received, having to be reprinted within a month of publication, and in some ways it was very conventional: its young hero died in the last chapter and in death he brought about harmony, persuading his father at last to accept his young lover. He also took care to have his ecstasies in the chapel at Eton and not in some pagan grove:

It happened that morning that the first lesson was the beautiful lament of David over his dead friend Jonathan; and Tim, listening to the history of those two friends long ago, felt his love for his friend almost a religion to him. 'Thy love to me was wonderful,' said the voice of the reader, 'passing the love of woman.' 'What woman could ever love him as I do?' thought Tim, as he looked naturally to the seat where Carol sat. At that moment a sunbeam from some hole high in the roof fell on the golden curly head which seemed transfigured; and as Tim's hungry eyes rested on the face of his friend, he turned towards him and smiled upon him in his place.

It was becoming clear that in going back to ancient Greece the new paganism might be going back to the Greek ideal of homosexual love. 1891 also saw the publication of *A Problem of Modern Ethics*, a treatise on homosexuality by John Addington Symonds which was later reprinted as an appendix to Havelock Ellis's study of sexual inversion. In 1892 Symonds told of 'men whose bodies you have

158

touched and handled' in *Our Life in the Swiss Highlands*, a book whose title was an obvious mockery of the Queen's literary efforts. From America came Oscar Wilde's *The Picture of Dorian Gray*, commissioned by Stoddart at the same time as *The Sign of Four* and published in *Lippincott's Magazine* in 1890. By the time it appeared as a book in April 1891 most reviewers had decided it was immoral. One said it was a thinly disguised account of the Cleveland Street scandal of 1889, when revelations made by good-looking telegraph boys had led to the uncovering of a male brothel frequented by the nobility and even, it was alleged, by members of the Royal Family. Accused of peddling 'moral putrescence', Wilde infuriated his critics by replying loftily that 'there is no such thing as a moral or an immoral book. Books are well written or badly written. That is all.'

Could there perhaps be worse things than the promiscuity of tele-graph boys? In 1886 Baron Richard von Krafft-Ebing's *Psychopathia Sexualis* had given clinical details of sadism and masochism and other sexual idiosyncrasies. *The Artist and Journal of Home Culture* provided an unwitting footnote to these findings when it suggested that painters should choose as a subject the whipping of Spartan boys at the altar of Artemis Orthia. 'The expression of steady and determined endur-ance under pain in a young face' would be a joy to behold. And William Sharp's most notable defiance of Mrs Grundy in *The Pagan Review* was not a description of the sexual act but an account of a pagan sacrifice of five youths and five maidens 'in a wide spirt of blood'. Just as the inability to be explicit about copulation had helped to push the new paganism into a hothouse of half-admitted homosexua-lity, so the restraints of the hothouse itself led to a darker eroticism that was seldom admitted or understood.

One man who understood it very well was Max Nordau, a doctor from Budapest who had studied Krafft-Ebing and now lived in Paris. In 1893 his book *Degeneration* claimed that much of the fashionable art and music and literature of the time was the work of men who should have been Krafft-Ebing's patients. It was sick and degenerate, produced by neurotics and fit only for neurotics. It betokened 'a Dusk of the Nations in which all suns and all stars are gradually waning and mankind with all its institutions and creations is perishing in the midst of a dying world'. The rhetoric was reminiscent of Nietzsche's threnody on the death of God and indeed Nordau had spurned God a decade earlier in *The Conventional Lies of our Civilization*, a book in which he had declared that 'Every separate act of a religious ceremony becomes a fraud and a criminal satire when performed by a cultivated man of the nineteenth century'. But to echo a writer was not to approve of him: Nietzsche was dismissed as 'a sufferer from sadism in its most pronounced form' and his works were consigned to the waste-paper basket of degeneration along with those of Wagner, Ibsen, Tolstoi, Zola, Baudelaire and many others. And the man who had infected Britain and America with these pernicious ideas, the man cast by Nordau as the high priest of decadence in the English-speaking world, was Oscar Wilde.

By now the enemies of the new movement were beginning to accuse it openly of homosexual tendencies. 'The New Morality might have gone elsewhere for its ideal than to Sodom and Gomorrah,' wrote *The Review of Reviews* grimly. Everyone knew what God had done to Sodom and Gomorrah: what would he do to this hydra-headed thing that called itself new paganism, new chivalry, new morality, new hedonism? The London *Christian Leader* said that *The Picture of Dorian Gray* 'portrays the gilded paganism which has been staining these latter years of the Victorian epoch with horrors'. By the time the English version of *Degeneration* came out at the beginning of 1895 Oscar Wilde's name stood for fashionable comedy rather than pagan horrors. *An Ideal Husband* was running in London at the Haymarket Theatre and *The Importance of Being Earnest* opened at the St James's Theatre on 14 February. The Marquis of Queensberry, who thought Wilde was corrupting his son Lord Alfred Douglas, attempted unsuccessfully to interrupt the performance. He then left a card at Wilde's club accusing him of 'posing as a sodomite'. Wilde brought an action for criminal libel and when it failed he was himself arrested and charged with acts of gross indecency with male persons. After a first trial at which the jury failed to agree a second ended on 25 May 1895 with a verdict of guilty. Wilde was sentenced to two years' imprisonment with hard labour and the pious rejoiced that God had cut off all the heads of the hydra at one stroke. In a sense they were right, for the downfall of Oscar Wilde was a turning point in moral attitudes as well as in literary fashions. However, the direction in which things turned was not to be quite what the orthodox had anticipated.

10 THE POWER OF EVIL

I<small>T WAS CLEAR FROM THE OUTSET THAT THE SINS OF</small> the world of literature were on trial along with those of real life. During the libel case Queensberry's lawyers read out passages from *The Picture of Dorian Gray* in an attempt to make Wilde reveal his sexual proclivities by identifying with his characters. On 6 April 1895, the day he was arrested, solicitors representing the publishers of the magazine *Chameleon* wrote to the newspapers saying its sale had been stopped because it was thought to have homosexual leanings. The trickle of such disclaimers became a flood and Edward Carpenter's *Homogenic Love*, which had been published in January, was killed stone dead. Other books, most of them far less overt, were abandoned or withdrawn. Within a week of Wilde's conviction the London *Christian World* was celebrating the defeat of paganism and decadence in a leading article entitled 'Culture and Gomorrah'. Sane and healthy-minded people must make a stand, declared *Blackwood's Magazine*, against 'the gilded and perfumed putrescence which is creeping over every branch of art'. The *National Observer* commented that *Degeneration* 'has made its appearance in its English dress at a very appropriate time. Herr Nordau is most indubitably right'.

But there was a difficulty. If all this was God's doing, if he had really arisen to scatter his enemies and cut off the heads of the hydra as the devout liked to think, he would hardly have chosen an atheist scientist like Nordau as his instrument. Alfred Hake's *Regeneration: a reply to Max Nordau* showed that many of the works Nordau dismissed under the heading of 'mysticism, a cardinal mark of degeneration' were in reality products of a religious revival which had offended him because it rejected clinical scientific thought. The publisher William Heinemann drove the point home when he followed up the success of *Degeneration* by bringing out *The Conventional Lies of our Civilization*, which had made little impression when it had first been published in English in Chicago in 1884. Nordau's attacks on 'The Lie of Religion' were not calculated to make the orthodox feel happy in his company. They would have been even more worried if they had known that Wilde himself was to invoke Nordau. In July 1896, petitioning to have his sentence reviewed on grounds of mental illness, he stressed that *Degeneration* had singled him out as 'a specially typical example of the intimate connection between madness and the literary and artistic temperament'. In the eyes of the conventionally pious the things that Wilde had done, both in his life and in his work, were not merely unbalanced but evil. His proper place was in hell, not in a lunatic asylum. Nordau was of little avail if he could be used to advance excuses instead of condemnation.

As far as Oscar Wilde himself was concerned there were limits even to the vindictiveness of the British public. Where his works were concerned the limits were less discernible and years after his trial, when he had become an object of pity or indifference rather than horror, *The Picture of Dorian Gray* was still being shunned as an immoral book. In 1908 *The Sunday Times* called it 'a *tour de force* of morbidity, interesting mainly because it gave a forecast of Oscar Wilde's own eclipse'. Critics compared it to Stevenson's *Dr Jekyll and Mr Hyde*, since both books were about incarnations of evil. In Dr Jekyll's case the evil in him became a second self, Mr Hyde, who grew steadily more monstrous until he took over Jekyll altogether. Dorian Gray was able to transfer the evil within him – or at any rate its physical manifestations – not to a second self but to his own portrait, which became foul and loathsome while he remained young and unmarked by his unspeakable sins. When he could bear the sight of the painting no longer he put a knife through it. The picture of Dorian Gray was then restored to its original beauty while the body of Dorian Gray, stabbed with his own knife, was invaded by all the foulness which had been on the canvas. Evil already possessed his soul and now it took over his body as well, just as it had in the end taken over the whole personality of Dr Jekyll.

At the time, in the eyes of ordinary outraged citizens, the portrayal of evil did not seem to be terribly relevant. They had been shocked by what they regarded as sins, offences against the law of God, and they had been repelled by what they regarded as indecencies, departures from normal wholesome behaviour. Such things must be punished if they took place in real life and condemned if they took

place in fiction. And that was all there was to it as far as the conventionally respectable were concerned. They thought of sin and indecency
as realities while dismissing evil as an outdated absurdity, a relic
of primitive imaginings. But already the ground was being cut from
under them as God's law slid into a vortex of Heraclitean fire carrying
man-made morals with it. In this uncertain and relativist universe
evil was to prove remarkably resilient, far more so than concepts like
sin and immorality and indecency which were its outward accoutre-
ments. The Wilde affair, which seemed a signal for society to nestle
back into its reassuring cocoon of respectability, was to prove part
of a process which would tear the cocoon to shreds. And one of the
aspects of the process was an increasing awareness of the power of
evil.

Something of that power was suggested in Arthur Machen's *The
Great God Pan*, published at the end of 1894 and greeted with howls
of disapproval which soon made it notorious. It was said to be 'a
most gruesome and *unmanly* book' and 'the most acutely and intention-
ally disagreeable we have yet seen in English'. Mudie's circulating
library refused to catalogue it or put it on display. It portrayed Pan
as ultimate and unbearable evil, 'before which the souls of men wither
and die and blacken, as their bodies blacken under the electric current'.
Other visions of evil were more conventional. *Studies of Death*, a book
of stories by Count Stenbock which also came out in 1894, included
'The true story of a Vampire', about a vampire who drained the blood
from a young boy and then vanished after kissing him on the lips.
There were obvious homosexual connotations and the censorious
might note that Stenbock had recently written an erotic story about
a werewolf for *Spirit Lamp*, Lord Alfred Douglas's undergraduate
magazine to which Oscar Wilde had contributed. Julian Osgood
Field's 'A Kiss of Judas', published at the end of 1894 in a collection
of tales entitled *Aut Diabolus aut Nihil*, featured a sinister blend of
vampire and werewolf, a corpse-like figure with the face of an animal.
A decent and wholesome Englishman who offended this creature ended
up nailed to a tree through the hands with his own knife. Another
vampire, appearing in the form of an unbelievably beautiful woman,
then killed him with a kiss.

It was ironic that these unpleasant images should be appearing
just when Wilde himself, their supposed originator and eventual scapegoat, had turned from the portrayal of evil to the portrayal of society's
foibles. Where had the visions of corruption and malevolence come

163

from? Dr Mayo had suggested half a century ago that they were linked with fears of being buried alive and now such fears were again being voiced. 'A concurrence of peculiar circumstances, beginning in May 1895, has directed public attention to the subject of premature burial,' declared William Tebb. In 1896 he published an authoritative work on the subject, written in collaboration with Colonel Edward Vollum, formerly Medical Inspector to the United States army. 'Ask any ten men and women at random what is the worst nightmare which oppresses the ordinary sane person,' commented the *Spectator*, 'and they will say the fear of being buried alive.' A disturbing number of funerals had been interrupted by knocking from within the coffin and the House of Commons had set up a Select Committee to inquire into the abuses associated with the issue of death certificates. A woman in Sheffield habitually carried hers around with her: it was signed by a doctor who had assumed she would die and had not bothered to find out whether she had actually done so.

It would have been comforting to think that evil was nothing but a shadow thrown by premature burial, a nightmare which would vanish if greater care was taken over death certificates. Unfortunately the nightmares themselves suggested otherwise. 'From the evidence of dreams we are more or less at liberty to believe that the dead and the living may exist together in a world of spirit in which the so-called living are less living than very many of the so-called dead,' declared Frederick Greenwood's *Imagination in Dreams and their study* in 1894. For centuries Christianity had denied the reality of this 'world of spirit': apart from the saints, who got special treatment, the dead would remain dead until all were raised at the Last Trumpet. But the notion of instant resurrection had always had its appeal and the advent of spiritualism had made it respectable. For most people eternity was no longer the sea into which the river of time would empty but the country through which it flowed. In dreams and in other unconscious imaginings the dead – especially dead parents – stood along the banks watching and judging. In Vienna Sigmund Freud was coming to appreciate their appalling power as he struggled to break their iron grip on the living. His work on the interpretation of dreams, which he was to publish in 1900, would make that power seem less malevolent, less calculated, but it would do little to reduce it.

As yet the English-speaking world knew nothing of Freud. Krafft-Ebing's work on sexual deviation attracted little attention when it came out in English in 1892 and the first of Havelock Ellis's *Studies in the Psychology of Sex* was widely condemned when it appeared in 1897. The only kind of sex which was acceptable, as Edward Carpenter pointed out bitterly in his doomed book on homogenic love, was 'matrimonial sex-intercourse and child-breeding'. Anything else was either a sin or an illness. Yet in the world of fantasy, in dreams and in tales of horror, things happened which were the work either of evil spirits or of perverted sexuality. Could it be that the lonely fantasies of masturbation, the images that had so alarmed Dr Dukes, were taking over from the collective fantasies of religion? Were they perhaps the same thing, were the demons and the avenging angels simply parental prohibitions and guilty desires in fancy dress? The horror story stood at the meeting of the ways, its ambiguous fascination explicable either in sexual terms as fear of parents or in religious terms as fear of the wrath of God and the works of the Devil. The proudly rational men and women of the 1890s were reluctant either to go back to belief in the wiles of Satan or to go forward to belief in the supremacy of sex.

This ambivalence was shown very clearly in the work of Ambrose Bierce, the most gifted American writer of horror stories in the 1890s. His portrayal of the vengeful things that rose from the tomb was remarkably and overtly Freudian: one of his characters 'found himself staring into the sharply drawn face and blank, dead eyes of his own mother ... he felt the cold fingers close upon his throat'. It seemed a signal for all the ghosts and vampires and werewolves to doff their grisly disguises and take their places in Freud's gallery of complexes. Yet Bierce also confessed to a profoundly religious dream which had haunted him since childhood and which lay behind all his best work. In it he found himself on an endless plain swept by some final and consuming fire. On it there stood a vast castle, its battlements and towers silhouetted against a dead sky, and deep inside this castle the black and shrivelled body of a man lay on a bed. Slowly it opened its eyes and he knew that he was himself the corpse. The horror of the dream lay not in this recognition but in the realization that the universe was empty and meaningless because God was dead: 'that hateful and abhorrent scrap of mortality, still sentient after the death of God and the angels, was I!' To the psycho-analyst such an outstandingly egocentric dream might suggest nothing worse than fear of a dead parent, but to the devout Christian it could presage cosmic disaster.

There was more reassurance in Bram Stoker's *Dracula*, one of the most popular of all horror stories, which was published in 1897. Here God was still very much alive and able to provide mankind with an impressive armoury of weapons against the power of vampires. The hero Jonathan Harker began by proclaiming his rationalist and Protestant contempt for the crucifix – 'as an English Churchman I have been taught to regard such things as in some measure idolatrous' – but he found his crucifix saved him when Count Dracula made his first attack. Professor van Helsing, called in because he was 'one of the most advanced scientists of his day', soon gave up relying on such clinical devices as blood transfusion and went to the British Museum to search out 'witch and demon cures'. The most potent of these was the body of God, the consecrated host. 'To superstition,' van Helsing declared in his shaky English, 'must we trust at the first; it was man's faith in the early, and it have its root in faith still'. He made Harker and his American friend Quincey Morris abandon Protestant scepticism and give credence to the beliefs of the Roman Catholic Church. Only thus were they able to rid the world of the menace of Dracula.

Algernon Blackwood was determined to bring the horror story out of these mediaeval shadows into the twentieth century. He created a character called John Silence, a 'Psychic Doctor' conversant with recent work on psychopathology and the paranormal. The John Silence stories, published in 1908, contained vivid accounts of spiritual possession laced with impressive jargon culled from the proceedings of the Society for Psychical Research. Yet their popularity was short-lived and Blackwood soon found that traditional tales of terror sold better. Montagu Rhodes James, who produced his first batch of *Ghost Stories of an Antiquary* in 1904 and the second in 1911, returned to the shadows and put the phenomenon of evil firmly back into its religious context. 'The technical terms of "occultism", if they are not very carefully handled, tend to put the mere ghost story upon a quasi-scientific plane and call into play faculties quite other than the imagination,' he wrote. His ghosts rose from the dark world of popish superstition and they obeyed no laws that either Freud or the Society for Psychical Research could propound. They came from the grave and they brought its putrefaction with them. 'I can tell you one thing,' ran a schoolboy's shuddering description of one of them, 'he was beastly thin: and he looked as if he was wet all over: and I'm not at all sure that he was alive.' These were not insubstantial spirits but things of horrifying power:

one, a dead child in its shroud, was able to tear a man's heart out.

In the real world the struggle between the Roman Catholic Church and the powers of darkness began in the spring of 1895, a fortnight before the Queensberry libel trial. A Parisian journalist calling himself Léo Taxil launched a periodical entitled *Le Palladium régénéré et libre – Directrice Miss Diana Vaughan*. Miss Vaughan was apparently descended from a seventeenth-century emigrant to America who had fornicated with a demon after signing a pact with Satan. In 1889, by order of Lucifer, she had been presented to her fiancé Asmodeus, another demon, in a Masonic lodge in Charleston Virginia. Taxil then revealed that after meetings with Beelzebub and Moloch she had renounced Satanism. The Roman Catholic authorities were glad to hear this and convoked a congress at Trent in northern Italy to declare war on the devilish practices of the Freemasons. It opened in September 1896 with a procession of nearly two thousand people. Thirty-six bishops attended, another fifty were represented by delegates and the Pope sent a telegram of approval. Diana Vaughan promised to address the congress and describe the various demons she had seen enthroned in American Masonic lodges. When she failed to appear doubts began to be voiced as to whether she really existed, but the Pope still believed in her and told his chaplain to write to her. Eventually, at a meeting in Paris on Easter Monday 1897, Taxil admitted it had all been a hoax.

Not everyone accepted his explanation. The papacy refused to believe it had been duped and the *Contemporary Review* ran an article on 'The Devil in Modern Occultism' suggesting that the real Satanists were not respectable Freemasons but practitioners of black magic who operated on the fringes both of Roman Catholicism and of the Church of England. Diana Vaughan had alleged that evil spirits were raised by the Order of the Golden Dawn, an occultist circle meeting in rooms near Euston Station in London, and when Arthur Edward Waite replied to these charges in his book *Devil Worship in France* he chose to dwell on the Satanic activities of the French occultists instead of questioning Miss Vaughan's existence. There were unpleasant stories coming out of Paris at this time, stories of secret cults where devils and werewolves were called up and where children were sacrificed at the Black Mass. Some of those recruited to the Golden Dawn were certainly meditating similar excesses. Aleister Crowley, who joined at the end of 1898, was convinced that he possessed magical powers and that he should use them in the service of evil. He regarded the strange sexual appetites revealed by Krafft-Ebing not as perversions but as magical acts which put men in touch with the powers of darkness.

Before Oscar Wilde's downfall his wife had joined the Golden Dawn but had been persuaded to break with it in case she brought discredit on her husband. Arthur Machen was a member and was making experiments which he described as 'halfway between psychology and magic'. The practice of strange rituals, the sense of belonging to an esoteric circle, gave an edge to the writing of fiction and sometimes fact and fantasy became interwoven. Machen wrote a novel in which a boy aspiring to mystic powers slept naked on thorns; Crowley made an aspirant sleep naked on a litter of gorse for ten nights after receiving thirty-two strokes with a gorse switch. Later Crowley and his aspirant dedicated acts of homosexual love to Pan on an altar on a desolate mountain top. Machen meanwhile became convinced that Crowley was hiring ruffians all over London to beat him up. Lord Alfred Douglas, who was editor of *Academy*, asked Machen to write for it on religious matters and soon there were accusations that the magazine had fallen into Roman Catholic hands. Douglas sued for libel and lost his case after Machen admitted writing that the Protestant Reformation was 'the most hideous blasphemy, the greatest woe, the most monstrous horror that has fallen on the hapless race of mortals since the foundation of the world'.

In Protestant eyes there was an obvious connection between popery and Satanism. Anyone superstitious enough to believe in the power of rituals and sacraments to ward off evil would be tempted to dabble with evil himself in the way doctors experimented with disease in order to test the efficacy of their remedies. How could you distinguish the experiment from the real thing, how could you tell whether papists were girding themselves against Satan or preparing to serve him, since both activities involved the same mumbo-jumbo? Worse still, how could you be sure that your Protestant brethren were not papists or Satanists in disguise? In 1894 Walter Walsh lectured to the Protestant Truth Society on 'The Secret Work of the Ritualists'. He claimed that the Church of England was 'literally honeycombed with secret societies', whose object was 'nothing less than that of bringing not only the Ritualists themselves but the whole Church of England into Popish bondage'.

Walsh's campaign against Anglo-Catholicism was greatly assisted by the revelations of Miss Povey, who had been an Anglican nun for seventeen years in convents founded by Father Ignatius Lyne. Her book *Nunnery Life in the Church of England*, telling of whippings and other harsh penances, was used to great effect by the Protestant Truth Society. John Kensit, the Society's secretary, mounted a display of penitential scourges, 'of well hardened and polished steel, each end of five chains neatly finished with a steel rowel', in his shop window in Paternoster Row. The proprietor of a neighbouring establishment selling such things confirmed that 'for every one he sold to a Catholic he sold three to Church of England people'. Satanists using gorse to induce mystic experiences were gentle compared with this. Father Ignatius was touring America when Miss Povey's book came out and it had an adverse effect on his reception there. At the beginning of his tour he had drawn enthusiastic crowds in New York and also in Boston, even though the Episcopalian Bishop of Boston had banned him from preaching in any Massachusetts church; but when he came back to New York his second mission there was 'a hard and trying ordeal ... those who had flocked to the first now held aloof because of public opinion'.

Public opinion was to harden still further. In a series of official pronouncements beginning in January 1895 the Pope rebuked the Catholic hierarchy in America for its liberal tendencies and in particular for taking part in 'promiscuous assemblies' such as the Parliament of Religions. The papacy, gulled by Taxil's lies, prepared to confront the devil-worshipping Freemasons of the United States. Progressive American Catholics were squeezed out of key positions and reconciliation with Protestants was discouraged. Catholic confidence was soaring – the number of Catholics in America went up from six million in 1880 to twelve million in 1900 – and Protestant fears were growing. In Britain there were similar fears. Figures published in 1897 suggested that Protestants were losing ground while Catholics, helped as in America by Irish immigration, were becoming more influential and more numerous. Walter Walsh's warnings about popish bondage found ready listeners when he returned to the attack in 1897 with *The Secret History of the Oxford Movement*. John Kensit became notorious for breaking up ritualist services in London churches and by 1898 even *The Times* was insisting that a stand must be made against Catholicism within the Church of England. 'If the Bishops cannot or will not make it,' it declared grimly, 'the people have Parliament to appeal to'.

There were those who felt that the time had come for a crusade

to defend Protestant enlightenment and Protestant liberty against
Catholic superstition and Catholic tyranny. Josiah Strong had already
sounded the clarion call for such a crusade and his book was now
at the height of its popularity. And while Strong talked of the Americans and the British standing together because of their shared religious
convictions and their Anglo-Saxon racial superiority, others put forward a less crude by equally persuasive view of the matter. Having
described the British writer Rudyard Kipling as 'the laureate of the
larger England, the great England whose far-strewn empire feels its
mystical unity in every latitude and longitude of the globe', the New
York critic William Dean Howells went on to claim that Americans
were inspired by equally lofty ideals, by 'a patriotism not less large
than humanity ... we have made a home here for all mankind. Upon
this hypothesis we may claim Mr Kipling, whether he likes it or not,
as in some sort American.'

When the Cubans rose in revolt against Spanish rule at the beginning of 1895 there was a chance to move from rhetoric to action.
A concerted press campaign throughout the United States demanded
intervention on behalf of the rebels. Here surely was a chance to show
'patriotism not less large than humanity' by helping the oppressed
to defy Catholic tyranny. But the Cuban revolt came at a time when
Anglo-American relations were strained, so that President Cleveland
faced what he called 'a tide of jingoism' against Britain as well as
against Spain. 'This folly puts an end to my good wholesome life
here,' wrote Rudyard Kipling, who had been living in Vermont for
the past three years. Fearing war between his native country and
his adopted one he took his family back to England in August 1896,
by which time the larger England whose laureate he had been called
was moving towards war with the Boers in South Africa. However,
the British were still capable of being inspired by American imaginings.
Stephen Crane, born in New Jersey five years after the end of the
Civil War and brought up by a devout father who laid down 'a rigid
iron rule for the guidance of all – total abstinence from novel-reading
henceforth and forever', nevertheless managed to produce the greatest
of all Civil War novels, *The Red Badge of Courage*. It attracted little
attention when it appeared in New York and Philadelphia magazines
at the end of 1894 but in London a year later it was hailed as a
work of genius for its picture of a raw recruit turning into a soldier.
'It is glorious,' said George Wyndham in the *New Review*, 'to see his
youth discover courage in the bed-rock of primeval antagonism after

170

the collapse of his tinsel bravado'. Crane had shown how men in battle, like women in love, were 'of the few to whom God whispers in the ear'.

Other critics made clear what it was God was whispering in British ears. News was coming in of an armed raid into Boer territory by Dr Jameson and Sir John Willoughby which ended in disaster but enraptured jingoists in Britain. The *Saturday Review* ran a piece entitled 'In the School of Battle: the Making of a Soldier', rejoicing that Crane's book had come 'at a time like the present, when England is showing that the heart of the nation is as sound after the long Victorian peace as it was in the days of the Armada, that the desperate if lawless enterprise of Jameson and Willoughby is as near to the general heart of the people as were the not very dissimilar enterprises of the old Elizabethan captains'. Major Martin Hume produced a piece called 'The Defeat of the Armada: an Anniversary Object-Lesson' in which he claimed that memories of this great victory were encouraging the British to hold their heads higher. 'For once we have cast aside our habitual reserve and self-depreciation and frankly glory in the qualities which have enabled our race to form the stately brotherhood of free and prosperous nations we call the British Empire.'

In April 1898 war broke out between the United States and Spain over Cuba. A few days later the British Colonial Secretary made a speech stressing the need for Anglo-American friendship. 'What is our next duty?' he asked amid loud cheers, 'It is to establish and to maintain bonds of permanent unity with our kinsmen across the Atlantic. They are a powerful and generous nation. They speak our language, they are bred of our race.' No formal alliance was signed but the two nations shared the same confident imperialism, the same religious fervour. 'I went down on my knees and prayed Almighty God for light and guidance,' President McKinley told his friends, 'and one night late it came to me.' He received divine instructions to annex the Philippines. The Treaty of Paris which ended the war with Spain in December 1898 accordingly ceded the islands to the United States, along with Puerto Rico and Guam, while Cuba was granted its independence. Voices were raised in Congress against the Treaty, claiming that annexation and subjugation were against everything America stood for, but the imperialists won the day. 'We will not renounce our part in the mission of the race, trustee under God of the civilization of the world,' cried Senator Beveridge of Indiana, 'He has marked the American people as his chosen nation to finally

171

lead in the regeneration of the world. This is the divine mission of America.'

Alfred Austin, who had succeeded Tennyson as Poet Laureate, published verses in *The Times* in praise of Jameson. They were jejune and jingoistic, closer to a juvenile adventure story than to poetry, and they failed to convey the full arrogance of British imperialism. It came across better in Kipling's 'Recessional', a poem in honour of the Queen's Diamond Jubilee in 1897. Here Kipling spoke directly to God, 'beneath whose awful hand we hold dominion over palm and pine', and made it clear that he was expected to be the God of war, 'Lord of our far-flung battle-line'. Early in 1898 Kipling went to South Africa to see things for himself and on his return he was hailed by Rider Haggard as one who had 'communed with the very spirit of our race'. Haggard, like Senator Beveridge, claimed 'the divine right of a great civilizing people'. When war with the Boers came in the autumn of 1899 Kipling went back to Africa and stood on the sidelines of battle as a privileged spectator. He was there for the relief of Ladysmith and when he got back to England there was the even greater excitement of the relief of Mafeking. Patriotism took strange forms: on 6 January 1900, at a remote spot in Wales, the mystic weapon known as the sword of Gorsedd was solemnly unsheathed, not to be returned to its scabbard until 'the triumph of the forces of righteousness over the hordes of evil'.

The dawn of a new century seemed to bring this triumph nearer. In 1895, after complaining that Wilde and other decadent writers were 'sapping manliness and making people flabby', Hugh Stutfield had concluded that 'the world seems growing weary after the mighty work it has accomplished during this most marvellous of centuries'. Now these *fin de siècle* literary languors could be dispelled. 'In 1900,' wrote W.B.Yeats, 'everybody got down off his stilts; henceforth nobody drank absinthe with his black coffee; nobody went mad; nobody committed suicide; nobody joined the Catholic church'. On the continent of Europe, it was true, the arts continued along the path which Nordau saw as leading to degeneration. Painting without representational intent, music without melody, writing without plot or moral values, all reflected the futility of human life in a universe stripped of meaning. But then in Europe even the new century was born into uncertainty, for the German Emperor officially decreed that it started in January 1900 while French scientists insisted that it must wait until January 1901. For the British an epoch ended on 22 January

172

1901 when Queen Victoria died. President McKinley ordered the flag on the White House to be flown at half-mast and when he was assassinated eight months later business was suspended in London on the day of his funeral. Fortified by these mutual courtesies the two nations moved into the twentieth century more convinced than ever of their divine mission. It was summed up in the ode that Archbishop Benson's son wrote for the coronation of the new king:

> Land of Hope and Glory, Mother of the Free,
> How shall we extol thee, who are born of thee?
> Wider still and wider shall thy bounds be set;
> God who made thee mighty make thee mightier yet.

Having mothered the free in Cuba – and less convincingly in the Philippines, where the Filipinos resisted fiercely – the United States did the same thing in Panama in 1903. The Colombians, who ruled Panama, refused to ratify a treaty whereby America leased land to build a canal linking the Atlantic and the Pacific. The American government incited a revolution in Panama, secured the Panamanians their independence and then got them to sign a treaty giving the United States the canal zone in perpetuity. 'I took Panama,' was the terse comment of Theodore Roosevelt, who had become President on the death of McKinley. Famous for his gospel of 'the strenuous life', Roosevelt had been an advocate of America's divine mission since 1895, when he had campaigned for intervention in Cuba. He had been a friend of Rudyard Kipling, who found his muscular Christianity a refreshing contrast after the 'colossal agglomeration of reeking bounders' he said President Cleveland had gathered around him. In later years, when Roosevelt visited England, he made a point of meeting leading writers and telling them how important it was to keep romance alive. 'The most priceless possession of the human race is the wonder of the world,' he declared, 'Yet latterly the utmost endeavours of mankind have been directed towards the dissipation of that wonder'.

There were those who had their doubts. George Bernard Shaw held the triumph of fiction directly responsible for the prevailing mood of belligerent jingoism. 'Ten years of cheap reading have changed the English from the most solid nation in Europe to the most theatrical and hysterical,' he wrote in 1901. Most of the cheap reading consisted of full-blooded adventure stories glorifying the strenuous life and the martial virtues. A.E.W. Mason's immensely successful novel *The Four*

173

Feathers, which came out in the same year as 'Land of Hope and Glory', was the story of a man redeeming himself not from sin but from a charge of cowardice. 'Dost never dream of adventures, Morice?' cried a character in one of Mason's later books, 'A life brimful of them and a quick death at the end?' Even *Dracula* joined in the chorus. 'A brave man's blood is the best thing on this earth when a woman is in trouble,' Van Helsing told a blood donor solemnly. And in the end Jonathan Harker's American friend Quincey Morris, 'a gallant gentleman', sacrificed his life in order to destroy Dracula.

Gallant gentlemen who had no vampires to impale or wars to fight turned to sport. One of the oddest results of the Wilde affair was the success of the Daily Telegraph National Shilling Testimonial to the cricketer W.G. Grace. 'Panic-stricken citizens hastened to contribute lest their sexual normality should be doubted – the connection was subtle but felt at the time to be real'. Already *Harper's Magazine* had asked 'Is American Stamina Declining?' and had insisted that sport was the remedy. 'Especially impress it on the weak, the poorly built and the over-studious, who are not good at any sport, that they are going to make very one-sided men and women, if they live that long, and get them out of doors in all weathers'. It was some consolation that when the Olympic Games were revived in Athens in 1896 the United States won nine of the twelve events. Henry Newbolt's poem 'Vitae Lampada', first published in Queen Victoria's Diamond Jubilee Year and constantly reprinted throughout the Edwardian era, told of a school cricket match and a battle in the desert, the two of them linked by a single cry: 'Play up! play up! and play the game!' It rallied the cricket team and it rallied the soldiers in the sand. And it was the cry which dying heroes 'flung to the host behind', so that those still left alive would be ready to follow their example. The same theme ran through H.A. Vachell's *The Hill*, which was hailed as 'a fine, wholesome and thoroughly manly novel' when it came out in 1905. It culminated in a lyrical celebration of the heroism of Henry Desmond, whom the book followed from his schooldays at Harrow to his death in battle:

To die young, clean, ardent, to die swiftly, in perfect health; to die saving others from death – or worse, disgrace – to die scaling heights; to die and to carry with you into the fuller, ampler life beyond untainted hopes and aspirations, unembittered memories, all the freshness and gladness of May – is not that cause for joy rather than sorrow?

174

There were some questionable assumptions underlying this rhapsody. The first and most obvious was that God approved of war and made the ampler life available to those killed by it. The second was that clean and ardent young men inspired by high sporting ideals would rather die in battle than have their high hopes tainted. They were 'magnificently unprepared,' as Frances Cornford later said of Rupert Brooke, 'for the long littleness of life'. This was all very well in Britain and America, where military service was still voluntary, but it was by no means certain it would survive the introduction of conscription. Another assumption seemed to be that any war in which Britain or America might become involved would be a just one, a genuine struggle against the hordes of evil. But if this was the case, if this struggle had an existence outside the hysteria and theatricality of those drunk with adventure stories, it was not likely to be won by playing the game. Evil had little respect for the courtesies of the games field. Even human enemies could sometimes be bad sports, as the British found when the Boers turned to guerrilla warfare. Kipling brought out a savage poem called 'The Islanders', attacking the comfortable delusion that sport was a breeding ground for heroes. The British were being humiliated by the Boers – 'a little people, few but apt in the field' – because they cared more for games and mock combat than for military preparedness. They must take war seriously, Kipling urged with bitter irony, 'as if it were almost cricket, as it were even your play'.

Sport was not the only route leading from fears of physical degeneracy to the excitements of war. In 1895, as anxiously heterosexual men rushed to give their shillings to the W. G. Grace fund, H. G. Wells gave expression to these same fears in *The Time Machine*. He saw the remote future as 'The Sunset of Mankind', a world without challenge and therefore without response. With nothing to fight for and nothing to fight against, men and women had become effete and enfeebled. 'We are kept keen on the grindstone of pain and necessity, and it seemed to me that here was that hateful grindstone broken at last!' When the Martians invaded the earth in *The War of the Worlds*, published in 1898, the pious preached repentance but an unnamed artilleryman preached defiance – defiance of God's wrath and also of man's conventions. What was the point of people living at all if they hadn't the guts to lay proper hold on life?

They haven't any spirit in them – no proud dreams and no proud lusts;

and a man who hasn't one or the other – Lord! what is he but funk and precautions? They just used to skedaddle off to work ... Lives insured and a bit invested for fear of accidents. And on Sundays – fear of the hereafter. As if Hell was built for rabbits!

There was certainly nothing rabbit-like about Bert Smallways, a suburban greengrocer's son who survived the breakdown of society in *The War in the Air*. Having shot his rival 'very accurately through the chest' he shot the man's friend 'much less tidily through the head' and then went to the nearest public house to establish his control of the neighbourhood at gun point. In 1903 Jack London's *The Call of the Wild* produced a canine counterpart to Bert Smallways in the shape of Buck, a family pet stolen from his California home and taken as a sledge dog to the wastes of Alaska. There he reverted to the wild. 'His development (or retrogression) was rapid. His muscles became as hard as iron, and he grew callous to all ordinary pain ... He could eat anything, no matter how loathsome or indigestible.' In the end he lived for the joy of the chase, 'running the wild thing down, the living meat, to kill with his own teeth and wash his muzzle to the eyes in warm blood.' 'There is an ecstasy that marks the summit of life, and beyond which life cannot rise,' the author commented, 'This ecstasy comes to the soldier, war-mad on a stricken field and refusing quarter; and it came to Buck, leading the pack, sounding the old wolf-cry.'

Heraclitus had said that war was father and king of all, producing some as gods and some as men. Did it make men into gods by means of this ecstasy beyond which life could not rise or by means of a hero's death carrying untainted hopes into an ampler life? Was hell built for rabbits and heaven for manly lovers of fair play or was there a pagan Valhalla for those who had reverted to the wild and put themselves beyond conventional ideas of good and evil? As long as the peace was kept, or broken only by minor wars which could be fought by a few brave volunteers, these questions could remain unasked. But if war should indeed become father and king of all, a fight to the finish which required unflinching sacrifice from every household in the land, they would have to be answered. And the answers could only come from God or from someone with unimpeachable authority to speak for him. God would need to whisper in everyone's ear, not just in the ears of a privileged ecstatic few.

11 THE WASTE LAND

THE TURN OF THE CENTURY BROUGHT MORE TALK OF cosmic change. 'Like most people of my generation,' wrote H.G. Wells in 1906 in the introduction to *The Future in America*, 'I was launched into life with millenial expectations ... it might be in my lifetime or a little after it, there would be trumpets and shoutings and celestial phenomena, a battle of Armageddon and the Judgment'. Once he had had high hopes of the Americans – 'these people can do anything,' he had cried – but now he saw only 'a dark disorder of growth' fouled by cruelty and indifference: 'little naked boys, free Americans, work for Mr Borden, the New York millionaire, packing cloths into bleaching vats, in a bath of chemicals that bleaches their little bodies like the bodies of lepers'. Before the final trumpeting there would have to be 'yet another Decline and Fall', that of the callous, careless, jangling civilization of America. In the same year he published *In the Days of the Comet*, in which a celestial phenomenon fulfilled his own millenial expectations. As the earth passed through the tail of a comet it was enveloped in a strange green vapour which sent all creatures great and small to sleep. 'The whole world of living things had been overtaken by the same tide of insensibility; in an hour, at the touch of this new gas in the comet, the shiver of catalytic change had passed about the globe.' The gas proved highly subversive, breathing socialism into men and women as they slept, so that on waking they overturned all existing authority. Many suspected that Wells was also looking forward to the collapse of existing sexual morality. No doubt the comet's undisclosed afflatus would lead men to share their women as well as their goods, commented one outraged reviewer.

Astronomers contributed to the book's success by predicting that in May 1910 the earth would pass through the tail of Halley's comet, an event awaited with some trepidation on both sides of the Atlantic. A charging rhinoceros might as well worry about colliding with a cobweb, wrote one scientist crisply. Nevertheless panic grew. There was talk of the wrath of God, of universal conflagration, of the human condition being transformed. In Pittsburgh a clergyman announced that the comet's arrival would herald Armageddon and the Second Coming. King Edward VII died on 6 May 1910, just as the tail was about to engulf the earth, and in the skies over Bermuda, as the official salute to the new king George V was being fired, 'the comet's tail flared a decided red end. The head, now distinctly visible, became a ball of fire'. Local people fell to their knees, convinced that this meant the new reign would bring the bloodiest of wars. Some sensed a growing power of evil, a cosmic force which demanded desperate forms of propitiation. In California a prospector named Paul Hammerton made a large wooden cross and crucified himself on it. As he was alone he was only able to nail his feet and one of his hands. When his rescuers came he implored them not to take him down but to complete the work.

The comet came and went without changing very much, though the newspapers followed the celestial happenings with banner headlines and farmers all across the United States retreated to their cyclone cellars. Nevertheless there were those who detected a mysterious transformation. 'In or about December 1910,' wrote Virginia Woolf, 'human character changed'. In her analysis, as in Wells's fiction, the result was the undermining of hierarchy: relations between master and man, between superior and inferior, became more relaxed. Domestic servants no longer lived for ever below stairs in a separate world but instead were 'in and out of the drawing-room, now to borrow the *Daily Herald*, now to ask advice about a hat'. From San Francisco a warning was sounded by Homer Curtiss, Secretary of the Order of Christian Mystics, and his wife Harriette. They revealed that astronomers at Harvard had found that 'the earth and this whole solar system has gone astray and is trailing off away from its path around the great sun Alcyone in the Pleiades towards the constellation Andromeda in the Milky Way ... there is a terrible commotion in the mental and astral worlds'. It was all very well to be told not to fear cobwebs, but what if the rhinoceros was out of control? The inevitable outcome would be 'a terrible mental revolt against all forms of restraint, both in government and religion'.

While some proclaimed that God was using comets or solar migrations to transform the human race others suggested that he was acting directly on the hearts and minds of men and women. 'We stand now on the threshold of one of those mysterious Thought Waves which often arise suddenly in the world's spiritual development and are the very breath of the Living God,' declared the Rev. F.W. Orde Ward in 1908. Mankind was learning that God's creation was Heraclitean and that God himself was not fixity but movement, the sum of the dimensions of an expanding universe: 'The universal acceptance of Christ as the kinetic centre of modern thought, even apart from theology, seems far and away the most characteristic feature of our age.' And since Orde Ward's grasp of modern thought extended to the geometry of curved surfaces, the mathematics of five dimensions and the interdependence of space and time, he could not be written off as a mere religious fanatic. Albert Einstein was only part of the way along the road from his Special to his General Theory of Relativity but Orde Ward had already glimpsed the sort of universe he was revealing and was determined to stake God's claim to it.

Philosophers too were beginning to take note of Heraclitus. Henri Bergson's *Evolution Créatrice* had appeared in 1907, two years after Einstein's Special Theory, and in 1911 William James's Harvard colleague Arthur Mitchell brought out an English translation. While Einstein considered time in relation to space Bergson considered it in relation to thought. Time was continuous and yet when human beings thought about it they split it into separate moments like a cinema film. In the cinema the separate frames were the reality and movement the illusion but in the real world it was the other way about. This meant that what Bergson called 'conceptual thought' was bound to distort reality. 'In vain we force the living into this or that one of our moulds. All the moulds crack.' Philosophy was both too proud and too humble, too ready to squeeze all reality into its moulds but also too ready to acknowledge something called the Unknowable, the Divine Mystery, when the moulds cracked. What was needed was a new kind of thought, a mould which would make everything knowable and so do for philosophy what Einstein was doing for physics.

Those who sought this new way of thinking felt they were embarking on a high adventure, a quest that would unlock the ultimate secrets of the universe. Orde Ward called his book *The World's Quest* and in London in the spring of 1909, at a meeting in Kensington Town Hall, the Quest Society was formed. Its motto was 'Seek and ye shall find' and its declared aims were 'to promote investigation and

179

comparative study of religion, philosophy and science on the basis of experience and to encourage the expression of the ideal in beautiful forms.' Another objective, not mentioned in the manifesto but soon made apparent in the pages of the Society's journal *Quest*, was to establish spiritualism as a scientific fact. G.R.S. Mead, first President of the Society and editor of the journal, wrote confidently of 'the rising psychic tide' which was engulfing traditional theologians and sceptical materialists alike: 'organized bodies, societies, associations and groups have sprung up like mushrooms in well-nigh every country ... as to the members of such bodies, they must be estimated in millions'. James H. Hyslop, Secretary of the Psychical Research Society of America, was one of Mead's staunchest supporters and one of the first to have his work published in book form under the Society's imprint.

The Quest Society's aspirations meant that serious scholarship was liable to be laced with eccentricity but they also gave the society an affinity with a wider public. 'The impulse which drives men to penetrate into the unexplored region of the Arctic and Antarctic zones finds its counterpart in the minds of those who feel the call to explore undiscovered fields in the region of Psychical Research,' declared *Quest*. A.E.W. Mason expressed much the same sentiment when he said that the best way for a man to know beyond a shadow of a doubt that he would go on living after death was to climb alone in the high Alps. Raymond Blathwayt, writing in the *Fortnightly Review* on 'England's Taste in Literature,' reported that 'Any writer who deals brightly and sincerely with anything that tends towards the rending of the veil hiding the invisible from the visible is certain of a respectful, I may say an enthusiastic, welcome ... upper-class women all over the country are coming under the spell of the mystic'. 'The novelist who succeeds,' wrote another critic, 'is he or she who gives expression and currency to the ideas and aspirations which are floating about the various classes of society'.

The ideas and aspirations in question were theosophy and spiritualism and other fashionable forays into the divine mystery. The new trends in science and philosophy which had discredited the theologians had consoled and encouraged ordinary men and women: 'with Lodge and other leading men of science a belief in the supernatural is not necessarily an indication of feeble intellect or an evidence of incapacity for advanced science.' Sir Oliver Lodge, a highly respected physicist and Principal of Birmingham University, was the author of *The Survival of Man*, in which he proclaimed personal immortality as a scientific

180

fact. He was even able to say what would be carried over into the world to come and what would be left behind: 'Essential belongings, such as memory, culture, education, habits, character and affections – all these, and to a certain extent tastes and interests, – for better for worse, are retained. Terrestrial accretions, such as worldly possessions, bodily pain and disabilities, these for the most part naturally drop away.' 'In consequence of the new evidence,' wrote Frederick Myers confidently, 'all reasonable men, a century hence, will believe in the Resurrection of Christ, whereas in default of the new evidence no reasonable men a century hence would have believed it.' So far from merely corroborating Christianity the new certainties transcended it: 'In the age of Christ Europe felt the first high authentic message from a world beyond our own. In our own age we reach the perception that such messages may become continuous and progressive'.

Blathwayt's article was a progress report. It came out in 1912, a quarter of a century after the *Fortnightly* had asked George Saintsbury to review the state of literature in Britian and America. Saintsbury had suggested then that society could only be saved from its dessicated scepticism and materialism by bathing long and well in the romance of adventure and passion: now it was time to see if the prolonged immersion had had the desired effect. It seemed it had. Blathwayt concluded that 'there is in this country a pretty general arrival at a belief in the after life' and he attributed it to the immense influence wielded by novelists. Saintsbury had made his plea for fiction to an England with relatively few public libraries; now there were hundreds of them, each lending out hundreds of thousands of novels a year. 'Those who decry the work of our Public Municipal Libraries on the ground that works of imagination are extensively read have a poor case to present,' one librarian was reported as saying. Sales were also up: 'novels which formerly sold less than 3,000 copies at six shillings a copy now sell 300,000 copies at sixpence a copy.' All this had stimulated 'a hankering after the unknown' which had completely replaced the old interest in devotional works. 'Theology is now a drug on the market,' Blathwayt added. Fiction had succeeded where faith had failed. Scepticism and materialism had been washed away.

Already the sceptics and the materialists had been confounded in open court. The Rev. Thomas Colley, rector of Stockton in Warwickshire, claimed to have frequent encounters with persons from beyond the grave and in 1907, after being called a fraud by a professional

181

conjuror, he sued for libel. The climax of the case came when Colley described from the witness box how he had been levitated some twenty feet in an attempt to 'grasp a white-attired Egyptian and try to keep him from getting back to invisibility' and how he had then been left clutching the 'psychic clothing' which the dead visitor had been wearing. The jury found in his favour and awarded him damages of £75 with costs. The figure was low – he had claimed £1,000 – but not so low as to be derisory. Although the verdict took into account other libels as well as the fraud charge there was no escaping the fact that the materialization of the dead had been accepted as evidence in a court of law. It seemed that the veil hiding the invisible from the visible was being rent in fact as well as in fiction.

All this made the frontier between reality and fantasy hard to define and even harder to defend. What Bergson and Einstein and other revolutionary thinkers were saying was so odd that most educated men and women regarded it as flying in the face of common sense. Common sense itself was soon to be a casualty, revealed as being neither common nor sense, but in the meantime it was easy to dismiss all aspects of the new thinking as manifestations of eccentricity. Just as the members of the Quest Society saw the Heraclitean view of the universe and the Bergsonian view of thought and the spiritualist view of eternity as converging on the same exciting truth, so their critics saw them all as aspects of the same crack-brained delusion. Neither the inspired minority nor the sceptical majority was very good at separating the pure metal from the dross. And this in its turn meant that the novelists and the story-tellers moved in a very uncertain world when they gave 'expression and currency to the ideas and aspirations floating about the various classes of society'.

Nevertheless Mead's Society was well named. The ancient image of the quest, challenging and mysterious and divinely ordained, promised the highest kind of adventure as well as the loftiest kind of reward. It could accommodate the intellectual and spiritual adventurers as well as the fictitious ones, people with millenial expectations and immortal longings as well as people who simply wanted a good yarn. And the most famous of all Christian quest legends, that of the Holy Grail, had recently become remarkably fashionable in the academic world. From Chicago to Cologne, from the Modern Language Association of America to the Imperial Academy in Vienna, scholars were showing an unprecedented interest in it and many significant contributions to its study had appeared during the past two decades. In 1908 Robert Eisler gave an important lecture to the Oxford International Congress for the History of Religions, tracing the connections between the Grail and ancient Orphic mysteries, and one of the first papers given to the Quest Society was 'The Romance of the Holy Graal' by A. E. Waite, Arthur Machen's associate in the Order of the Golden Dawn. Machen took little interest at first, telling Waite that all the highest things could be found in Holy Church 'without reference to the Quest of the Sangraal', but he later wrote *The Secret Glory*, a story about a schoolboy entrusted with the Grail, and also *The Great Return*, in which a town was redeemed by its power. He was taken to task by the *Times Literary Supplement* for having the bad taste to allow the Holy Grail to appear to 'common farmers, village grocers and the like'.

Waite's paper led him into lengthy controversy with Miss Jessie Weston, who took exception not only to his pretentious spelling but also to his suggestion that the story of the Grail was mere romance. She pointed out that in mediaeval times, when the legend was first written down, 'more was believed, more was known, than the official guardians of faith and morals cared to admit ... this undercurrent of yearning and investigation was concerned with the search for the source of Life – Life physical, Life Immortal'. She went on to argue that the Grail was an ancient symbol of female sexuality while the lance which figured so prominently in the legend was patently phallic. Neither had anything to do with Christ's blood. They were memories of a pagan ritual in which men overcame death without the help of the crucified Christ. She later published in *Quest* a story called 'The Ruined Temple' in which a traveller came upon the remains of a Phoenician altar sacred to Adonis. He fell asleep and found himself facing a slab on which lay a corpse: 'this was not a dead man; it was *Death Itself*'. Then, after a mystical re-enactment of the ancient Grail ritual with a chalice filled with blood and a spear which became 'a quivering shaft of flame', he found that he had conquered death and was 'drawing closer, closer, to the very Fount of Life itself'.

Miss Weston was to publish two authoritative accounts of the Grail ritual, *The Quest of the Holy Grail* in 1913 and *From Ritual to Romance* in 1921. In 1922 her second book was to be acknowledged by the expatriate American poet T. S. Eliot as the principal inspiration for his poem 'The Waste Land'. Eliot appreciated the significance of the Grail story as a convergence of fantasy and reality. He understood the pagan roots from which it sprang as well as the Christian aspirations which had been grafted onto it. Others were less percipient. As the shadow cast by fiction upon the real world lengthened, as the Edwardian cult of heroic adventure darkened into the First World War cult of heroic self-sacrifice, devotees turned increasingly to the Grail legend. It was after all not just about the personal redemption of a hero but about restoring a whole society to health. The Grail was guarded by a wounded or sick King in a castle in the midst of a Waste Land. The King's mysterious weakness could only be cured and the Waste Land brought back to life if a brave knight could be found to undertake the quest. In August 1914 the relevance of the legend seemed clear, at least in the world of fantasy, as Watson talked of God's curse on a degenerate world and as Sherlock Holmes looked forward to men dying in order that England might be cleaner and better and stronger.

In reality the Grail legend was not primarily about fighting or about dying. The knight's business was not to lay down his life but to ask a certain question, the nature of which was not revealed. It was a ritual of testing, of initiation, but not of sacrifice. If it was a fertility rite it was not the sort in which a god or a hero had to die before the earth would bring forth its bounty. There was no propitiation of the forces of evil. In one early German version the Grail was said to have been the talisman of those angels who had refused to take sides in the conflict between God and Satan. The two great adversaries who had waged war in heaven must both take blame for the desolation of the Waste Land. Even the iconoclastic Nietzsche was closer than conventional Christians to the Grail story: it looked back to a world before good and evil just as he looked forward to one beyond good and evil. His ideas were at last beginning to be taken seriously in Britain and America. In 1909 the *Westminster Gazette*, a Christian journal, said that whatever his faults he was at least 'at war with frivolity and the mere craving for pleasure and ease which infects the modern world'. *Quest* suggested that his evolutionary theory of morals was the necessary counterpart to Bergson's thinking. An unchanging view of good and evil was as outdated as a fixed concept of the universe: 'The virtues of yesterday are no use today save as stepping-stones towards higher ideals.' When the quest reached its goal, when all the strands of the new thinking came together, the resulting transformation of human character would be far more fundamental than the whimsical fancies of Virginia Woolf.

Most readers on both sides of the Atlantic were more interested

184

in present adventuring than in future transformation. Hilaire Belloc scored a success with *Hills and the Sea*, a collection of short pieces about two men who pitted themselves against the elements. When their leaky boat was hit by a gale 'there were no men on earth save these two who would not have got her under a try-sail and a rag of storm-jib with fifteen reefs and another; not so the heroes. Not a stitch would they take in.' Their valiant stupidity was duly rewarded: 'when they slept the Sea Lady, the silver-footed one, came up through the waves and kissed them in their sleep; for she had seen no such men since Achilles ... The high gods, which are only names to the multitude, visited these men.' Even the most eccentric member of the Quest Society would have hesitated to write such stuff, yet Belloc's readers loved it. And they loved it partly because of its hint of auto-biography, because these fantastic things might just have happened in real life to Belloc and his trusty companion.

It seemed that fortune not only favoured the brave but touched them with some kind of divinity. In some strange way they would redeem society simply by being brave. The *Fortnightly* followed up Blathwayt's account of literary tastes with a poem in which Laurence Binyon called upon the young and valiant to bring about this unspeci-fied and miraculous transformation:

> High-beating hearts, to your deep vows be true!
> Live out your dreams, for England lives in you.

Although Binyon did not yet know it five high-beating hearts had just lived out a dream which was to have an immense impact in Britain and America. Captain Scott and his four companions died of exposure and frostbite in the Antarctic early in 1912 and a year later, when news came of the discovery of their bodies, they became instant heroes. Of Scott it was said that 'his dominant thought was the placing of his country in the van of heroism. The dream in his far-away blue eyes was scarcely so much success as sacrifice.' Lieutenant Oates, one of his companions, was said to have 'embraced Death, the bride whom he had gone out to seek in the wilderness, with all the purpose of his strong heart.' In life the two men had been very different. Scott had been a harsh and incompetent leader and towards the end, when Oates was in agony from gangrene, he told him he was 'a terrible hindrance'. At last, almost delirious with pain, Oates left the tent and disappeared into the blizzard. It was an act of desperation, a form of suicide committed by a man driven beyond endurance by

Scott's hectoring, and when the details emerged from the diaries his mother made it clear that she regarded Scott as her son's murderer.

Nobody was interested in the recriminations of Mrs Oates. 'Greater love hath no man than this,' Christ had said, 'that a man lay down his life for his friends.' Everyone was sure this was what Oates had done. As for Scott, he was a man inspired, a prophet who had foreseen what wonders his heroism would work. 'Had we lived,' he wrote in his 'message to the public' from the tent in which he died, 'I should have had a tale to tell of the hardihood, endurance and courage of my companions which would have stirred the heart of every Englishman.' His Scottish friend J.M. Barrie hastened to correct the narrow word 'Englishman'. 'Almost every Briton alive,' he wrote to *The Times*, 'has been prouder these last days because a message from a tent has shown how the breed lives on'. Members of the search party who had found the bodies said it was 'a ghastly sight' but Barrie revamped their accounts to suit his own imaginings. 'Scott and his comrades emerge out of the white immensities, always young,' he told an audience at St Andrew's University. King George V set aside precedent and paid his tribute in person at the memorial service at St Paul's Cathedral in London. What Queen Victoria had been unable to do even for the greatest of her subjects her grandson was prepared to do for the members of an unsuccessful polar expedition, one of whom had helped to drive another to suicide.

Barrie's vision of immortal explorers emerging from white immensities was a new and more powerful version of Mead's doctrine that the quest for adventure and the quest for eternal truth were two sides of the same coin. But there had been an ominous change in the coin's superscription. It was not now about quest but about sacrifice. 'We are showing that Englishmen can still die with a bold spirit fighting it out to the end,' Scott had written. His expedition had become not a quest but a combat, a battle which must be fought out to the end. Against whom was he fighting with such a bold spirit? Not against his rival Amundsen, for he and his expedition had already reached the Pole and returned from it. Not against the elements, unless desolation and icy winds could be personified or regarded as demonic. Yet the image was one of conflict rather than search. Scott was not like the Grail hero, facing mysterious dangers in order to resolve an enigma which transcended good and evil. He was like a soldier on the field of battle, ready to lay down his life because there were still good and evil in the world and the one must triumph over the other.

The road that led from the fictitious self-sacrife of Henry Desmond to the presumed self-sacrifice of Scott and Oates was already well marked out. In 1908, when the archaeologists dug up the temple of Artemis Orthia where Spartan youths had been ritually flogged, *The Times* pointed out that this gruesome practice had been a relic of earlier human sacrifices – the goddess had had to be content with the blood of the living instead of the blood of the dead – but it also reminded its readers that such 'rigorous discipline' was necessary in societies dedicated to war. If the ordeal was a substitute for one kind of sacrifice it was also a preparation for another. 'You can bear a spot of pain, Pete old lad, can't you?' said bluff Dr Wadd to Peter Ackerley as he prepared to lance his poisoned hand with a pair of borrowed scissors, 'Or do you want an anaesthetic?' The boy told him to go ahead and when his palm was slit he turned pale but did not cry out. 'It was what my father would have called "a jolly good show",' commented his brother later after Peter had been killed in battle. In 1909 Charles Doughty's verse drama *The Cliffs* showed a ceremony in which those about to die for their country kissed a basket of earth and then had some sprinkled on their heads to show that they looked forward to the hero's grave for which they were destined. Like Christ in the garden of Gethsemane they must come willingly to the sacrifice and contemplate their approaching agony without flinching.

Strictly speaking such comparisons were blasphemous. Christianity taught that the crucifixion was 'a full perfect and sufficient sacrifice, oblation and satisfaction for the sins of the whole world'. There was no need for a repeat performance and when Paul Hammerton tried to give one he was pronounced insane. And if the re-enactment of Christ's suffering was madness and impiety in the eyes of traditional theologians it was even more of an absurdity in the eyes of those who trod the converging paths of the new thinking. *Quest* had called yesterday's virtues, 'stepping-stones towards higher ideals' and the supposed virtue of self-immolation was surely one of them. If Myers was right and messages from the world beyond were becoming continuous and progressive, if there was an easier route to immortality than the one carved out on Calvary, what point was there in the idea that he who would save his life must lose it? If the ferment of the past few years meant anything at all, if mankind really was experiencing a thought wave breathed out by the living God, then the signposts of the new thinking might possibly point to a hero's quest but not to a hero's death.

Towards the end of the Boer War, as H.A.Vachell was meditating Henry Desmond's death in battle, Thomas Hardy had produced a poem announcing the demise of the god of war, Kipling's 'Lord of our far-flung battle-line'. 'The Battle-god is god no more,' he had proclaimed triumphantly. Now, a decade later, he published in the *Fortnightly Review* in March 1912 a more ambitious poem entitled 'God's Funeral: an allegorical conception of the present state of Theology'. In suitably ponderous stanzas he described how he had seen, at twilight on a darkling plain, a line of mourners who bore the now defunct ruler of the universe to his last resting place. They blamed themselves for his birth as well as for his death – 'Whence came it we were tempted to create One whom we can no longer keep alive?' – and they wept bitterly for the happy assured days that were gone, the days when life had been lapped and cradled in the certainty of the divine presence. The language and imagery were predictable enough – the darkling plain was very like those Matthew Arnold and Ambrose Bierce had glimpsed, while the penitence of the mourners echoed Nietzsche's insistence that man was the murderer of God – but there were also some topical touches. *Peter Pan*, first produced in 1904, was fast becoming an annual favourite and as Hardy's mourners lamented that they could no longer keep God alive his readers might perhaps have recollected the call for children in the audience to shout out their belief in order to save the dying Tinkerbell. Now God had fallen victim to an insufficiently enthusiastic audience. His shrivelled form lay like a deflated child's balloon, lacking the breath of faith which alone could give it substance and reality.

The parallel could be pushed further, for it seemed that the young and trusting were as ready to save God from the theologians as the excited and adventurous had been to save Sherlock Holmes from Conan Doyle. Hardy noted that all the mourners were aged – 'lined on the brows, scoop-eyed and bent and hoar' – while in the background youths and maidens protested that this premature interment of the deity was a hideous mistake. 'Still he lives for us!' they cried, pointing to a gleam of light on an otherwise dark horizon. But their elders refused to see it and continued on their funereal way. Thirty years ago Nietzsche had greeted the image of God's death as 'a glimpse of things which put me in advance of all other men' but now the position was reversed. Orthodoxy itself, 'the present state of theology', was unable to keep God alive and only the young, the unconventional,

188

the advanced, were sure of his existence.

Those who had followed the new developments in science and philosophy found it easy to interpret Hardy's metaphor. The god of the old men was dead, the god who had been thought to preside over a fixed and unchanging universe, and a dynamic god of Heraclitean fire now lived in the hearts and minds of the young. Grail enthusiasts could go further. For them the god who had died was the one who had set good against evil by waging war in heaven. The ancient vision of a world not polarized into good and evil could therefore be recaptured: perhaps the Waste Land could be restored. More practical men and women concentrated on the reality of peace rather than on its spiritual or intellectual foundations. In America a World Peace Foundation was established, endowed with a million dollars by the industrialist Edwin Ginn. It was followed by the Church Peace Union, which included Catholics, Protestants and Jews. The steel magnate Andrew Carnegie was so sure of its success that when he funded it he stipulated what further use should be made of his money once war had been abolished.

On the other hand Marxist Socialists, for whom religion was the opium of the people, wished to slay the God of war not with capitalist millions but with international working-class solidarity. In October 1912, while Hardy's readers were still considering the rights and wrongs of God's funeral, the Church of England Congress considered the rights and wrongs of Socialism. Did British Socialism follow Karl Marx or Jesus Christ? While one lay speaker regretted that 'members of religious bodies, including the Established Church, were coquetting with Socialism', the Bishop of Hull insisted that not all Socialists were 'predatory, revolutionary, materialistic and anti-Christian'. When the Second Socialist International met three weeks later to inveigh against the escalating war in the Balkans only thirteen out of more than four hundred delegates were British and none was American.

In the Balkans the god of battles was by no means dead. On 18 October 1912 the Archbishop of Sofia held high a crucifix bearing the ancient promise 'In this sign shalt thou conquer' and the King of Bulgaria called on 'all those who love justice and progress' to support a crusade against the Ottoman Turks. The British and Foreign Bible Society distributed copies of the New Testament to Bulgarian troops, earning shouts of 'Three cheers for England!', but *The Times* remarked sourly that 'neither Europe nor the Christians in the Ottoman Empire need thank King Ferdinand for introducing sectarian issues into what is mainly a political and racial struggle'. The Archbishop of Canterbury was ready to back his own country's war preparations – his wife had recently launched one of Britain's most powerful battleships – but he did not care for King Ferdinand's god of war. He instructed his clergy instead to pray to the God of peace, 'that the course of this world may be so peaceably ordered by thy governance that thy Church may joyfully serve thee in all godly quietness'. In the United States the World Peace Foundation and the Church Peace Union began to make preparations for a World Peace Congress in Switzerland on 2 August 1914. The Socialist International planned to meet in Belgium at the end of July and the orgy of peacemaking would be completed by an international peace congress in Vienna and by a Catholic Peace Conference at Liège in Belgium on 4 August.

August 1914 brought not peace but the sword. German armies entered Belgium and attacked Liège on the day the Catholic Peace Conference was to have met. European nations mobilized their forces, trains were commandeered, delegates to the congresses were unable to reach their destinations. The bureau of the Second International met in Brussels to hear French delegates announce that their German comrades had failed to hold their government in check and so it was the duty of all Frenchmen to fight for their country and for civilization. British Socialists followed suit and *The Times* was soon able to proclaim that 'the International Socialist League has been crushed out of existence'. The god of war was proving more than a match for the Marxists, even if he was only a figment of bourgeois imagining.

Some of his other opponents put up a more determined fight. Mead wrote a *Quest* editorial declaring that governments would now put the welfare of the world above their own petty interests. 'Humanity as a whole would have at long last acted morally for the first time in its history,' he concluded. As late as April 1915 he could still convince himself that 'the devotion of the nation in its public prayers is taking a higher form of petition than ever before. There is much to show that the majority have become ashamed of the old "god of battle" order of procedure.' When the Archbishop of Canterbury preached on 2 August 1914, as Britain stood on the brink of war, he praised the international peace movements and studiously avoided any talk of a divine call to arms. Nevertheless he proclaimed that 'the thing which is now active in Europe is not the work of God but of the Devil'; and it was this insistence on the diabolical nature of

190

the enemy that was to prove the divine warlord's greatest strength.

As soon as the British entered the war they took charge of all transmission of news across the Atlantic. Most American newspapers gave the impression that God was on Britain's side and the British press assured its readers that they had the unbounded sympathy of their transatlantic cousins. 'The American citizen who in the crowd before Buckingham Palace cried out to King George "New York is with you" did not misrepresent the feelings of this country,' wrote the American correspondent of *The Times*. Carnegie issued a public apology, eagerly copied in the British press, because his attempts to avert war had been unduly friendly towards the German Kaiser. 'We advocates of heavenly peace and foes of hellish war must not fail to expose and denounce the guilty originators thereof,' he wrote, 'I feel that Britain was in honour bound to protect Belgium'. The World Peace Foundation was stopped in its tracks and its director David Starr Jordan held a breakaway congress in Chicago and enlisted the aid of the motor millionaire Henry Ford. 'We're going to get the boys out of the trenches before Christmas,' Ford declared, 'I've chartered a ship and some of us are going to Europe'. Cardinal Gibbons gave his support to the venture but withdrew it after he had been mauled by the press. When Ford and his peace delegates finally crossed the Atlantic in December 1915 the British navy made sure that they were unable to influence British opinion or get anywhere near the boys in the trenches.

The lord of the far-flung battle-line seemed to be giving the British powerful support. On 23 August 1914, according to an account written by a British officer, an angel on a white horse with a flaming sword stopped the German advance at Mons. Other stories told of skies filled with angels on outstretched wings and of a figure in golden armour recognized as St George by the British and as St Michael by the French. 'The radiant forms of the spiritual hierarchies can only be made manifest to mortal eye in a form which the beholder can interpret,' declared the *Occult Review* by way of explaining these differences of interpretation. The *Evening News* pointed out that the tales of supernatural assistance seemed to spring from 'The Bowmen', a story by Arthur Machen which it had published at the end of September 1914. One critic said that a typed copy of 'The Bowmen' had been sent to him with a statement that it had been taken down 'from the lips of a wounded soldier in a London hospital'. When Machen insisted that he had made the whole thing up he was accused of irreverence and disloyalty. 'To have entered upon a scene of such awful havoc and desolation for a story of mystery is in itself, I think, an act very near to sacrilege,' wrote Harold Begbie in his book *On the side of the angels: a reply to Arthur Machen*.

If God and his angels were on the side of the British it followed that Satan and his legions were on the side of the Germans. Shortly before the war a group of British theologians had published a symposium entitled *Is there a Hell?*, pointing out that 'mankind has abandoned the conception of hell as a real pit full of fire and brimstone'. The Devil was a myth and the only punishment in store for sinners was the absence of God. But now it was necessary to re-invent the Devil and all his works. Ironically enough it was an admirer of Germany who was one of the first to do so, in a letter to *The Times* four days after war broke out. It was tragic, he wrote, that the British should find themselves at war with a people so much like themselves. 'It makes one despair of human intelligence unless it is believed that this calamity may be ascribed to an anti-human, devilish influence which has found its instrument in the extraordinary arrogance of the Emperor William.' 'The idea that a monarch of modern Europe could fulfil in his person an ancient prophecy of the coming of Antichrist is astounding to twentieth century thought,' wrote the *Occult Review*, 'yet this conception is coming home to us today'. *The Faith and the War*, a collection of essays by church leaders in Britain, asserted among other things that Germany had abandoned Christianity and reverted to paganism. *The Times* claimed to have known for some time that the Germans had re-established the worship of Odin and the Chancellor of the Exchequer proclaimed that their aim was the destruction of Christianity.

It was to be expected that churchmen would back the secular authorities and portray the conflict as a holy war against the forces of evil. What was more surprising was the alacrity with which unconventional thinkers came round to the same view. The very people who had been least conformist in peace were most fervent in war. By November 1914 Bergson was alleging that the values for which the Allies stood were in line with the creative evolutionary processes of the universe whereas those of the Germans were opposed to them. Miss Weston turned away from the Grail that stood beyond good and evil and wrote instead of a chalice which sacrilegious Germans had filled with swine's flesh in a church near Verdun. From this and other incidents she deduced that a failure to defeat and punish Germany would be 'an act of treason against humanity'. Orde Ward used his religious and scientific insights to develop a theory that conflict was as central to the moral universe as energy was to the physical one. 'Without conflict there would be no rest, without evil no good ... We can no more stop war than we can stop the tides or the stars in their courses ... We should recognize in the Spirit of War the Spirit of Love ... We have no choice but to fight and fight for ever'. The resurrected god of battle and the newly revealed dynamic Heraclitean god had become one and the same. Algernon Blackwood joined Orde Ward in the pages of *Quest* to greet the war as a miracle, a triumph of spiritual values over the material world. The Dean of St Paul's hoped that it had come in time to save the British from 'godless civilization, a disease of which nations die by inches'.

Angelic helpers and questing heroes and novelists' miracles were not enough for the warring nations. They needed something more sublime and they found it in Christianity's ultimate fantasy, the re-enactment of Christ's passion. *The Treasury*, a journal run by a clergyman later made chaplain to King George v, carried an article called 'The Precursor': 'before God permitted this passion of the human race in which, reverently be it said, the Lord Christ is once more crucified in all Christianity and the forces of evil are let loose in hideous conflict against the powers of good, He sent his precursor'. The precursor was Captain Scott, whose voice in the great white wilderness of Antarctica had repeated the Baptist's cry in the wilderness of Judaea. Even before the outbreak of war Scott's deeds had been described as 'equally as great as any committed on a battlefield' and now it seemed that his death had pointed the way ahead to the sacrificial slaughter just as the death of John the Baptist had pointed the way to Calvary. *The Last Crusade*, Orde Ward's collection of patriotic verses, was hailed as 'profoundly religious'. It opened with 'The Eternal Passion', a vision of Christ sharing the agonies of British soldiers: 'He suffers and delights to die, In awful pangs and seeks his Calvary.' Other poems described the Germans as the murderers of God, casting down his cross and dancing on the broken body.

Orde Ward's recurring phrase, 'Our Lord is crucified again in France', was soon taken up by other writers who had the English Channel between them and the battlefield. But in the horror and desolation of Flanders Wilfred Owen had a more ironic version of the fantasy:

For 14 hours yesterday I was at work – teaching Christ to lift his cross by numbers, and how to adjust his crown; and not to imagine he thirst till after the last halt; I attended his Supper to see that there were no complaints; and inspected his feet that they should be worthy of the nails. I see to it that he is dumb and stands to attention before his accusers. With a piece of silver I buy him every day and with maps I make him familiar with the topography of Golgotha.

There were other bridges from fantasy to reality. British soldiers were subject to Field Punishment Number One: they could be tied to a post for several hours a day, sometimes within range of enemy fire. Although this was popularly known as 'crucifixion' an artist illustrating it in a War Office manual was told peremptorily to change his drawing and make the post look 'entirely unlike the Cross'. Those at home might perhaps draw comfort from the notion that their loved ones had played the part of the Son of God but in the field the metaphor had its dangers, especially if it suggested that Christ's tormentors were not the Germans at all but his superior officers.

The real value of the fantasy lay not in comforting the bereaved but in influencing public opinion in neutral countries, above all in America. Owen Wister, an able publicist of the Allied cause, produced *The Pentecost of Calamity*, saying that an American declaration of war would be 'a great stride in national and spiritual maturity' and painting the familiar picture of Germans exulting in fiendish cruelties while martyred Belgians and Frenchmen were transfigured and brought to glory. At the beginning of 1917 Winston Churchill and sixty-four other public figures signed an appeal to Christians in America not to support moves for a negotiated peace because 'the just God who withheld not His son from the cross would not look with favour upon a people who put their fear of pain and death above the holy claims of righteousness and justice'. But the British did not have it all their own way. A group of pro-German intellectuals led by Professor Yandell Henderson of Yale sponsored C.L. Droste's *Germany's Golgotha*, yet another image of Christ re-crucified: 'As during the last days of July 1914 Germany prayed in its Gethsemane and there was kissed by its Iscariot in the shape of England, so it now finds itself on its Golgotha, with the prayer of supreme beauty on its lips: "Father, forgive them, for they know not what they do".'

Nevertheless most Americans accepted that it was the Allies who were imitating Christ. As early as January 1915 a Massachusetts preacher told his flock that they should 'catch the spirit of battle' because they had been anointed by God as champions of Christian civilization. A few weeks later a British clergyman said that the war had halted what he called 'the German conspiracy' in the United States and in May, after the sinking of the *Lusitania* by a German submarine had resulted in the loss of 128 American lives, a Baptist minister in Pennsylvania proclaimed that the German government was in league with hell. But he also prayed that America should not be drawn into the fighting and when the *New York Times* conducted a survey of opinion on the issue most of the ministers of religion who were polled said that the Germans were guilty of murder but few called for war. Nevertheless well over a hundred clergymen took part in New York's Preparedness Parade of May 1916. 'I advocate it because of its moral and spiritual value,' wrote one of those pressing for compulsory military training, 'It will make our young men better Americans, better citizens and better Christians.' After the United States declared war on Germany in April 1917 American religious leaders took part eagerly in the great game of reading God's mind. 'He is the most powerful, the most active and the most important of all who are influencing the war,' wrote one, 'He is delaying victory to either side in the deadlock until men shall comprehend that the war is being waged between spiritual principles and vital philosophies rather than between mere armed forces.'

Spiritualists did not need to be so presumptuous. Instead of asking God why the war had happened they could ask the dead. Mrs Elsa Barker, whose *Letters from a Living Dead Man* had caused a stir in America in 1913, got in touch with her deceased friend Judge Hatch again and was told that 'it is because man has not made moral progress corresponding to his material progress that evil elemental beings who fear for their rule in the elemental kingdom have come so near to succeeding in their attacks on the human race'. At a spiritualist séance in March 1916 Sir Olive Lodge was told by his dead friend Frederick Myers that 'man has made the earth plane into such a hotbed of materialism and selfishness that man again has to atone by sacrifice of mankind in the prime of their physical life'. Through Myers he was able to speak to his son Raymond, who had been killed in action, and an account of these conversations was later published under the title *Raymond, or Life and Death*. As the killing grew more monstrous the need to believe in personal survival became more desperate. Hereward Carrington, a psychic investigator who had once been extremely sceptical, now seemed totally convinced. His book *Psychical Phenomena*

195

and the War listed cases in which relatives had received messages from the fallen and insisted that 'These experiences can be repeated in the lives of every mourner if they will only put aside prejudice'. The *Occult Review*, now enjoying unprecedented popularity, poured scorn on 'the orthodox who believe that those who have passed over are dead and asleep and unable to communicate with us'. On the contrary, it declared confidently, most of those killed were 'probably helping to form a Britain or Empire beyond the grave, a better Britain or Empire than exists now on the material plane'.

The idea of posthumous patriotic empire-building might seem grotesque but it was less damaging than the fantasies which centred on Christ. 'I've been a Christian all my life,' one recruit remarked in 1914, 'but this war is a bit too serious.' Here in a single sentence was the cold truth of the matter. The war required men to disobey Christ's greatest commandment and if they were to do so as free human beings, rather than as beasts driven to the slaughter, then they must decide what it was that was too serious, what it was that forced them to set Christian morality aside. Nor was it only Christian morality that must go. They must also defy the God of the Old Testament, as Wilfred Owen saw very clearly in 'The Parable of the Old Man and the Young'. He looked back beyond the crucifixion to the earlier sacrifice Jehovah had demanded of Abraham, the sacrifice of his son Isaac. Abraham had been told at the last minute to sacrifice a ram instead but now, as the hideous ritual was played out again in the trenches, the old man refused to obey the divine command because the ram represented his pride. And so he slew his son 'and half the seed of Europe, one by one'. Abraham had been shown that it was not necessary to sacrifice man to the supposed needs of God but nobody was going to stop the world's rulers from sacrificing God to the supposed needs of man.

In the summer of 1916, in a cottage in New Hampshire, Aleister Crowley crucified a frog which he had baptized as Jesus of Nazareth. 'Give thou place to me, O Jesus,' he cried, 'thine aeon is passed; the Age of Horus is arisen by the Magick of the Master, the Beast that is Man'. He now regarded himself as the Great Beast, the Antichrist who would take over the dominion of the world. His gesture in the name of the supposed powers of evil was puny beside those being made in the name of the alleged powers of good. 'The state, the nation, national honour, became the idols and both sides voluntarily sacrificed their children to these idols,' wrote the psychologist Erich

Fromm many years later. 'The ubiquity of human sacrifice,' said Arthur Koestler, 'is one of the earliest manifestations of the paranoid trend in the human psyche.' But human sacrifice, as anthropologists have shown, has always required that the victim be sinner as well as saviour. He must himself be in some sense guilty of the sin he is expiating. And it was unthinkable that the war dead should be seen in this way. They must be idealized, apotheosized, even deified, in order that the carnage should be raised to a level higher than mere human sacrifice. The reversal of roles was complete: just as it was man rather than God who demanded the sacrifice so it must be God rather than man who was the victim. Christ must be re-crucified in the human imagination whether or not he liked it, whether or not he survived it.

When the killing at last came to an end the full power of the re-crucifixion myth was revealed. From being an offensive and rather silly idea in the minds of people like Orde Ward it had become a national necessity. On 11 November 1920, the second anniversary of the armistice, a soldier who had been so badly mangled that his identity was unknown was buried in Westminster Abbey while King George v stood in mute respect before his coffin. 'Oh, 'tis Christ that passes,' declared a versifier in *The Times*, 'In thee, poor soldier, who didst die for me.' A year later a similar ceremony took place at Arlington National Cemetery in the presence of President Harding. Honoured above all men the two unidentified corpses took on a glory that was more than human.

Such were the fantasies of war. Sir Philip Gibbs, who covered the London ceremony for the *Illustrated London News*, had just published a book called *The Realities of War*. He had described unknown warriors as they actually were – 'bodies, and bits of bodies, and clots of blood, and green, metallic-looking slime . . . Scraps of flesh, booted legs, blackened hands, eyeless heads'. Now he had to feel respectful and uplifted as putrefied remains were honoured by those who had commanded the carnage. He did his best, speaking of 'remembrances, ghosts, pities, subconscious and unuttered thoughts,' but his piece lacked the pious assurance which was expected of him. Nor was he alone. All over the country the two aspects of the dead, the disembodied memories held sacred by the bereaved and the appalling realities which haunted the survivors, had to live cheek by jowl. In the same house there might be those who woke from nightmares with the smell of dead men in their nostrils and those who knew only a face in a fading photograph and saw it transfigured and sanctified.

Slowly the pious and the orthodox realized what it was they had done. Already an angry clergyman had complained about men in battle thinking of death as 'a hideous foe'. 'The war has brought back again much that underlay the old pagan conception of death,' he thundered, 'It has not brought the idea of death as a friend.' He was displeased to learn that men who had seen rats eat their dead comrades – 'they go into a man at one place, they come out at another' – found it difficult to think of death as a blessed reunion with God. Those who peddled the fantasy of Christ re-crucified implied that the imitation of Christ gave a Christ-like ability to rise again from the dead, or at least to inherit the eternity he had promised. Those who had survived the slaughter had their doubts. They insisted that the dead be honoured – anyone who failed to observe the Armistice Day silence was liable to be roughly handled – but they did not do so out of respect for Christian doctrine. 'The leaders of the Church seem to have no idea of the extent to which the great mass of the people are hostile to, and not merely out of contact with, organized religion,' wrote Canon Green of Manchester in November 1919. The faithful continued to sing that 'a thousand ages in thy sight are like an evening gone' but in truth it had taken little more than five years for the shadows to lengthen in the quiet places which God inhabited. Whatever name they went by – the human soul, the human spirit, the human imagination – these places would never be the same again after the assaults that had been made upon them. The gun carriages that rolled to Westminster and to Arlington were part of God's funeral procession.

POSTSCRIPT

On the day after the Arlington ceremony T.S. Eliot left England for Lausanne to be treated for what he called 'an emotional derangement'. 'It is a commonplace,' he later remarked, 'that some forms of illness are extremely favourable, not only to religious illumination, but to artistic and literary composition'. In Lausanne he wrote the first draft of 'The Waste Land'. Readers familiar with Miss Weston's book and with *The Golden Bough* would find, he explained, 'certain references to vegetation ceremonies'. In the first section, originally called 'The death of Saint Narcissus' but later changed to 'The Burial of the Dead', he found himself discussing horticulture with a man called Stetson who had been with him in an ancient battle long ago. 'That corpse you planted last year in your garden,' he inquired, 'Has it begun to sprout? Will it bloom this year?'

Ezra Pound thought it was 'a damned good poem, about enough to make the rest of us shut up shop.' Eliot said it was 'a personal and wholly insignificant grouse against life, a piece of rhythmical grumbling' and he shrugged off attempts by critics to interpret it as 'criticism of the contemporary world'. The contemporary world had other and more exciting fantasies to explore. *The Strand Magazine*, Sherlock Holmes's happy home, had published an article by Sir Arthur Conan Doyle claiming that fairies had been photographed by two little girls at Cottingley in Yorkshire. That story was hardly cold before Doyle was in the news again, this time commenting on the fact that Lord Carnarvon had died in Cairo shortly after he had opened up the tomb of the Pharaoh Tutankhamun. 'An evil elemental may have caused Lord Carnarvon's illness,' Doyle told reporters, 'One does not know what elementals existed in those days, nor what their power might be. The Egyptians knew a great deal more about those things than we do.' At the precise moment of Carnarvon's death all the lights

199

in Cairo went out and no satisfactory explanation of the power failure was forthcoming, even though Lord Allenby as High Commissioner took the matter up with the English engineer in charge of the electricity supply. At home in England, also at the precise moment of death, Carnarvon's favourite dog howled a terrible howl and expired.

There were others as well as outraged pharaohs who might have been expected to call up an evil elemental. Carnarvon had infuriated the press on both sides of the Atlantic by giving exclusive coverage of his expedition to *The Times*. 'The tomb is not his private property,' raged the *Daily Express*, 'By making an exclusive secret of the contents of the inner tomb he has ranged against him the majority of the world's most influential newspapers.' But it did not occur to anyone that the anger of an excluded reporter might have been more deadly than that of an exhumed monarch. The craving was not just for supernatural powers but for supernatural beings to wield them. And so was born the fantasy of pharaoh's curse, even though most of the other members of the expedition lived out their lives happily enough. Soon the fantasies which fed the popular press were dwarfed by those which ruled the destinies of nations. Italian fascism made myth the basis of political action and in the beer-halls of Munich the Nazis nursed the obscene nonsense of racialism. Russia was governed by the Marxist conviction that capitalism was an agent of fantasy, 'a sorcerer who is no longer able to control the powers of the nether world he had called up by his spells', while the capitalist world in its turn dismissed as fantasy the supposedly inexorable historical forces which the Marxists recognized.

In this counterpoint of thinking and imagining the constant, the universal, seemed to be respect for the heroic dead. There was a war memorial at the heart of most communities, whatever might have happened to their churches and their centres of social and political cohesion. And so Eliot's image of a corpse sprouting and blooming in the garden was hardly welcome. Yet it was the one sane thing in a world gone mad, the one reality in a welter of fantasy. Early in the war Arnold Bennett had seen 'wheat absolutely growing out of a German' and by the summer of 1919 the Imperial War Graves Commission found that 'vegetation is fast covering up all traces of the dead.' 'It is a tremendous fact to bear in mind,' observed *The Times*, 'that there are more dead soldiers lying in isolated areas than constituted the whole of the Expeditionary Force of 1914 ... The French peasant is not going to allow these vast areas to remain uncultivated'. The armies had completed the planting of corpses and now the owners of the gardens and the fields and the woodlands were returning to plant other things and reap a richer harvest. The war memorials announced piously that the heroes had died in order that others might live; the ancient fertility cults had proclaimed the same truth in a way which was, quite literally, more down to earth. It was not an accident that the early twentieth century had seen a revival of interest in these rituals and that Eliot had now woven them into one of the most important poems of the post-war years. The waste land of which he wrote was a place of desolation but it was not without hope. It was the land in which the human imagination had once been nurtured and in which it might yet become whole again.

NOTES

A BIBLIOGRAPHY OF ALL THE TOPICS COVERED IN THIS book would far outrun the available space. I have tried to provide a bibliographical outline by indicating in note form the source material on which the book is based and the principal secondary works consulted. In order to eliminate figures in the text each note is keyed to the final words of the paragraph to which it relates. First references are in full, subsequent references are abbreviated. Place of publication is London unless otherwise stated. Wherever possible references to periodicals are to dates rather than to volume or part numbers. The following abbreviations are used for sources to which frequent reference is made:

AR – Annual Register; CR – Contemporary Review; FR — Fortnightly Review; H – Hansard's Parliamentary Debates; LQV(1) – A.C.Benson and Viscount Esher (eds), *The Letters of Queen Victoria 1837–1862,* 3 vols, 1907; *LQV(2)* – G.E.Buckle (ed.), *The Letters of Queen Victoria 1862–1885,* 3 vols, 1926–28; *M&B* – W.F. Monypenny and G.E.Buckle, *The Life of Benjamin Disraeli Earl of Beaconsfield,* rev'd edn, 2 vols, 1929; *NC — Nineteenth Century; QR – Quarterly Review; R – Reasoner; S – Spectator; SR – Saturday Review; T – The Times; WR – Westminster Review.*

INTRODUCTION

p.1 '*. . . and reality reigned.*' R.C.K.Ensor, *England 1870–1914,* Oxford 1936, pp. 137–38.

p.3 '*. . . an unimaginable fantasy.*' Kathleen Coburn and Bart Winer (eds), *Collected Works of Coleridge, Volume 7, Biographia Literaria,* London and Princeton 1983, i, 304; ii, 18.

p.4 '*. . . a wider meaning.*' *Ibid.,* i, 305; John Bullitt and W.Jackson Bates, 'Distinctions between Fancy and Imagination in eighteenth-century English criticism', *Modern Language Notes 60,* 1945, pp. 8–15.

p.5 '*. . . been a fantasy.*' Sir A.C.Doyle, *Complete Sherlock Holmes Long Stories,*

1929, pp. 131–32; W.Winwood Reade, *The Martyrdom of Man*, The Thinker's Library No. 25, 1932, p. 447.

p.6 *'... into the fantastic.' AR*, 1871, pp. 57–58.

p.6 *'... storm has cleared.'* Sir A.C.Doyle, *Complete Sherlock Holmes Short Stories*, 1928, p. 1086.

CHAPTER 1

p.9 *'... he concluded.'* W.Marsh, *Antichrist detected*, 1841, p. 11.

p.9 *'... from the earth.'* J.Morley, *Life of Gladstone*, 2 vols, 1905, i, 140; Owen Chadwick, *The Victorian Church*, 2 vols, 1961, 1970, i, 158; Morley, *Gladstone*, i, 174; *QR*, July 1837, p. 268; Christopher Ricks (ed.), *The Poems of Tennyson*, 1969, pp. 582–98; William Plomer (ed.), *Selections from the Diary of the Rev. Francis Kilvert*, 1944, pp. 82–83.

p.10 *'... in anxious uncertainty.'* John Keble, *National Apostasy considered in a sermon preached in St Mary's Oxford*, 1833.

p.10 *'... had passed away.'* Sir Charles Lyell, *Principles of Geology*, 3 vols, 1830–33, iii, 384; *Poems of Tennyson*, pp. 597–98.

p.11 *'... of all things.'* E.B.Elliott, *Horae Apocalypticae*, 4 vols, 1844; 2nd edn 1846, 3rd edn 1847.

p.11 *'... at all abroad.'* W.E.Gladstone, *First Letter... on the Neapolitan Government*, 1851, p. 9n.; W.Marsh, *The Cholera*, 1831, p. 16; *Poems of Tennyson*, p. 583.

p.12 *'... be long delayed.' Antichrist detected*, p. 11.

p.12 *'... fires of hell.' T*, 9 March 1842, p. 7; 10 March 1842, p. 7; 17 March 1842, p. 5; 18 March 1842, p. 15.

p.13 *'... buried beneath it.'* J.Cumming, *Apocalyptic Sketches*, 1849, p. 482.

p.13 *'... tormentors and tormented.'* G.P.Pinamonti, *Hell opened to Christians*, Derby 1844; W.G.Ward, *Everlasting Torments Unscriptural*, n.d. (1871).

p.14 *'... a nearby collier:' H*, lxiii, 1320–64.

p.14 *'... residing in Rochdale.' Ibid.*, 1346.

p.15 *'... darkness after death.' Ibid.*, 1347.

p.15 *'... senses of mankind?' Poems of Tennyson*, p. 596.

p.16 *'... distress the susceptible.'* Dorothy Thompson, *The Chartists*, 1984, pp. 291, 295.

p.16 *'... MEET THY GOD!' Memoirs of William Miller*, Boston Mass. 1853; Edwin S.Gaustad (ed.), *A Documentary History of Religion in America to the Civil War*, 1982, p. 373.

p.16 *'... the great day:' Memoirs of Miller*, pp. 255–56.

p.17 *'... a revolutionary outbreak.' T*, 31 October 1844, p. 5.

p.17 *'... continue to deepen.'* W.Marsh, *A Few Plain Thoughts on Prophecy*, 1843, pp. 92, 96.

p.19 *'... colder and darker.' L'Artiste*, Paris 31 March 1844.

p.19 *'... is called Infidelity.' R*, Vol. i, No. 1, p. 1; No. 17, p. 238.

p.20 *'... his British audience.'* Horace Mann, *Religious Worship in England and Wales*, 1853; Chadwick, *Victorian Church*, i, 369. See also K.S.Inglis,

'Patterns of Worship in 1851', *Journal of Ecclesiastical History*, December 1960, pp. 74–86 and W.S.Pickering, 'The Religious Census of 1851 – a useless experiment?', *British Journal of Sociology*, September 1967, pp. 382–407.

p.20　'... *of itinerant preachers.*' F.Thistlethwayte, *The Great Experiment*, Cambridge 1961, p. 17; C.Dickens, *American Notes*, J.S.Whitley and A. Goldman (eds), 1972, p. 290; *T*, 13 April 1838, p. 3.

p.20　'... *assign a termination.*' *R*, Vol. ii, No. 39, p. 93; *T*, 6 September 1847, p. 4.

p.21　'... *superstition and unreason.*' Karl Marx and F.Engels, *The Manifesto of the Communist Party*, authorized English translation 1933, pp. 14, 20.

p.21　'... *old God yet.*' *T*, 11 November 1947, p. 5.

CHAPTER 2

p.22　'... *this latest exhumation:*' *H*, cxi, 1076; *T*, 13 August 1847, p. 1; 27 August 1847, p. 1.

p.22　'... *and sell them.*' *T*, 6 September 1847, p. 3.

p.23　'... *he concluded.*' *T*, 4 September 1847, p. 6; 6 September 1847, p. 1; *R*, Vol. ix, No. 8, p. 87; No. 7, p. 74.

p.24　'... *of the dead.*' E.Stone, *God's Acre*, 1858, p. 9; John Morley, *Death, Heaven and the Victorians*, 1971, p. 33; S.Baring-Gould, *Further Reminiscences*, 1925, p. 21.

p.25　'... *gushed and spurted.*' *Blackwood's Magazine*, April 1847, pp. 432–40.

p.25　'... *mercies of God.*' *T*, 16 September 1847, p. 1; 5 October 1847, p. 1; 21 October 1847, p. 1; 11 November 1847, p. 1.

p.26　'... *a successful termination.*' *T*, 11 November 1947, p. 5; 24 February 1848, pp. 4–5.

p.26　'... *to revolutionary demands.*' *R*, Vol. ii, p. 196; iv, pp. 182, 267, 303; *H*, xcvi, 754–55; *English Review*, March 1848, pp. 90–96.

p.27　'... *deepening apocalyptic darkness.*' *H*, xcviii, 287, 1330; J.Cumming, *The True Charter*, 1850, p. 120.

p.27　'... *charm against drowning.*' Thompson, *Chartists*, p. 329; Charles Greville, *A Journal of the Reign of Queen Victoria from 1837 to 1852*, 3 vols, 1885, iii, 256; Alfred Cobban, *The Debate on the French Revolution*, 2nd edn 1960, p. 376.

p.28　'... *audacity of Voltaire.*' *Edinburgh Review*, October 1849, pp. 338–39, 356; A.Saintes, *History of Rationalism in Germany*, tr. J.R.Beard 1849, pp. v–vi; *English Review*, December 1848, pp. 357–58. See also M.A. Crowther, *Church Embattled: Religious Controversy in Mid-Victorian England*, Newton Abbot 1970.

p.30　'... *part of it.*' J.Cumming, *Apocalyptic Sketches*, 1849, p. 494.

p.30　'... *of any kind.*' Gaustad, *Doc. Hist.*, pp. 342, 440–42.

p.31　'... *from their persecutors.*' Arthur E.Bestor, *Backwoods Utopias*, Philadelphia 1950, pp. 238–42; *Bible Communism: a compilation from the Annual*

Reports and other publications of the Oneida Association, New York 1953, p. 65; *T,* 23 October 1844, p. 5; 15 October 1845, p. 6; Robert Mullen, *The Mormons,* 1967, p. 57.

p.31   '... *made them all!'* J.P.Nichol, *View of Astronomy,* 1848, p. 41.

p.32   '... *that of Jehovah.'* Harold Beaver (ed.), *The Science Fiction of Edgar Allan Poe,* 1976, pp. 395–96; 307; 308–9.

p.33   '... *of the telegraph.'* E.M.Goulburn (ed.), *Replies to 'Essays and Reviews'... with a preface by the Lord Bishop of Oxford,* 1862, preface pp. xii–xiii; Emma Hardinge, *Modern American Spiritualism,* New York 1869, ii, 29.

p.34   '... *as a necromancer.'* Ruth Brandon, *The Spiritualists: The Passion for the Occult in the Nineteenth and Twentieth Centuries,* 1983, p. 3; Hall Caine, *My Story,* 1908, p. 231; *The Spirit World,* May 1853, p. 3; *The Congressional Globe,* Washington 1854, vol. xxviii, pt 2, p. 923; *Spiritual Magazine,* June 1864, pp. 255–60.

p.34   '... *more perfect condition.'* *The Spiritual Herald,* April 1856, p. 65; Eliab Capron, *Modern Spiritualism,* Boston and New York 1855, pp. 378–79; S.C.Hewitt (ed.), *Messages from the Superior State; communicated by John Murray through John M.Spear in the summer of 1852, containing important instructions to the inhabitants of the earth,* Boston 1852, p. 119.

p.35   '... *his imminent arrival.'* Brandon, *Spiritualists,* p. 32.

p.35   '... *of Christian orthodoxy.'* *Poems of Tennyson,* p. 907; Charles Tennyson, *Alfred Tennyson,* 1949, pp. 243, 253–56; *T,* 2 May 1851, p. 4.

p.36   '... *the new dispensation:'* J.Cumming, *The Seventh Vial,* 1870, pp. xiv–xv; F.G.Kenyon (ed.), *The Letters of Elizabeth Barrett Browning,* 2 vols, 1897, ii, 193–94.

p.36   '... *but the beginning.'* Elizabeth Barrett Browning, *Letters to her sister 1846–59,* 1929, p. 221.

p.37   '... *already taken place.'* *Cornhill Magazine,* August 1860, pp. 222–23; J.Cumming, *The Great Tribulation,* 1860; P.S.Desprez, *Apocalypse Fulfilled,* 1854.

p.37   '... *the same time:'* *Revue des Deux Mondes,* Paris 15 February 1861, pp. 812–56; *T,* 10 November 1860, p. 8; 16 February 1861, p. 10.

p.38   '... *in American spiritualism.'* *Replies to 'Essays and Reviews',* pp. xi–xiii.

p.38   '... *image of God.'* *LQV(1),* ii, 602–3; J.Cumming, *From Life to Life,* 1861, p. 9; *Spiritual Magazine,* October 1864, p. 470.

CHAPTER 3

p.39   '... *he committed suicide.'* Arturo Castiglioni, *A History of Medicine,* tr. E.B.Krumbhaar 2nd edn New York 1947, pp. 723–24.

p.40   '... *death of pain.'* *T,* 30 March 1844, p. 8.

p.40   '... *first battle won.'* *WR,* July 1871, p. 203.

p.41   '... *his religious master.'* *T,* 18 February 1841, p. 3; Gaustad, *Doc. Hist.,* p. 474.

p.42   '... *not properly birched.'* *T,* 10 January 1845, p. 5; 7 April 1845,

p. 6; E.Channing, *History of the United States*, 7 vols, New York 1905–32, vi, 18; Dickens, *American Notes*, pp. 282, 287.

p.42 '... *became their equals.*' Philippe Ariès, *Centuries of Childhood*, Penguin Books 1986, p. 254; G.B.Hill (ed.), *Boswell's Life of Johnson*, rev'd edn L.F.Powell, 6 vols, Oxford 1934–50, i, 46.

p.44 '... *not at all.*' Frances Power Cobbe, *Broken Lights*, 1864, p. 152.

p.45 '... *going to heaven.*' *R*, 29 May 1850, p. 86.

p.45 '... *the Protestant mind.*' (Anon), *The Bible History of Satan*, 1858, pp. 25, 32; Rev. J.Furniss, *Books for children and young persons: Book X The Sight of Hell*, Dublin 1861, pp. 17–18, 20; Rev. T. Livius, *Father Furniss and his work for children*, 1896, pp. 116, 114.

p.46 '... *for its salvation.*' *T*, 20 November 1845, p. 2; *Essays and Reviews*, 1860, p. 93.

p.46 '... *punished its authors.*' *S*, 7 April 1860, pp. 331–33; *WR*, October 1860, pp. 293–332; *QR*, January 1861, p. 302.

p.47 '... *was at stake.*' *Revue des Deux Mondes*, Paris 15 May 1861, pp. 403–24.

p.47 '... *of everlasting damnation.*' *Essays and Reviews*, p. 206; *T*, 9 June 1863, p. 14; Margaret Goodman, *Sisterhoods in the Church of England*, 1863, p. 25; *S*, 27 February 1864, p. 229.

p.48 '... *one with dogma.*' *T*, 1 July 1861, p. 8; 14 March 1864, p. 12; 17 March 1864, p. 7; John Keble, *A Litany of Our Lord's Warnings*, 1864, p. 8; *T*, 22 September 1864, p. 7.

p.49 '... *celebrate total victory.*' *H*, clxxvi, 1544; *Everlasting Punishment: a sermon preached... by the Rev. E.B.Pusey*, Oxford 1864; *T*, 17 July 1875, p. 13; 20 January 1876, p. 10; 21 January 1876, p. 10; 22 July 1876, p. 10; 17 February 1876, p. 10.

p.49 '... *of popular belief.*' *Alfred Tennyson*, pp. 259–60, 262; *T*, 21 February 1876, p. 5; 23 February 1876, p. 5; 28 February 1876, p. 10.

p.49 '... *curb his haughtiness.*' *Spirit World*, May 1853, p. 7; Rev. Norman Macleod, *The Recognition of Friends in Heaven*, 1863; Rev. Richard Cunningham Shimeall, *The Unseen World*, New York 1870, pp. 37, 214; *Spiritual Herald*, July 1856, p. 197.

p.50 '... *endorsement of it.*' *Spiritual Magazine*, December 1860, pp. 549–50; November 1861, p. 500; S.E.Gay, *Spiritual Sanity*, 1879, p. 16.

p.51 '... *to aphrodisiac flagellation.*' Peter Fryer (ed.), *Forbidden Books of the Victorians*, 1970, pp. 130–31, 23–24; Donald Thomas, *Swinburne: the Poet in his World*, 1979, pp. 18–19. See also Iain McCalman, 'Unrespectable Radicalism: Infidels and Pornography in early Nineteenth-Century London', *Past and Present*, August 1984, pp. 74–110.

p.51 '... *or by fire.*' Kilvert, *Diary*, pp. 253, 293, 97–98; Christopher Devlin (ed.), *Sermons and Devotional Writings of Gerard Manley Hopkins*, Oxford 1959, p. 241.

p.51 '... *up the attempt.*' Edward Royle, *Victorian Infidels: the Origins of the British Secularist Movement 1791–1866*, Manchester 1974, pp. 270–71;

H, clxi, 697, 1936–40; clxiii, 953–75; clxvii, 1024–26; clxix, 223, 1285–1302.

p.52   '... *a future world*.' Derek Hudson (ed.), *Munby: Man of Two Worlds*, 1974, pp. 64, 67.

p.53   '... *a continuing cannonade*.' Gertrude Himmelfarb, *Darwin and the Darwinian Revolution*, 1959, pp. 347, 332, 185; *Poems of Tennyson*, p. 912.

p.53   '... *of all things*.' The *Oxford Dictionary of Quotations*, 3rd edn Oxford 1979, p. 172.

p.54   '... *known at Eton*.' Hudson, *Munby*, pp. 198–99; R.L.Green (ed.), *The Diaries of Lewis Carroll*, 2 vols, 1953, i, 220; Cecil Y.Lang (ed.), *The Swinburne Letters*, 6 vols, New Haven and London 1959–62, i, 55.

p.54   '... *it was born*.' Frances Power Cobbe, *Darwinism in Morals and other essays*, 1872, pp. 173–74.

p.55   '... *and no Hereafter*.' *Ibid.*, pp. 312, 314.

p.55   '... *steeds into riders*.' *Ibid.*, pp. 333–34.

CHAPTER 4

p.57   '... *cost and pain*.' *Cornhill Magazine*, July 1860, p. 84.

p.57   '... *were suitably chagrined*.' J.D.Crowley (ed.), *Hawthorne: The Critical Heritage*, 1970, p. 315; *Centenary Edition of the Works of Nathaniel Hawthorne, Volume IV*, Ohio State University 1968, p. xxi.

p.58   '... *from a reed*.' *Ibid.*, p. xxxiii.

p.59   '... *those of Christianity*.' Chadwick, *Victorian Church*, ii, 36.

p.60   '... *a physical reality*.' S.Baring-Gould, *Curious Myths of the Middle Ages, Second Series*, 1868, p. 371.

p.61   '... *a new mythology*.' B.Torrey and F.H.Allen (eds), *The Journals of Thoreau*, 14 vols, New York 1906, ii, 145; H.D.Thoreau, *Walden*, Everyman's Library 1908, p. 185.

p.62   '... *of our race*.' S.S.Smith and H.Hayford (eds), *Journals and Notebooks of R.W.Emerson, Volume XIV*, Cambridge Mass. 1978, p. 194; L.A.Allardt, D.W.Hill, R.H.Bennett (eds), *Journals and Notebooks of R.W. Emerson, Volume XV*, Cambridge Mass. 1982, pp. 155, 222; Cobbe, *Darwinism in Morals*, p. 201.

p.62   '... *of Swinburne's talk*.' E.C.Stedman (ed.), *An American Anthology*, Boston, New York, Chicago, San Francisco 1900, pp. 334–35; Swinburne, *Correspondence*, i, 233–34; H.Cabot Lodge (ed.), *The education of Henry Adams*, Boston and New York 1918, p. 141.

p.63   '... *make it grow*.' *SR*, 4 August 1866, p. 147; Swinburne, *Correspondence*, i, 173–74; ii, 72–76.

p.64   '... *the schoolmaster's tune*.' *Ibid.*, i, 103–4, 288, 276n.; Bernard Falk, *The Naked Lady*, 1934, p. 227; *SR*, 4 August 1866, p. 145.

p.64   '... *as a wolf*.' S.Baring-Gould, *The Book of Werewolves*, 1865, pp. 107–8.

p.65   '... *throughout the world*.' Cobbe, *Darwinism in Morals*, pp. 269–70, 271; *AR*, 1890, p. 8.

p.65   '... *almost supernatural being:*' T.E.Kebbel (ed.), *Selected Speeches of*

Lord Beaconsfield, 3 vols, 1882, iii, 606, 612; *Punch*, 23 February 1867, p. 77; 15 June 1867, pp. 246–47.

p.65 '... *gets the chance.*' *M&B*, ii, 292–93.

p.66 '... *brigantine ever materialized.*' *AR*, 1867, pp. 107–8; *M&B*, ii, 307–8.

p.66 '... *of the universe.*' R. Payne, *Karl Marx*, 1968, pp. 398, 62–64, 349–50.

p.67 '... *gods die too.*' Reade, *Martyrdom of Man*, pp. 51, 328.

p.67 '... *makes men die!*' *Ibid.*, pp. 328, 417, 446, 137–40.

p.68 '... *its moral influences.*' *Ibid.*, p. 447; *Daily Telegraph*, 27 April 1875; Frances Power Cobbe, *Hopes of the Human Race, Hereafter and Here*, 1874, pp. ix–x.

p.69 '... *so astonishingly popular.*' *Ibid.*, 11n.; Guillaume Figuier, *The Day after Death; or, Our Future Life according to Science*, 1872, pp. 1, 113, 217.

p.70 '... *clash by night.*' *FR*, October 1867, p. 417; K. Allott (ed.), *The Poems of Matthew Arnold*, 2nd edn rev'd M. Allott 1979, pp. 253–57.

p.70 '... *had yet seen.*' Christopher Middleton (ed.), *Selected Letters of Friedrich Nietzsche*, Chicago and London 1969, pp. 67, 68.

p.70 '... *India into Greece.*' *Ibid.*, p. 22; Friedrich Nietzsche, *The Birth of Tragedy*, Section 20, cited in John Cruickshank, *Aspects of the Modern European Mind*, 1969, p. 76.

CHAPTER 5

p.73 '... *at Cumming's lectures.*' Harcourt Bland, *A Reply to Dr Cumming's Lectures*, Glasgow 1855; 'The End of the World', Correspondence between Rev. Dr Cumming and H. Bland, Comedian, Glasgow 1855; J. Cumming, *The End; or, the Proximate Signs of the close of this Dispensation*, 1855; 'Investigator', *The Rev. Dr Cumming and his Critics*, 1860; Rev. J. F. Witty, *What have we, and what has Dr Cumming, to do with 1867?*, Sheffield 1862, p. 3.

p.73 '... *of the apocalypse.*' Cumming, *The End*, pp. 137, 251.

p.73 '... *what it was.*' Chadwick, *Victorian Church*, i, 467–70, 482; *LQV(1)*, iii, 314.

p.74 '... *a beautiful creation.*' Rev. C. G. Finney, *Memoirs*, New York 1876, p. 437; Philip Schaff, *America: a Sketch of its Political, Social and Religious Character*, ed. Perry Miller, Cambridge Mass. 1961, pp. 29, 36, 39–40, 181, 80–81.

p.74 '... *when he came.*' Robert Baird, *Religion in America*, New York 1856, pp. 264, 365–66.

p.75 '... *of God's presence.*' Isabel Bishop, *Aspects of Religion in the United States*, 1859, p. 1; J. C. Pollock, *Moody without Sankey*, 1963, p. 29; Perry Miller, *Life of the Mind in America*, New York 1965, pp. 90, 89; Finney, *Memoirs*, pp. 442–44.

p.76 '... *rise in America.*' Finney, *Memoirs*, p. 444; Schaff, *America*, p. 43; John Weiss, *Life and Correspondence of Theodore Parker*, 2 vols, New York 1864, ii, 125–54, 161.

p.76 *'... a slave revolt.'* Bishop, *Aspects of Religion,* p. 188; *T,* 12 October 1841, p. 4.

p.76 *'... held in subjection.'* Weiss, *Parker,* i, 463.

p.77 *'... Atlantic with him.'* *Ibid.,* i, 463; *LQV(1),* iii, 323–24; Finney, *Memoirs,* pp. 449ff.

p.77 *'... fervour of 1857–58.'* Gaustad, *Doc. Hist.,* pp. 393–95.

p.78 *'... the apocalyptic scenario.'* Weiss, *Parker,* ii, 315, 301; Rev. Richard Cunningham Shimeall, *The Political Economy of Prophecy,* New York 1866, pp. 157–62. (For an account of the Emperor's being invited to a lecture proving he was Antichrist see Augustin Filon, *Souvenirs sur l'Impératrice Eugènie,* 1920, p. 259. I am indebted to Dr W.H.C.Smith for this reference); Gaustad, *Doc. Hist.,* p. 448.

p.79 *'... a safe distance.'* Weiss, *Parker,* ii. 438, 423, 405; *T,* 4 October 1860, p. 6; 9 November 1860, p. 6; 4 August 1860, p. 9.

p.79 *'... the old one.'* Wendell Glick (ed.), *Henry D. Thoreau: Reform Papers,* Princeton 1973, pp. 135, 152; P.M.Angle and E.S.Miers, *Tragic Years 1860–1865: A Documentary History of the American Civil War,* 2 vols, New York 1960, i, 33.

p.80 *'... in Charleston harbour.'* Sir Sidney Lee, *King Edward VII,* 2 vols, 1925–27, i, 98, 101–4; *T,* 20 November 1860, p. 6.

p.80 *'... that stirring tune?'* Angle and Miers, *Tragic Years,* i, 160, 189; *Reminiscences of Julia Ward Howe 1819–1899,* Boston 1899, pp. 274–75.

p.81 *'... from the North.'* Morley, *Gladstone,* i, 705.

p.81 *'... sway of slaveholders.'* Angle and Miers, *Tragic Years,* ii, 721.

p.82 *'... of the Lord.'* *Ibid.,* ii, 1007, 1022–23.

p.83 *'... jaws of hell.'* *T,* 25 May 1864, p. 8; Kebbel, *Speeches of Disraeli,* iii, 606, 617; Chadwick, *Victorian Church,* ii, 7, 25; *AR,* 1867, p. 347; J.B.Mozley, *Eight Lectures on Miracles,* 1865, p. 165; H.P.Liddon, *The Divinity of Our Lord and Saviour Jesus Christ,* 1867, p. 231; Chadwick, *Victorian Church,* ii, 65.

p.84 *'... the Last Trumpet.'* J. Cumming, *The Sounding of the Last Trumpet,* 1867, pp. 224, 233, 228; *AR,* 1866, pp. 172–75; *T,* 2 January 1867, p. 11; Cumming, *Last Trumpet,* p. 413.

p.84 *'... class and class.'* Hudson, *Munby,* p. 235; *T,* 3 January 1867, p. 7; 4 January 1867, p. 10; G.W.E.Russell (ed.), *Letters of Matthew Arnold,* 2 vols, 1895, i, 346; *AR,* 1867, p. 307.

p.85 *'... and be sober.'* *M&B,* i, 260, 262; E.L.Woodward, *The Age of Reform,* Oxford 1958, p. 181; Russell, *Letters of Arnold,* i, 378–79; *AR,* 1867, p. 139.

p.85 *'... voice of God.'* H.M.Schueller and R.L.Peters (eds), *The Letters of John Addington Symonds,* 3 vols, Detroit 1967–69, i, 687–88; *M&B,* ii, 291, 605, 606; Benjamin Disraeli, *Tancred or the New Crusade* (Bradenshaw edition of the novels of Benjamin Disraeli, Volume X), 1927, p. 141.

p.86   '... *a summer street.*' *T*, 4 May 1868, p. 10; *M&B*, ii, 317; *LQV(2)*, i, 512, 529.

p.86   '... *formally in Convocation.*' *AR*, 1868, p. 124; J.W.Draper, *History of the Intellectual Development of Europe*, 2 vols, New York 1864; Chadwick, *Victorian Church*, ii, 86–87, 89.

p.87   '... *less imaginative weapons.*' Morley, *Gladstone*, ii, 40; *T*, 20 November 1871, p. 9; *M&B*, ii, 511, 513.

p.87   '... *of visiting Englishmen.*' H.House and G.Storey (eds), *Journals and Papers of Gerard Manley Hopkins*, Oxford 1959, pp. 200–1; *AR*, 1870, p. 127; Swinburne, *Correspondence*, ii, 124–26; *LQV(2)*, ii, 61, 104.

p.88   '... *ruled by Germany.*' *Ibid.*, ii, 101; *FR*, January 1871, p. 66; *CR*, January 1871, p. 224; *T*, 9 February 1871, p. 6; *Blackwood's Magazine*, May 1871, pp. 539–72; *T*, 19 June 1871, p. 9.

p.88   '... *recaptured the city.*' *FR*, August 1871, p. 155; *LQV(2)*, ii, 126; House and Storey, *Journals of Hopkins*, pp. 210–11.

p.89   '... *form of government.*' C.C.Abbott (ed.), *Letters of Gerard Manley Hopkins to Robert Bridges*, Oxford 1935, pp. 27–28; Swinburne, *Correspondence*, ii, 151; *Newspaper Warfare! The Grand Ink Battle between Figaro and Reynold's Newspaper*, 1872; Philip Guedalla (ed.), *The Queen and Mr Gladstone*, 2 vols, 1933, i, 304; Elizabeth Longford, *Victoria R.I.*, 1964, p. 384.

p.89   '... *unnoticed and uncontradicted.*' *T*, 9 November 1871, p. 6; *LQV(2)*, ii, 164–65.

p.90   '... *to save us.*' *LQV(2)*, ii, 171; *T*, 11 December 1871, p. 9; *LQV(2)*, ii, 179; *T*, 30 December 1871, p. 7; Lee, *Edward VII*, i, 329.

p.90   '... *offered them up.*' *T*, 11 December 1871, p. 5; Kilvert, *Diary*, p. 158; *T*, 24 November 1871, p. 5.

p.91   '... *grasp of reality.*' *Ibid.*, 13 February 1872; Guedalla, *Queen and Gladstone*, i, 321; *M&B*, ii, 523.

CHAPTER 6

p.92   '... *of the world.*' *T*, 19 June 1871, p. 9; 4 April 1872, p. 5; 25 June 1872, pp. 7–8.

p.93   '... *met and mastered.*' H.Grisewood (ed.), *Ideas and Beliefs of the Victorians*, 1949, p. 76; *Poems of Tennyson*, pp. 1755–56.

p.93   '... *noted Charles Dodgson.*, *CR*, May 1872, p. 738; *T*, 8 April 1871, p. 5; Chadwick, *Victorian Church*, ii, 25; *AR*, 1872, p. 370; Green, *Diaries of Lewis Carroll*, ii, 334.

p.94   '... *of public prayers.*' Eliza Lynn Linton, *Joshua Davidson*, 1872, pp. 267–74; *FR*, August 1872, pp. 125–35.

p.94   '... *of the universe.*' John Burke (ed.), *Jowitt's Dictionary of English Law*, 2 vols, 2nd edn 1977, i, 33; Kilvert, *Diary*, p. 204; *WR*, July 1872, pp. 97–98.

p.95   '... *and scientific scepticism.*' Rev. F.G.Lee, *The Other World; or Glimpses of the Supernatural*, 2 vols, 1875; *T*, 19 April 1876, p. 4.

p.96   '... *he warned.*' Winthrop S.Hudson, *Religion in America*, 3rd edn New York 1981, pp. 249, 265–66, 268–69.

p.96   '... *witnessed in Manchester.*' *Ibid.*, p. 267.

p.97   '... *a nightmarish fanaticism.*' Allen W.Trelease, *White Terror: the Ku Klux Klan Conspiracy and Southern Reconstruction*, Westport Conn. 1979, pp. 19, 51, 88, 202; Angle and Miers, *Tragic Years*, i, 462.

p.97   '... *English-speaking peoples.*' Robin May and Joseph G.Rosa, *Cowboy: the Man and the Myth*, 1980.

p.98   '... *on the rocks:*' *T*, 5 February 1874, p. 9; 16 February 1874, p. 9.

p.98   '... *lie too deep.*' *CR*, August 1874, p. 358.

p.99   '... *were being fulfilled.*' J.Cumming, *The Seventh Vial, or the Time of Troubles Begun*, 1870.

p.99   '... *Scrap Books, etc.*' *Notes and Queries*, 4th series vol. xi (26 April 1873), p. 355; *The end of the world and other remarkable prophecies*, 1872, pp. 4, 5.

p.100   '... *of the age.*' Charles Piazzi Smyth, *Our Inheritance in the Great Pyramid*, 1864, unnumbered page following title page.

p.100   '... *of biblical apocalypse.*' Smyth, *The Great Pyramid and the Royal Society*, 1874 (for his account of his differences with the Royal Society); *Great Pyramid*, 3rd edn 1877, pp. 569, 582.

p.100   '... *nations into infidelity.*' Smyth, *Great Pyramid*, 2nd edn 1874, p. 485.

p.102   '... *year of destiny.*' *"The End of the World" in 1881–2, according to Mother Shipton, the Great Pyramid of Ghizeh and other Ancient Prophecies related to Russia and Turkey*, 1880, pp. 5–6; *Palatine Note-Book*, Manchester April 1881, pp. 64–66; *"The End of the World" in 1881–2*, pp. 42–44.

p.102   '... *frightful to witness.*' *Ibid.*, pp. 50, 58; C.A.Grimmer, *The Voice of the Stars*, London and Manchester 1880, pp. 7, 9, 11.

p.102   '... *of his sovereign.*' *M&B*, ii, 633, 657; *LQV(2)*, ii, 290.

p.103   '... *Battle of Armageddon.*' *M&B*, ii, 665, 670, 685; *CR*, June 1876, p. 26.

p.103   '... *of Gloucester anxiously.*' Joyce Coombs, *Judgment on Hatcham: the History of a Religious Struggle 1877–1886*, 1969, pp. 63–64; *AR*, 1877, p. 50; *NC*, July 1877, pp. 753–73.

p.104   '... *walls of heaven.*' *CR*, January 1874, p. 326.

p.104   '... *inherit eternal life.*' *T*, 25 March 1874, p. 12.

p.104   '... *then publicly burned.*' *Ibid.*, 1 February 1875, p. 5; 4 February 1875, p. 12; 20 February 1875, p. 9.

p.105   '... *their very midst.*' *Ibid.*, 14 October 1874, p. 5; *AR*, 1878, pp. 127–28.

p.105   '... *one for undertakers.*' *T*, 20 May 1875, p. 10; 14 June 1875, p. 12; 17 June 1875, p. 12; 18 June 1875, p. 13.

p.106   '... *a draper's shop.*' *Ibid.*, 22 March 1875, p. 11; *LQV(2)*, ii, 385–86; *T*, 19 March 1875, p. 8; 21 June 1875, p. 9; 22 June 1875, pp. 6, 8; 23 June 1875, p. 12.

p.106   '... *politics of fantasy.*' *M&B*, ii, 731; *T*, 23 July 1874, p. 10.

p.107 '... *told the Queen.*' Kinley Roby, *The King, the Press and the People*, 1975, pp. 197–98; Allen Andrews, *The Follies of King Edward VII*, 1975, pp. 126–35; Anon (S.O.Beeton, A.A.Dowty, E.Jerrold), *Edward the Seventh*, 1876; Lady Betty Balfour (ed.), *Personal and Literary Letters of Robert, first Earl of Lytton*, 2 vols, 1906, ii, 3–6.

p.107 '... *Canal, four millions.*' *M&B*, ii, 789; *Punch*, vol. lxix, p. 245 (11 December 1875); *AR*, 1876, pp. 27–28.

p.108 '... *a political clown.*' *LQV(2)*, ii, 480, 567–68; R.T.Shannon, *Gladstone and the Bulgarian Agitation 1876*, 1963, p. 64; R.W.Seton-Watson, *Disraeli, Gladstone and the Eastern Question*, reprint 1971, p. 203.

p.109 '... *than ever before:*' Shannon, *Bulgarian Agitation*, pp. 200, 14; *CR*, October 1876, pp. 855–65.

p.109 '... *cast its spell.*' *H*, ccxxxvii, 769; *Daily News*, 13 March 1878, pp. 3–4; Longford, *Victoria*, p. 412; *T*, 13 September 1878, p. 9.

p.110 '... *were 'somewhat fanciful'.*' Kilvert, *Diary*, p. 327; *M&B*, ii, 1276, 1371.

p.110 '... *for the reduction.*' Herman Ausubel, *In Hard Times: Reformers among the late Victorians*, Westport Conn. 1960, p. 22; *T*, 7 February 1881, p. 5; Ausubel, *Hard Times*, p. 29.

p.110 '... *faculty of wonder.*' Morley, *Gladstone*, ii, 198; *NC*, August 1878, p. 910.

p.111 '... *a new dawn.*' *LQV(2)*, iii, 73; Morley, *Gladstone*, ii, 223.

CHAPTER 7

p.113 '... *struggle against science.*' J.W.Draper, *History of the Conflict between Religion and Science*, New York 1873, pp. 352.

p.114 '... *of modern science.*' *Ibid.*, pp. v, xi, xv, 327, 367; *T*, 20 August 1874, pp. 4–5; *AR*, 1874, pp. 375–77.

p.114 '... *had been written:*' Countess of Caithness, *Old Truths in a new light*, 1876, pp. 9, 12; Edward Maitland, *England and Islam*, 1877, pp. 198–99.

p.114 '... *I can speak!*' Edward Maitland, *Anna Kingsford: her life, letters, diary and work*, 2 vols, 1896, i, 107.

p.115 '... *the high towers.*' *Ibid.*, i, 250–52, 1–11, 279.

p.115 '... *of my vision.*' *Ibid.*, i, 282; Maitland, *England and Islam*, p. 98; Maitland, *Kingsford*, i, 415, 427.

p.116 '... *of the Enlightenment.*' *Ibid.*, i, 229, 236–38, 215, 15; ii, 3–4, 50.

p.117 '... *branch in Paris.*' John Symonds, *Madame Blavatsky*, 1959, p. 76; S.B.Liljegren *Bulwer-Lytton's novels and Isis Unveiled*, Cambridge Mass. 1957, pp. 11–13; Symonds, *Blavatsky*, p. 66; Josephine Ransom, *The Direction of the Theosophical Society by the Masters of Wisdom*, 1942, p. 15; Maitland, *Kingsford*, ii, 119; James Webb, *The Flight from Reason*, 1971, p. 181.

p.117 '... *were at work.*' *T*, 18 April 1878, p. 4.

p.117 '... *in June 1881.*' Symonds, *Blavatsky*, pp. 103, 108–10, 150.

p.118 '... *from the tomb?*' *Ibid.*, p. 90; *SR*, 25 June 1881, p. 823; Helen

Zimmern, *Schopenhauer*, 1876, p. x; Lady Betty Balfour, *Letters of Lytton*, ii, 275–76; *CR*, February 1876, pp. 369–76.

p.119 '... *its varied contributors:*' *Metaphysical Society Papers*, n.d. (1880?), contains 44 papers given between 1869 and 1879.

p.119 '... *gulf of Doubt.*' *NC*, March 1877, p. 1; *Tennyson's Poems*, p. 1239.

p.119 '... *of seven o'clock.*' Martin Gardner (ed.), *The Annotated Snark*, rev'd edn 1974, p. 45; R.A.J,Walling (ed.), *The Diaries of John Bright*, 1930, pp. 456–57; Sir T.Wemyss Reid, *Life, Letters and Friendships of Richard Monckton Milnes, first Lord Houghton*, 2 vols, 1890, ii, 359.

p.120 '... *ever under it.*' *NC*, May 1877, p. 539; September 1877, p. 273.

p.120 '... *was a Boojum.*' Gardner, *Annotated Snark*, pp. 55–56, 93–96, 16.

p.121 '... *of all crimes:*' Middleton, *Nietzsche Letters*, pp. 178, 173.

p.121 '... *have killed him.*' Nietzsche, *The Gay Science*, cited in Cruickshank, *Modern European Mind*, pp. 80–81.

p.122 '... *not itself still.*' Maitland, *Kingsford*, i, 416; *Dictionary of American Biography*, new edn 1957–64, vi, 593–96.

p.122 '... *remained equally unfulfilled.*' Hopkins, *Letters to Bridges*, pp. lxxi, 116; *AR*, 1881, pp. 5, 6, 9, 11, 14–15; *Diaries of Bright*, pp. 456–57.

p.123 '... *body was gone.*' *Ibid.*, p. 460; *T*, 3 December 1881, p. 6.

p.123 '... *to be apprehended.*' *T*, 10 December 1881, p. 6; 9 December 1881, p. 8; *AR*, 1882, pp. 11–12; *T*, 20 July 1882, p. 6.

p.124 '... *of five years.*' *T*, 26 September 1882, p. 10; 25 October 1882, p. 5.

p.124 '... *by Professor Smyth.*' *Proceedings of the Society for Psychical Research, 1883*, pp. v–xvii; *H*, cclxvi, 1234–65.

p.125 '... *storm of hissing.*' Swinburne, *Correspondence*, v, 13; A.F.Hort (ed.), *Life and Letters of F.J.A.Hort*, 2 vols, 1896, ii, 290, 291; *T*, 6 March 1883, p. 12.

p.126 '... *Uncle Tom's Cabin.*' Josiah Strong, *Our Country*, ed. Jurgen Herbst, Cambridge Mass. 1963, pp. 218, 133, 225–26, ix.

p.126 '... *Darwin looked forward.*' Himmelfarb, *Darwinism*, pp. 343, 407; *H*, cclxv, 216–19.

CHAPTER 8

p.128 '... *the tennis lawn.*' S.Colvin (ed.), *The Letters of Robert Louis Stevenson*, 4 vols, 5th edn 1919, ii, 39, 213n., 49–51; *SR*, 11 November 1882, pp. 633–34.

p.129 '... *as the sciences:*' Colvin, *Letters of Stevenson*, i, 53–54, 224; ii, 123.

p.129 '... *flowing and emasculated.*' *Longman's Magazine*, November 1884, p. 142.

p.130 '... *the surrounding darkness:*' *FR*, July 1891, p. 109.

p.130 '... *anticipated – darkness still.*' *Ibid.*, p. 111.

p.130 '... *of its destiny.*' *T*, 20 November 1891, p. 6; 27 November 1891, p. 10.

p.131 '... *books and dreams.*' *FR*, March 1887, p. 417; *WR*, December 1887,

NOTES TO PAGES 132–142

pp. 840–49; *CR,* April 1890, p. 485; April 1894, pp. 225–26; November 1887, pp. 683–93; Amy Cruse, *The Victorians and their Books,* 1935, pp. 308–9; *CR,* li, February 1887, p. 173.

p.132 '...*fiction's onward march.' WR,* October 1872, pp. 333–77; *CR,* March 1881, p. 398; William James, *Principles of Psychology,* 2 vols, 1890, i, 125.

p.132 '...*to better things.' The Bookseller,* 28 February 1867, pp. 121–23; *Five Years Penal Servitude by One who has Endured it,* 1877, p. 67.

p.133 '...*well-trained athletic schoolboys.' CR,* March 1881, pp. 385–402; *Boy's Own Paper,* vols i–iv, 1879–82.

p.133 '...*and scriptural readings.'* Altick, *Common Reader,* pp. 361–62.

p.134 '...*the contemporary idealist.'* Thomas Hughes, *The Manliness of Christ,* 1879; Colvin, *Letters of Stevenson,* i, 224, 209.

p.134 '...*daubed with dishonour.' Ibid.,* ii, 228–29.

p.135 '...*touch of life.' Ibid.,* ii, 274–76.

p.135 '...*danger and adversity.' CR,* April 1887, pp. 473, 477; Colvin, *Letters of Stevenson,* i, 285–86.

p.136 '...*to vital spirits.' Congressional Record,* Vol. xiii, pt 1, Washington 1882, pp. 834, 856; Rupert Hart-Davis (ed.), *The Letters of Oscar Wilde,* 1962, pp. 112–15.

p.136 '...*been there before,' CR,* February 1887, p. 175; Colvin, *Letters of Stevenson,* ii, 274–76, 228; Kenneth S.Lynn (ed.), *Huckleberry Finn: Texts, Sources and Criticism,* New York 1961, pp. 199, 202, 141.

p.137 '...*made for health.'* Richard Jefferies, *Bevis: the Story of a Boy,* illustrated edn 1932, pp. 478–79; *T,* 7 November 1884, p. 11; Maurice Hewlett, *The Forest Lovers,* 1898, p. 240.

p.138 '...*periodical Christian Union.'* Hudson, *Religion in America,* p. 311.

p.138 '...*no real grievance.' CR,* November 1887, pp. 731–32.

p.138 '...*foot in Ireland.' AR,* 1882, pp. 10, 21; *LQV(2),* ii, 293, 298–9; *T,* 13 January 1880, p. 6.

p.139 '...*of its power.' LQV(2),* iii, 438; *T,* 11 February 1886, p. 6.

p.139 '...*had been fulfilled.' Poems of Tennyson,* p. 699.

p.140 '...*an earlier age.' Ibid.,* pp. 1362, 1365; *S,* 18 December 1886, pp. 1706–7; *NC,* January 1887, p. 18. For an illuminating discussion of the confrontation between Tennyson and Gladstone see Charles Morgan, *Liberties of the Mind,* 1951, pp. 18–34.

p.140 '...*appreciated by Whitman.' The Collected Writings of Walt Whitman: The Correspondence, Volume IV 1886–89,* New York 1969, p. 58; J.D.Jump (ed.), *Tennyson: the Critical Heritage,* 1967, pp. 348–49; Robert Buchanan, *A Look Round Literature,* 1887, p. 345.

p.141 '...*of the Will.' Poems of Tennyson,* pp. 1365, 1369.

p.142 '...*a well-intentioned earthquake.' T,* 26 February 1887, p. 7; Middleton, *Letters of Nietzsche,* pp. 262–63.

p.142 '...*to be achieved.' T,* 24 February 1887, p. 9.

CHAPTER 9

p.143 '... *of the world.*' *FR*, February 1887, p. 224; June 1887, pp. 885–92; May 1887, p. 656; December 1886, p. 802.

p.144 '... *had begotten them.*' James Thomson, *Satires and Profanities*, 1884, p. 108.

p.144 '... *dreams are true.*' Himmelfarb, *Darwinian Revolution*, pp. 336–37, 190; *Poems of Tennyson*, pp. 257–58.

p.145 '... *and some free.*' G.T.W.Patrick (ed.), *Heraclitus of Ephesus: The Fragments on Nature*, Baltimore 1889, p. 1; O.Kulpe, *The Philosophy of the Present in Germany*, tr. G.T.W.Patrick and M.L.Patrick, 1913; *Heraclitus: Fragments*, p. 95.

p.145 '... *of the diamond.*' Middleton, *Letters of Nietzsche*, p. 335; W.H.Gardner and N.H.Mackenzie (eds), *The Poems of Gerard Manley Hopkins*, 4th edn 1967, pp. 105–6.

p.146 '... *current scientific orthodoxy.*' *FR*, June 1887, p. 884; *AR*, 1888, p. 79.

p.147 '... *matter for contrition.*' *FR*, January 1890, p. 116; Grant Allen, *The Evolution of the Idea of God*, 1897, pp. 433, 438; Reade, *Martyrdom*, pp. 446–47.

p.147 '... *his invariable laws.*' *T*, 9 August 1894, p. 6; 10 August 1894, p. 12; 11 August 1894, p. 11; 18 August 1894, p. 12.

p.148 '... *you at dinner.*' Chadwick, *Victorian Church*, i, 102, 112.

p.148 '... *devout was undented.*' *Ibid.*, ii, 224; *T*, 27 December 1888, p. 10; 31 December 1888, p. 12; 9 January 1889, p. 9; 22 March 1889, p. 10; 29 March 1889, p. 12; 30 March 1889, p. 12; 2 April 1889, p. 4; Chadwick, *Victorian Church*, ii, 224, 232.

p.149 '... *only true centre.*' Rev. J.H.Barrows (ed.), *The World's Parliament of Religions*, 2 vols, Chicago 1893, i, 14, 21–22, 62, 112, 25.

p.150 '... *on American soil.*' *Ibid.*, i, 442, 592; ii, 1250–51; i, 185, 160.

p.150 '... *supposed to rest.*' *Ibid.*, i, 45; *T*, 9 January 1894, p. 8.

p.151 '... *even Tennyson's expectations.*' Maitland, *Kingsford*, ii, 291.

p.152 '... *far from orthodox.*' Hart-Davis, *Letters of Oscar Wilde*, p. 291n.; Doyle, *Complete Long Stories*, pp. 131, 178, 137.

p.152 '... *of ordinary mortals.*' Doyle, *Complete Short Stories*, pp. 556, 569.

p.153 '... *was not supernatural.*' *Ibid.*, p. 55.

p.154 '... *own superhuman powers.*' *Ibid.*, pp. 121, 3.

p.154 '... *of social co-operation.*' *Blackwood's Magazine*, June 1895, p. 833; A.E. Hake, *Regeneration: a reply to Max Nordau*, 1895, p. 235; *FR*, February 1891, pp. 317, 319.

p.155 '... *satyr he was.*' Edward Carpenter, *Days with Walt Whitman*, 1906, p. 6; *Towards Democracy*, Manchester and London 1883, pp. 97, 98, 23; Henry Havelock Ellis, *The New Spirit*, 1890, p. 28; *My Life*, 1940, p. 82.

p.155 '... *but on sexuality.*' *FR*, March 1894, p. 390.

p.156 '... *to the next.*' *T*, 30 August 1890, p. 4.

p.156 '... *under another name.' The Pagan Review*, No. 1, Rudgwick Sussex 15 August 1892; *FR*, March 1894, p. 384.

p.157 '... *in human affairs.'* Peter Green, *Kenneth Grahame*, 1959, p. 123; *CR*, November 1887, p. 690.

p.157 '... *over fifteen thousand.' Ibid.*, February 1887, p. 177; Altick, *Common Reader*, p. 237.

p.158 '... *early morning swim.'* C.Dukes, *The Preservation of Health as it is affected by Personal Habits such as Cleanliness, Temperance etc.*, 1885, pp. 150, 155, 161; Timothy d'Arch Smith, *Love in Earnest*, 1970, p. 87.

p.158 '... *in his place.'* Howard O.Sturgis, *Tim*, 1891, p. 159.

p.159 '... *That is all.'* Smith, *Love in Earnest*, pp. 13, 27; H.Montgomery Hyde, *The Cleveland Street Scandal*, 1976; Colin Simpson, Lewis Chester, David Leitch, *The Cleveland Street Affair*, Boston 1976; *FR*, March 1891, p. 480.

p.159 '... *admitted or understood.'* Smith, *Love in Earnest*, p. 182; *Pagan Review*, August 1892, pp. 5–18.

p.160 '... *was Oscar Wilde.'* Max Nordau, *Degeneration: translated from the second German edition*, 1895, p. 2; *The Conventional Lies of our Civilization*, Chicago 1884, p. 63; *Degeneration*, pp. 450, 317.

p.160 '... *orthodox had anticipated.'* Smith, *Love in Earnest*, pp. 110, 155; 'Stuart Mason' (Christopher Millard), *Oscar Wilde: Art and Morality*, 2nd edn 1912, pp. 137–38; Hart-Davis, *Letters of Wilde*, 1962, pp. 380, 382, 383, 384, 389.

CHAPTER 10

p.161 '... *most indubitably right.'* Mason, *Oscar Wilde*, pp. 203–19; Smith, *Love in Earnest*, p. 59; Mason, *Oscar Wilde*, p. 139; *Blackwood's Magazine*, June 1895, p. 843–44. The *National Observer* review of *Degeneration* is quoted, together with others, at the end of Heinemann's 1895 edition of *Conventional Lies*.

p.162 '... *instead of condemnation.'* Hake, *Regeneration*, p. 78; Nordau, *Conventional Lies*, pp. 55ff.; Hart-Davis, *Letters of Wilde*, p. 402.

p.162 '... *of Dr Jekyll.'* Mason, *Oscar Wilde*, p. 201.

p.163 '... *with a kiss.'* S.Aidan Reynolds and William Charlton, *Arthur Machen*, 1963, pp. 43–46; Arthur Machen, *The Great God Pan*, 1894, p. 93; Eric, Count Stenbock, *Studies of Death*, 1894, pp. 120–47; *The Spirit Lamp*, Oxford June 1893, pp. 52–68; Julian Osgood Field, *Aut Diabolus aut Nihil*, 1894, pp. 145–226.

p.164 '... *actually done so.' S*, 14 September 1895, p. 232; William Tebb and Edward Perry Vollum, *Premature Burial*, 1896, pp. 242–43.

p.164 '... *to reduce it.'* Frederick Greenwood, *Imagination in Dreams and their study*, 1894, p. 113.

p.165 '... *supremacy of sex.'* Edward Carpenter, *Homogenic Love*, Manchester 1895, p. 45.

p.165 '... *presage cosmic disaster.*' *The Collected Works of Ambrose Bierce*, 12 vols, New York 1966, iii, 20, 29–30; x, 127–31.

p.166 '... *menace of Dracula.*' Bram Stoker, *Dracula*, 1897, pp. 5, 26, 280–81, 337.

p.167 '... *man's heart out.*' M.R.James, *More Ghost Stories of an Antiquary*, 1911, pp. v, 15.

p.167 '... *been a hoax.*' Henry Charles Lea, *Léo Taxil, Diana Vaughan et l'Église Romaine: histoire d'une mystification*, Paris 1901, pp. 18–24.

p.168 '... *powers of darkness.*' *CR*, May 1897, pp. 694–710; A.E.Waite, *Devil-Worship in France*, 1896; Robert Baldick, *The Life of J.-K.Huysmans*, Oxford 1955, pp. 140, 154; John Symonds, *The Great Beast: the Life and Magick of Aleister Crowley*, 1971, p. 16.

p.168 '... *of the world.*' Ellic Howe, *The Magicians of the Golden Dawn 1887–1923*, 1972, p. 50, 52; Reynolds and Charlton, *Arthur Machen*, pp. 70–79; Arthur Machen, *The Hill of Dreams*, 1907, pp. 113–15; Jean Overton Fuller, *The Magical Dilemma of Victor Neuburg*, 1965, pp. 148–50; Reynolds and Charlton, *Arthur Machen*, pp. 73, 106–7.

p.168 '... *into Popish bondage.*' Walter Walsh, *The Secret Work of the Ritualists*, 1894, pp. 43, 11.

p.169 '... *of public opinion.*' Sister Mary Agnes (Miss J.M.Povey), *Nunnery Life in the Church of England*, 1890, p. 99; Walter Walsh, *Secret History of the Oxford Movement*, 1897, pp. 38–39; Father Michael, O.S.B., *Father Ignatius in America*, 1893, pp. 101–3, 237.

p.169 '... *to appeal to.*' Hudson, *Religion in America*, pp. 257–61, 249; *CR*, February 1897, pp. 276–79; *Dictionary of National Biography Supplement 1901–1911 Volume II*, 1912, pp. 389–90; *T*, 17 September 1898, p. 9.

p.170 '... *some sort American.*' R.L.Green (ed.), *Kipling: the Critical Heritage*, 1971, pp. 192–93.

p.171 '... *in the ear.*' Allan Nevins, *The Letters of Grover Cleveland*, Boston and New York 1933, p. 419; Charles Carrington, *Kipling*, 3rd rev'd edn 1978, pp. 283, 297; R.W.Sallman and L.Gilkes (eds), *Letters of Stephen Crane*, 1960, pp. 5, 43n.; S.Bradley, R.C.Beatty and E.H.Long (eds), *The Red Badge of Courage; an annotated text*, New York 1962, p. 196.

p.171 '... *the British Empire.*' *SR*, 11 January 1896, p. 44; *FR*, August 1897, pp. 286–96.

p.172 '... *mission of America.*' *T*, 14 May 1898, p. 12; Charles S.Olcott, *Life of McKinley*, Boston 1916, ii, 110–11; *Congressional Record*, Vol. XXXIII, pt 1, Washington 1900, pp. 704–12.

p.172 '... *hordes of evil.*' *T*, 11 January 1896, p. 9; 17 July 1897, p. 13; M.Cohen (ed.), *Rudyard Kipling to Rider Haggard: the record of a Friendship*, 1965, pp. 34–37; *AR*, 1900, p. 2.

p.173 '... *the new king:*' *Blackwood's Magazine*, June 1895, p. 842; Bernard Bergonzi, *The Turn of the Century*, 1973, p. 39; *AR*, 1899, p. 76; 1901, pp. 9, 25.

p.173 '... *of that wonder.*' Carrington, *Kipling*, pp. 277–78; Green, *Grahame*, pp. 301–2.

p.174 '... *to destroy Dracula.*' *The Works of Bernard Shaw*, Vol. IX, 1930, p. xxii; R.L.Green, *A.E.W.Mason*, 1952, p. 60; Stoker, *Dracula*, pp. 152, 389.

p.174 '... *death in battle:*' Evelyn Sharp, *Unfinished Adventure*, 1933, p. 57; *Harper's Magazine*, July 1889, pp. 241–44.

p.174 '... *rather than sorrow?*' H.A.Vachell, *The Hill*, 1905, p. 313.

p.175 '... *even your play.*' *T*, 4 January 1902, p. 9.

p.175 '... *hold on life?*' H.G.Wells, *The Time Machine*, 1895, p. 27.

p.176 '... *built for rabbits!*' H.G.Wells, *The War of the Worlds*, 1898, p. 195.

p.176 '... *the old wolf-cry.*' H.G.Wells, *The War in the Air and particularly how Mr Bert Smallways fared while it lasted*, 1908, pp. 336–67; Jack London, *The Call of the Wild*, 1903, pp. 61, 90, 91.

CHAPTER 11

p.177 '... *one outraged reviewer.*' H.G.Wells, *The Future in America*, 1906, pp. 9, 354, 78, 154, 355; *The Days of the Comet*, 1906, p. 189; *Experiment in Autobiography*, 2 vols, 1934, ii, 480.

p.178 '... *complete the work.*' *T*, 10 February 1910, p. 11; Brian Harpur, *The Official Halley's Comet Book*, 1985, pp. 44, 51, 44.

p.178 '... *government and religion.*' *Ibid.*, p. 40; *Collected Essays by Virginia Woolf*, 2 vols, 1966, i, 320; Harriette and Homer Curtiss, *The Philosophy of War*, Los Angeles and San Francisco 1914, pp. 33, 38 (passage written May 1909, revised September 1914).

p.179 '... *claim to it.*' Rev. F.W.Orde Ward, *The World's Quest*, 1908, pp. 1, 223; *'Falling Upwards': Christ the Key to the Riddle of the Cosmos*, 1911, p. 5; *Quest*, p. 1.

p.179 '... *doing for physics.*' Henri Bergson, *Creative Evolution*, tr. A.Mitchell, 1911, pp. x, 322–23.

p.180 '... *the Society's imprint.*' *Quest*, October 1909, pp. 29–43; April 1912, p. 401; James H.Hyslop, *Psychical Research and Survival*, 1913.

p.180 '... *classes of society.*' *Quest*, January 1916, p. 320; R.L.Green, *A.E.W. Mason*, 1952, p. 59; *FR*, January 1912, p. 161; *AR*, 1904, p. 36.

p.181 '... *continuous and progressive.*' *FR*, January 1912, p. 166; Sir Oliver Lodge, *The Survival of Man*, 1909, p. 339; F.W.H.Myers, *Human Personality and its Survival of Bodily Death*, 2 vols, 1903, ii, 288, 281.

p.181 '... *been washed away.*' *FR*, January 1912, pp. 166, 170, 167, 161.

p.182 '... *as in fiction.*' *T*, 27 April 1907, p. 14; 1 May 1907, p. 4.

p.183 '... *and the like.*' Emma Jung and Marie-Louise von Franz, *The Grail Legend*, tr. Andrea Dykes, 1971, pp. 401–7; *Quest*, October 1909, pp. 125–39, 91–107; Reynolds and Charlton, *Arthur Machen*, pp. 101, 103–4, 116.

p.183 '... *of Life itself.*' *Quest*, October 1909, pp. 170–74; April 1910,

p. 524; Jessie L. Weston, *The Quest of the Holy Grail*, 1913, p. 138; *Quest*, October 1916, pp. 127–39.

p.184 '... *of Virginia Woolf.*' Jung and von Franz, *Grail Legend*, pp. 150–51; D.S. Thatcher, *Nietzsche in England 1890–1914*, Toronto 1970, p. 41; *Quest*, April 1911, pp. 417–37.

p.185 '... *his trusty companion.*' Hilaire Belloc, *Hills and the Sea*, 1906, pp. x, xii–xiii.

p.186 '... *her son's murderer.*' *FR*, June 1912, p. 116; *The Treasury*, January 1916, pp. 323–29; Roland Huntford, *Scott and Amundsen*, 1979, p. 559.

p.186 '... *another to suicide.*' Huntford, *Scott and Amundsen*, pp. 554–55; Andrew Birkin, *J.M. Barrie and the Lost Boys*, 1979, p. 209.

p.186 '... *over the other.*' Huntford, *Scott and Amundsen*, p. 543.

p.187 '... *agony without flinching.*' *T*, 1Q June 1908, p. 10; J.R. Ackerley, *My Father and myself*, 1968, p. 53; Charles M. Doughty, *The Cliffs*, 1909, pp. 223–24.

p.188 '... *substance and reality.*' James J. Gibson (ed.), *The Variorum Edition of the Complete Poems of Thomas Hardy*, 1979, pp. 97–99; *FR*, March 1912, pp. 397–99.

p.189 '... *of his existence.*' Ibid.

p.189 '... *had been abolished.*' Ray Abrams, *Preachers Present Arms: a study of the war-time attitudes and activities of the churches and clergy in the United States 1914–1918*, Philadelphia 1933, p. 9.

p.189 '... *none was American.*' *T*, 5 October 1912, p. 3; Georges Haupt, *La Deuxième Internationale 1889–1914*, Paris and the Hague 1964.

p.190 '... *on 4 August.*' *T*, 19 October 1912, p. 6; 19 November 1912, p. 4; 22 October 1912, p. 5; *AR*, 1911, p. 4; *T*, 15 October 1912, p. 6; Abrams, *Preachers Present Arms*, p. 9.

p.190 '... *of bourgeois imagining.*' *T*, 29 July 1914, p. 7; 26 September 1914, p. 6.

p.191 '... *warlord's greatest strength.*' *Quest*, October 1914, pp. 160–63; April 1915, p. 519; *T*, 3 August 1914, p. 8.

p.191 '... *in the trenches.*' *T*, 6 August 1914, p. 5; 29 August 1914, p. 5; Louis P. Lochner, *America's Don Quixote*, 1924, pp. 4–19.

p.192 '... *to Arthur Machen.*' John Terraine, 'A Comfortless Mythology', *T*, 11 November 1978, p. 8; Ralph Shirley, *The Angel Warriors of Mons*, 1915, p. 15; Arthur Machen, *The Bowmen and other Legends of the War*, 1915; *The Treasury*, October 1915, p. 46; Harold Begbie, *On the side of the angels: a reply to Arthur Machen*, 1915, p. 12.

p.192 '... *destruction of Christianity.*' *Is there a Hell? A Symposium by Leaders of Religious Thought*, 1913, p. 4; *T*, 8 August 1914, p. 9; *Occult Review*, September 1914, p. 355; F.J. Foakes-Jackson (ed.), *The Faith and the War*, 1915, p. 234; Cate Haste, *Keep the Home Fires Burning: propaganda in the First World War*, 1977, pp. 79–83.

p.193 '... *die by inches.*' Henri Bergson, *The Meaning of the War*, 1915, pp. 37–38; Jessie L. Weston, *Germany's Crime against France*, 1915, pp. 17,

27; *Quest*, January 1917, pp. 256, 259, 262; January 1915, pp. 244–49, 203–6.

p.193 '... *the broken body.*' *The Treasury*, January 1916, pp. 323–29; *Quest*, April 1917, pp. 452–53; F.W.Orde Ward, *The Last Crusade: Patriotic Poems*, 1917, pp. 7, 19.

p.194 '... *topography of Golgotha.*' Harold Owen and John Bell (eds), *Wilfred Owen: Collected Letters*, 1967, p. 562.

p.194 '... *his superior officers.*' John Hughes, 'The evidence for war objectors' "crucifixion"', *Sunday Times*, 19 October 1975, p. 11.

p.194 '... *what they do.*' *Ibid.*; Owen Wister, *The Pentecost of Calamity*, 1915, pp. 98, 121; Abrams, *Preachers Present Arms*, p. 41; C.L.Droste, *Germany's Golgotha*, New York 1917, p. 22.

p.195 '... *mere armed forces.*' Abrams, *Preachers Present Arms*, pp. 27; *CR*, March 1915, pp. 339–45; Abrams, *Preachers Present Arms*, pp. 28, 37–38, 59.

p.196 '... *the material plane.*' *Occult Review*, January 1916; Sir Oliver Lodge, *Raymond*, 1916, p. 249; Hereward Carrington, *Psychical Phenomena and the War*, 1918, p. 251; *Occult Review*, January 1916, p. 39.

p.196 '... *needs of man.*' C.E.Montague, *Disenchantment*, 1922, p. 71; Edmund Blunden (ed.), *The Poems of Wilfred Owen*, 1931, p. 57.

p.197 '... *he survived it.*' Symonds, *Great Beast*, pp. 203–4; Erich Fromm, *The Anatomy of Human Destructiveness*, 1977, pp. 243–44; Arthur Koestler, 'What's Wrong With Us?', *Observer Review*, 28 April 1968, p. 25; Nigel Davies, *Human Sacrifice in history and today*, 1981.

p.197 '... *more than human.*' *T*, 26 October 1920, p. 10.

p.198 '... *transfigured and sanctified.*' Sir Philip Gibbs, *The Realities of War*, 1920, p. 84; *Illustrated London News*, 20 November 1920, p. 806.

p.198 '... *God's funeral procession.*' *The Treasury*, May 1917, p. 100; Laurence Housman (ed.), *War Letters of fallen Englishmen*, 1930, p. 214; *T*, 18 November 1919, p. 9.

POSTSCRIPT

p.199 '... *bloom this year?*' Valerie Eliot (ed.), *The Waste Land: facsimile and transcript*, 1971, pp. xxii, 95.

p.200 '... *howl and expired.*' *Ibid.*, pp. xxii, 1; Edward L.Gardner, *Fairies: the Cottingley Photographs and their sequel*, 2nd edn 1951, p. 9; Leonard Cottrell, *The Lost Pharaohs*, 1976, pp. 180–81.

p.201 '... *become whole again.*' *T*, 4 June 1919, p. 11.

INDEX

A Study in Scarlet 151, 153, 155
'Abide with me' 21, 23, 35
abolitionists 75; *see also* slavery
absolute space 129
absolute time 129
acts of God 94; *see also* earthquakes; natural disasters
Adam and Eve 43; *see also* creation myth
adventure 141, 186
adversity 135
afterlife, belief in 68
age of miracles 122
Age of Reason 1
Allen, Grant 146, 147, 156
Allies, First World War 194
Albert, Prince Consort 35, 85, 95
  death of 38
America 16
anaesthesia 39, 40, 44; *see also* pain, death of
anarchists, American 138
anarchy 69, 84
ancient Egypt 64, 101
angels 5–6, 9, 11
Angels of Mons 5, 6, 191
Anglican creed 23
Anglo-American friendship 171
Anglo-Catholicism 168
Antichrist 9, 11, 12, 16, 26, 29, 32, 33, 36, 37, 73, 192
anti-Catholic riots 84

Anti-Interment in Towns Association 22
apocalypse 13, 72
appearance 2, 30, 112
Apollo 67, 69, 70, 155
architecture 9
Ariès, Phillipe 42
Armageddon 16, 36, 177
Armistice Day 198
Aristotle 70
Artist and Journal of Home Culture 159
Arthur, President 135
Arundel, Earl of 26
asceticism 134, 153, 155
Ashley, Lord 14, 15; *see also* Shaftesbury, Earl of
aspiration, Christian 183–4
astral body 117
atheism 2, 9, 12, 96, 148
  American 19
aurora borealis 87
Austin, Alfred 172

Baird, Robert 74
Balfour, Arthur 124, 130, 131
Balkan Question 108
Balkan War 189
Ballantyne, R.M. 132
Bank Holidays 92
barbarity 40
Baring-Gould, Sabine 24, 60, 64, 82
Barrie, J.M. 18, 186
Bath, Marquis of 106

'Battle Hymn of the Republic' 81, 95
Beaconsfield, Lord 109, 110, 115
    death of 122
    see also Disraeli, Benjamin
Beard, J.R. 28
Beecher, Henry Ward 95–6, 97
Belloc, Hilaire 185
Bennett, Arnold 200
Benson, Bishop (later Archbishop)
    124–5, 148, 149, 150
Bergsonian view of universe 182
Berkley, Theresa 50
Bible Communism 30, 32
biblical authority 10, 42, 147
biblical criticism 46
biblical revelation 146
Bierce, Ambrose 165, 188
bigotry 26
birching 42
Birth of Tragedy, The 70, 71; *see also*
    Nietzsche, Friedrich
Bishop, Mrs 74, 76
black Americans 41–2
black magic 167
Black Mass 167
Blackwood, Algernon 166, 193
Blackwood's Magazine 24, 34
blasphemy 12, 17, 32, 125
Blathwayt, Raymond 180, 181, 185
Blavatsky, Helena 116, 117, 118
blood 34
bodily resurrection 44
Boer War 170, 171, 188
Book of Werewolves 64
bourgeois society 21
boy vagabonds 136–7
Boy's Own Paper 132, 133
Bradlaugh, Charles 124
bravery 185
Bright, John 119, 122, 123
British Association for the
    Advancement of Science 52, 83,
    113, 147
British and Foreign Anti-Slavery
    Society 76

British and Foreign Bible Society
    189
Brooke, Rupert 175
Brotherhood of Luxor 116
Brougham, Lord 26–7
Brown, John 75, 79
Browning, Elizabeth Barrett 36, 56,
    71, 95
Brownson, Orestes 30, 77, 78
Buccleuch, Duke of 83
Buchanan, Robert 140
Buddha 117
Buffalo Bill 97
Bulwer-Lytton, Edward 116
Buren, Martin van 8
burial grounds 22
Burne-Jones, Edward 125
Burns, Anthony 75

Caine, Hall 33, 131
Caithness, Countess of 114, 115, 117
Call of the Wild, The 176
Cambridge, Duke of 90
Cambridge Ghost Society 125
capitalism 21
Capron, Eliab 34
Carlyle, Thomas 48
Carnegie, Andrew 131, 189, 191
Carpenter, Edward 154, 161, 165
Carrington, Hereward 195
Carroll, Lewis 119, 120; *see also*
    Dodgson, Charles
catalepsy 24
catastrophes 12
Catholic Book Society 12
Catholic tyranny 170
Catholicism, American 169; *see also*
    Irish immigration
cause and effect 129
chaos 143
Chartism 12, 15, 27
child sacrifice 167
childbirth 40
children, employment of 14, 15
chivalry 10, 158

chloroform 40, 42
Christ 155
  agony of 43, 187
  death of 144
  passion of 193
  resurrection of 145
  suffering of 40
'Christ aux Oliviers, Le' 18
Christian military duties 82
Christian morality 57
Christian orthodoxy 61
Christian Science 119
Christian World 161
Christianity 2, 5, 20
  American 16
church attendance 19, 148
Church of England 9, 10, 11, 26,
  44
Church of England Union 189, 190
Church Peace Union 189, 190
civilization, Christian 40
class conflict 52, 98
Cleopatra's Needle 109
Cleveland, President 170
Cleveland Street scandal 159
Cobbe, Frances Power 44, 55, 56, 61,
  64, 68, 69, 71, 76, 78
Coleridge, Samuel Taylor 2, 4
Coley, Rev. J. 104
collective unconsciousness 3
Colley, Rev. Thomas 181–2
common sense 182
Communism 20, 30, 88
Communist Manifesto 20, 21, 28
companionship in arms 158
comparative religion 47, 64, 69
compassion 15
competition 52
conceptual thought 179
conflict 52, 193
Congress of the Communist League
  20
consciousness 30
  general 32
Conservatism 86, 87

*Conventional Lies of our Civilization,
  The* 161
Cook, Rev. Flavel Smith 48–9
Cornford, Frances 175
Cornhill Magazine 36, 56
corporal punishment 42
Cory, William 158
cosmic change 177
cosmic disaster 165
cosmic synthesis 146
cowardice 174
creation 2, 4, 10, 53, 114
creation myth, Jewish 59
creative evolutionary process 192
creative intelligence 10
creativity 4
Crane, Stephen 170
Crawford, Lord 123–4
Crime and Punishment 135
Crimean War 35
'Crossing the Bar' 119
Crowley, Aleister 167
  as Antichrist 196
crucifix 43–4
cruelty 15, 137
Cuban revolt 170
Cumming, Dr John 13, 27, 29, 32,
  35, 36, 72, 73, 78, 83, 84, 95, 122

danger 135, 138
Daniel, Book of 16
Dante 53, 69
darkness 8, 13, 18, 21, 139, 141, 167
Darwin, Charles 52, 53, 58, 93, 126
dawn of reason 26
Day of Judgement 23
Day of National Prayer and
  Humiliation 73
Day of National Prayer and
  Supplication 89–90
Day of Pentecost 149
de Nerval, Gerard 18
de Sade, Marquis 54
death 2, 23
  fear of 24

death (*contd.*)
  pagan conception of 198
degeneracy 7
democracy 135, 139
Derby, Lord 84, 85
Descent of Man, The 93
desire, guilty 165
desire, physical 155
despair 17.
Desprez, P.S. 37
Devil 13, 45
  belief in 49
  disproof of 54
  as myth 192
devils 24
dialectical materialism 28, 29
dialectics 29
Diamond Jubilee 172, 174
Dickens, Charles 20, 42, 95
Dilke, Sir Charles 20, 89, 90, 105,
  111
Dionysus 62, 69, 144, 145, 155
disasters 101
disbelief 94
discipline 187
disembodied souls 35
disestablishment 86
Disraeli, Benjamin 65–6, 82, 84, 85,
  91, 100, 102–3, 106, 107
Divine Mystery 179
divine retribution 12
divine right of civilized nations 172
divine truth 148
divine wisdom 116
divinity 185
Dodgson, Charles 54, 93, 120; *see also*
  Carroll, Lewis
Doré, Gustave 53
Dostoevsky, Fëdor 135, 136
Douglas, Lord Alfred 160, 163, 168
Douglass, Frederick 41
dove, symbolism of 127
'Dover Beach' 69, 84
Doyle, Sir Arthur Conan 4, 6, 151,
  199

Dr Jekyll and Mr Hyde 162
Dracula 166, 174
Draper, Professor John William 86,
  113, 114
dreams 1, 4, 32, 54, 165
  interpretation of 198
Dwellers of the Threshold 116, 117,
  152
Dyer, Oliver 31

earthquakes 12, 13, 14, 120
  Cannes 141–2
Eastern mythology 64
Eastern Question 114
eccentricity 182
Ecclesiastical Commissioners 148
economic necessity 29
ecstasy 176
Edinburgh, Duke of 85
Edinburgh Review 28
Edward VII 178; *see also* Wales,
  Prince of
Edwards, Amelia 131
Einstein, Albert 31, 122, 146, 179,
  182
Eisler, Robert 183
elementals 200
Elijah 72
Eliot, T.S. 136, 183, 199, 200, 201
Elliott, Rev. Edward Bishop 11, 98
Ellis, Havelock 144, 154–5, 158, 165
emancipation of slaves 81
Emerson, Ralph Waldo 30, 60, 79
emotionalism 20
end of the world 99
Engels, Friedrich 20, 21, 66
England and Islam 114, 115, 117
English Review 26, 28
Ensor, Sir Charles 1, 2, 4
eroticism 159
Essays and Reviews 46, 51, 86
eternal punishment 47, 48
ether 39
Euston scandal 22
Evangelical Alliance 113

evil 15, 43, 162, 184, 186
  belief in 54
  power of 178
  supremacy of 144
expanding universe 122, 179; *see also*
  relativity, theory of
evolution 52

fact 1
faith 28
  decay of 9
faith healing 118
fallen angels 44
fallibility 141
fanaticism 9, 29, 31, 75
fancy 4
fantasy 1, 2, 3, 4, 6, 8, 47, 54, 71,
  99, 130, 165, 193
  politics of 110
  religious 87
  and thought 111
fear
  of death 24
  of the dead 24
Fenian Brotherhood 76
Fenian outrages 84, 85, 122
Fergusson, James 62
fertility cults 60, 62, 65, 184, 201
fiction 129, 130, 181
  popular 6
Fields, James 80, 81
Figuier, Guillaume 68–9
fin de siècle 172
financial crisis, 1857 77
Finney, Charles 75, 77
fire 13
  as cleansing agent 16
First World War 6, 190–4
flagellation 169
  erotic 50–1
Foote, G.W. 125
Ford, Henry 191
Forrest, General Nathan 96
fortitude 42
Four Feathers, The 173–4

Four Horsemen of the Apocalypse
  10, 35
Fowle, Thomas 93
Fox, Katherine and Margaretta 32
Franco-Prussian War 87
Frazer, Sir James 156
Free Religious Association 68, 69
Freemasonry 167, 169
Freethinker 125
French Revolution 8, 9, 11, 27, 29
Freud, Sigmund 3, 65, 164
Fromm, Erich 196

gallantry 5, 174
Galton, Francis 93–4
Genesis, Book of 10, 13, 43, 52, 101
geologists 13
George v 178, 186, 197
German metaphysics 28, 29, 59
German philosophy 46
ghosts 24, 165
Gladstone, William Ewart 9, 11, 81,
  86, 89, 90, 91, 100, 108, 110,
  111, 122, 134, 138, 140
God 2
  absence of 13, 17, 18, 192
  anger of 18, 165, 175, 178
  of battle 6, 188, 190, 193
  commandments of 29
  death of 18, 37, 121, 143, 159,
    165
  image of 7, 38
  imminent 141, 145
  knowledge of 9–10
  as movement 179
  of peace 190
  plan of 113
  transcendental 141, 145
  will of 29
godhead 32
'God's Funeral' 188
golden age 53
Golden Bough, The 156, 199
Golden Jubilee 135, 139, 143
goodness 145, 184, 186

Gordon, General 134; *see also* heroism; self-sacrifice
Goschen, George 130
Gosse, Edmund 135
Goya, Francisco 1, 2, 5, 11, 18, 27
Grace, W.G.; as heterosexual hero 174
Grahame, Kenneth 156
Great Exhibition 35
Great God Pan, The 163
Great Pyramid 99–100, 101, 102
Greece 67
Greek mythology 60
Green, Thomas Hill 129
Greenwood, Frederick 164
Greville, Charles 27
Grosvenor, Lord Robert 73
guardian angels 5

Haden, Francis Seymour 105
Haggard, Rider 131, 136, 151, 159, 172
Hake, Alfred 161
Hallam, Arthur 9, 35; *see also* 'Morte d'Arthur'; Tennyson, Alfred Lord
Harrison, Frederic 46, 49, 88
hatred 153
Hawthorne, Nathaniel 57–8
heaven 1, 2, 4, 13, 55
  glories of 23, 33
Hegel, Georg 29
hell 1, 2, 4, 13, 25, 55
  destruction of 44
  harrowing of 43
  as kingdom of pain 44
  torments of 13
Hell Opened to Christians 13, 14, 44–5
hellfire 12
Heraclitean creation 179
Heraclitean fire 145, 149, 163, 189
Heraclitean theory of the universe 146, 182
Heraclitean thought 150, 154

Heraclitus 144, 145, 146, 155, 176, 179
heresy 30
  German 37
heroism 6, 134, 155, 174, 175, 185, 187
Hewlett, Maurice 137
Hiawatha 34, 61
hierarchy, undermined 178
Hindley, Charles 99
Hindu revivalism 117
Hindu Vedanta 117
Holmes, Parson 10,11
Holmes, Sherlock 4, 5, 18, 151–3, 184, 188
Holy Grail 183, 184
holy war 192
Holyoake, George Jacob 19, 20, 21, 23, 25, 26, 27, 28, 44, 45
Homogenic Love 161
homosexuality 158, 160, 168
Hopkins, Gerard Manley 51, 88, 122, 145
horror stories 24, 165
Hort, Professor F.J.A. 125
Houghton, Lord 48, 52, 53, 54, 119
Howe, Julia Ward 80, 81, 95, 149
Howells, William Dean 170
Huckleberry Finn, 136; *see also* boy vagabonds
Hughes, Thomas 133
human sacrifice 187, 197
Hume, Daniel 34, 36
Hunting of the Snark, The 119–20
hymnody 82
Hymns Ancient and Modern 82

ideas, history of 3
illusion 5, 7
imagination 1, 2, 3, 4, 52, 53, 130, 139
  and knowledge 130, 145
  and reason 5
'Imaginatio' 4

immortality 2, 5, 55, 64, 163, 187
  personal 180
immutability of species 147
imperial destiny 101, 109
imperialism 92, 172
impiety 187
indecency 163
Indian culture 61
individuality 130
industrial decline 98
Inferno 53
infidelity 9
Ingersoll, Robert Green 96, 126
initiation 184
initiation rites 42
inner consciousness 31
Inquisition 26
insubordination 15
intellectualism 131
International Socialist League 190
Ireland 19
Irish immigration to US 95, 169
irrationality 8, 144
Isis Unveiled 117, 118

James, Henry 132, 136
James, Jesse 136
James, William 132, 179
Jesuits 26
Jevons, Professor 132
jingoism 109, 171
  belligerent 173
Joan of Arc 116

Kant, Immanuel 29
Keble, John 10, 48
Kelvin, Lord 147
Kensit, John 169
Kilvert, Francis 51, 90, 94, 109
King Solomon's Mines 131
Kingsford, Anna 115, 151
Kipling, Rudyard 170, 172, 188
Knights of the Round Table 158
Knowles, James 118
Koestler, Arthur 197

Krafft-Ebing, Baron Richard von
  159, 164, 168
Ku Klux Klan 96, 97, 153

'Land of Hope and Glory' 174
Last Judgement 1, 2, 4, 6
lawlessness 97
Lee, Frederick George 94
Leopold, Prince 85
Lévi, Eliphas 115
lewdness 56
Liberal Party 86
liberty 135
life after death 5, 33, 120
life before birth 32
Lincoln, Abraham 79, 80, 81
  assassination 82
Linton, Mrs Lynn 93
'Locksley Hall' 139
'Locksley Hall Sixty Years After'
  139, 141, 151
Lodge, Sir Oliver 180
London 12
London Cemetery Company 23, 25
London, Jack 176
Long, Crawford 39
Longfellow, Henry Wadsworth 2,
  23, 33, 34, 61, 79, 85
love 52, 53
Lusitania, sinking of 195
lycanthropy 64
Lyell, Charles 10
Lyne, Father Ignatius 169
Lyte, Rev. Henry Francis 2, 21, 31,
  33, 35
Lytton, Lord 107, 117, 118

Mach, Ernst 129
Machen, Arthur 163, 168, 183, 191
Maden, Mrs 51, 52
Mafeking 172
magic 57
Maitland, Edward 114, 115, 116,
  121, 123, 124, 125
male brothels 159

Mallock, William 120
man as God's image 58, 59
Manliness of Christ, The 133
Marble Faun, The 57–8
martyrdom 134
Marsh, Rev. William 11, 12, 15, 98
Marx, Karl 20, 21, 28, 52, 126
Marxism 200
Marxist Socialists 189
masochism 159
Mason, A.E.W. 173, 180
Massachusetts Quarterly Review 61
masturbation 157, 165
materialism 4, 33, 96, 155, 181
materialization of the dead 182
Mayo, Dr 24, 25, 164
McKinley, President 171, 173
Mead, G.R.S. 180
Merrett, Frederick 104
Metaphysical Society 119
Mexico 17, 60, 62
Michelson, Albert Abraham 121–2
Mill, John Stuart 95
millenial expectations 177
Miller, William 16, 18
Milton, John 13, 43, 58
mining 14
miracles 83, 85
Momerie, Dr Alfred Williams 147–8,
    149–50
monarchists 90
money markets 137
monsters 1, 11, 24, 54
Moody, Dwight 75, 105, 106
moral law 55
moral progress 195
moral responsibility 55
moral universe 193
moral values 29
moral will 55
morality 107
Morgan, Henry Lewis 61
Morley, Edward 122
Morley, John 63
Mormon Church 30, 32

Mormon fanaticism 144
'Morte d'Arthur' 9, 10
mortification of the flesh 42
Morton, W.T.G. 39
Moses 72
Müller, Friedrich Max 59, 61
Munby, Arthur 52, 53, 84
muscular Christianity 173
Murray, John 34
Myers, Frederick 181
mysticism 25, 161
myths 2
    and religion 47
myth-making 6

Napoleon iii 77, 78–9
    as Beelzebub 77
    as beast of the Apocalypse 78
    overthrow of 87
National Association of Spiritualism
    50
national crimes 17
natural disasters 120–1
natural law 94
natural selection 93
nature 53, 70
necromancy 33, 115
neo-paganism 155, 156
neuroticism 159
new hedonism 156
new paganism 155, 156
Nichol, John Pringle 31
Nietzsche, Friedrich 70, 71, 121, 129,
    141, 144, 145, 155, 159, 160,
    184, 188
nihilism 122
Nineteenth Century 119
nitrous oxide 39
Nordau, Max 159, 161, 162, 172
novel reading 132; *see also* fiction;
    public libraries
Noyes, John 30

Oates, Lieutenant 185, 186, 187; *see
    also* self-sacrifice, heroic

oath-taking 51
observation 153
occult 124, 166
Occult Review 196
occultism 166
Odger, George 89, 90
O.K. Corral 135; *see also* Wild West
old dispensation 126, 127
Olympic Games 174
O'Mahoney, John 76
Oneida Community 30, 32; *see also*
    utopian communities
'Onward, Christian soldiers' 24
order 146
Order of Christian Mystics 178
Order of the Golden Dawn 167, 168
Origin of Mind, The 66
Origin of Species, The 52, 53, 66, 78
orthodoxy 23, 188
Our Lady of Lourdes 77
Owen, Wilfred 193, 196

pagan conception of death 198
pagan ecstasy 56
pagan fantasy 66
pagan gods 58
Pagan Papers 156
Pagan Review 156, 159
pagan rituals 59
pagan sacrifice 159
paganism 155
    nostalgia for 58
pain 42, 43, 50
    death of 40, 44; *see also* anaesthesia
    infliction of 41; *see also* whipping
    necessity for 53
    and paganism 57
Painter's Church of England Gazette 20
Palmerston, Lord 73
Pan 62, 69, 155
    death of 37, 56
    rebirth of 144
'Pan in Wall Street' 62
Pandora 43, 53

pantheism 28, 31, 32, 62
papal infallibility 113
papal tyranny 46
paradise 8, 10
Paradise Lost 13, 43, 58
Paradise Regained 58
paranoia 197
paranormal 166
parental prohibition 165
Paris Commune 88, 93
Parker, Ely Samuel 61
Parker, Theodore 61, 62, 71, 75, 76,
    77–8
patriotism 172
peace 189
People's Charter 27
penitence 156
penny dreadfuls 132
pestilence 11
Peter Pan 18, 153, 158
phallic symbolism 60, 62
'Phantasia' 4
pharaoh's curse 200
phoenix 126–7
Phoenix Park murders 138
physical degeneracy 175
physical desire 135
piety 48
Pinamonti, Father 13, 44
Plato 2, 70, 112, 144
Plevna, fall of 108
Poe, Edgar Allen 24, 31–2, 34
Poems and Ballads 62
poetic genius 2
Polk, President 41
political corruption 137
politics
    and religion 86
Pope, Alexander 65
popery, and satanism 168
popular culture 101
portents 99
Picture of Dorian Gray, The 159, 160,
    161, 162
positivism 88

Pound, Ezra 199
Povey, Miss 168–9
prayer 17, 94
premature burial 164; *see also* Dr
    Mayo; vampire myths
Prince of Darkness 54
Principles of Geology 10
progress 52
    inevitability of 140
progressive idealism 86
prophecy 17, 72
    of apocalypse 29
Protestant Enlightenment 170
Protestant hysteria 77
Protestant Reformation 74
Protestant scepticism 166
Protestant Truth Society 168
Protestantism 11, 30
    and fanaticism 11
    and science 113
pseudo-Catholicism 102
psycho-analysis 3, 54
public libraries 131
Public Worship Regulation Act 102
punishment 13
pure love 158
Pusey, Professor Edward 47, 48, 59,
    86

Quimby, Phineas 118
Queensberry libel trial 167; *see also*
    Douglas, Lord Alfred; Wilde,
    Oscar
Queensberry, Marquis of 160
Quest 187, 190
Quest Society 179, 180, 182

racialism 200
Radical Club 68
radicalism 75, 138
rational religion 143, 146
rationalism 1, 12, 19, 28, 29, 33
Reade, Winwood 4–5, 6, 18, 66, 67,
    69, 146, 147, 152
realism 131

reality 1, 2, 3, 7
reason 1, 2, 28, 153
    god of, *see* Apollo
    goddess of 27
Reasoner, The 19, 23, 26, 44, 51
recrucifixion fantasy 197, 198
redemption 43
Regeneration 161, 162
reincarnation 68–9
relative universe 163
relativity, theory of 146
religion, history of 3
religious conversion 19
religious fantasy 87
religious fervour 19
religious observance 17
religious prejudice 52
religious revival 73, 75, 76
    hymns 82
Religious Tract Society 132, 133
reproductive urge 155
republicanism 89
Resurrection of Christ 181
resurrection of the body 23, 24, 104
    instant 164
retribution 52
revealed religion 10
Revelation, Book of 10, 12, 16, 36,
    99, 118
revolution 8
    threat of 15
    of 1848 21
Revue des Deux Mondes 37, 46
Richter, Jean Paul 18, 152
riots 73, 122
ritual of death 156
Rochdale Secular Society 51
Rogers, Henry 28
Roman Catholicism 37, 40, 44, 74,
    167
    and superstition 11, 95
Roman mythology 60
romance 131
Roosevelt, President 173
Rossetti, Dante Gabriel 33, 63, 88

Rubáiyát of Omar Khayyám 59
rural distress 110
Russia 108

sacrifice 17, 176, 186, 196
sacrilege 24
sadism 159, 160
Saintsbury, George 130–1, 154, 181
Salisbury, Lord 101, 147
Salt, Henry 50
sanctity 24
Sankey, Ira 105, 106
Satan 43, 53
satanism 63, 166, 168
scepticism 181
Schaff, Philip 74, 75, 77
Schiller, Friedrich 58
schoolboy love 158
Schopenhauer, Arthur 18, 145
science 67, 155
    and democracy 139
    as enemy 93
    and religion 82–3
scientific determinism 67
scientific heresy 146
scientific laws 113
scientific method 112
scientific progress 86, 96
scientific research 10
scientific scepticism 95, 143
scientific truth 52
séances 33, 36, 145
Second Coming 16, 37, 72, 100, 134
Second International 189
Second Reform Bill 84
self-control 42
self-immolation 187
self-sacrifice 6, 156, 157
    heroic 184
self-transcendence 151, 154
sexual deviation 164, 165
sexual instinct 156, 157
sexual inversion 158
sexual morality 177
sexuality 56, 155

Shaftesbury, Earl of 83; *see also*
    Ashley, Lord
Shaw, George Bernard 173
Shimeall, Rev. Richard 78
Shipton, Mother 99, 101, 123
Sight of Hell, The 45
Silence, John, 166
Simpson, Professor James 40, 42
sin 11, 29, 43, 163
sinners, punishment of 15
Skelton, Sir John 65, 91
slavery 41, 75
    and religion 41
'Sleep of Reason, The' 1, 2, 11, 54,
    144; *see also* Goya, Francisco
Smith, Joseph 30
Smith, Sydney 9
Smyth, Professor Charles Piazzi 99–
    100, 101, 102, 109, 115, 134
social breakdown 98
social co-operation 154
social regeneration 154
socialism 12, 15
Society for Psychical Research 24,
    166
Socrates 70, 144, 146, 155
Socratic tradition 69, 98
soldiers of Christ 82
soul 15
    in hell 51
    sacrifice of 5
    sleep of 2
Southey, Robert 27
space 31
Spirit Lamp 163
spirit rapping 32, 118
Spirit World 33–4, 49
spirits, evil 33
Spiritual Magazine 38, 50
spiritualism 32–4, 36, 44, 49–50, 164,
    180
Sparta 187
Spencer, Herbert 52, 95
spiritual evolution 66
spiritual science 118

spirituality 150
sport 174
St Paul 42, 44, 50, 64
starvation 11
Stead, W.T. 108
Stedman, Edmund Clarence 62, 110
Stevenson, Robert Louis 128–9, 134, 135, 136, 141, 143, 157
stoicism 42
Stoker, Bram 166
Stone, Elizabeth 23
strikes 15, 84, 106
Strong, Josiah 170
Sturgis, Howard Overing 158
Stutfield, Hugh 172
Subirous, Bernadette 77, 94
suffering 40
superhuman 153, 154, 155
superman 155
supernatural 38, 153, 154, 180
superstition 1, 11, 12, 18, 59, 94
surgery 39–40; see also anaesthesia, pain
survival 195
   of the fittest 53
sword of Gorsedd 172
Symonds, John Addington 85, 134, 143, 146, 158

Taylor, Bayard 62
Temple, Frederick, Bishop of Exeter 86
Tennyson, Alfred 9, 10, 15, 35, 44, 49, 92, 119, 138, 141, 144, 150
terrorism, Irish 138
Theosopical Society 116
theosophy 180
Thompson, Sir Henry 104, 105
Thomson, James 144
Thoreau, Henry David 60, 71, 79, 82
thought 111
Tiberius 56
time 31
Time Machine, The 175
Tinkerbell 18, 153, 188

tithe payments 148
Tom Brown's Schooldays 133
tomb of the unknown soldier 197
Tooth, Rev. Arthur 103
trade depression 106
transcendentalism 30, 60
Treasure Island 128, 131
Trelawny, Sir John 51
Turkey 108
Tutankhamun 199
Twain, Mark 136
Tyndall, Professor John 95, 113, 114, 144
tyranny 11

ultimate reality 2
ultimate sacrifice 156
ultimate truth 61, 149
unbelief 10, 11, 17
Unconscious Cerebration 54
unconscious mind 56
underworld 15
union of man and beast 64
Union Jack 132
universal archetypes 3
universal law 146
universe, nature of 31
Unknowable 179
unreality 141
USA 19, 74
   Catholicism 169
   divine mission of 173
utopian communities 30

valour 185
vampire myths 24–5, 50, 163, 165, 166
Vanity 33
Varney the Vampire 24
Victoria, Queen 11, 35, 38, 40, 85, 95, 101, 110
   assassination attempt 138
   death of 173
Virgil 69
violence 138, 153
   as creative force 145

virtue 34, 57, 184
  redemption from 63

Waite, A.E. 183
Walden 60
Wales, Prince of 80, 85, 89, 105, 106, 117, 141
  as pagan prince 107
walking dead 24
Walsh, Walter 169
war 15, 145, 175
War of the Worlds, The 175
Ward, Rev. F.W.Orde 179, 193
'Waste Land, The' 183, 189, 199; *see also* Eliot, T.S.
Wells, H.G. 130, 175, 177
Wells, Horace 39
werewolves 163, 165
Weston, Jessie 183, 192
whipping 41–2
whipping brothels 50, 63
white supremacy 96
Whitman, Walt 140, 141, 154

wickedness 34
Wilberforce, Samuel 32, 35, 37, 46, 48, 52, 53, 59, 65, 78
Wild Bill Hickok 97
Wild West 97, 136
Wilde, Oscar 136, 154, 159, 160, 162, 163, 168
William IV 9
Williams, Rowland 47
Wilson, Henry Bristow 47
Woolf, Virginia 178, 184
Wordsworth, William 9, 32, 58
working-class revolt 16
World Peace Foundation 189, 190
World's Parliament of Religions 148–9
worship 17

Yeats, W.B. 172
Young, Edward 31

Zeus 43, 66
Zimmern, Helen 118